Electric Motorcycles
and Bicycles

ALSO BY KEVIN DESMOND
AND FROM MCFARLAND

Electric Trucks: A History (forthcoming, 2019)

Electric Airplanes and Drones: A History (2018)

Electric Boats and Ships: A History (2017)

*Innovators in Battery Technology:
Profiles of 95 Influential Electrochemists* (2016)

*Gustave Trouvé: French Electrical Genius
(1839–1902)* (2015)

Electric Motorcycles and Bicycles

A History Including Scooters, Tricycles, Segways and Monocycles

KEVIN DESMOND

Foreword by ED BENJAMIN

McFarland & Company, Inc., Publishers
Jefferson, North Carolina

LIBRARY OF CONGRESS CATALOGUING-IN-PUBLICATION DATA

Names: Desmond, Kevin, 1950– author.
Title: Electric motorcycles and bicycles : a history including scooters, tricycles, segways and monocycles / Kevin Desmond ; foreword by Ed Benjamin.
Description: Jefferson, North Carolina : McFarland & Company, Inc., Publishers, 2019 | Includes bibliographical references and index.
Identifiers: LCCN 2018051291 | ISBN 9781476672892 (softcover : acid free paper) ∞
Subjects: LCSH: Electric motorcycles—History. | Electric bicycles—History. | Inventors—History. | Electric vehicles. | Transportation—Technological innovations.
Classification: LCC TL448.E44 .D47 2019 | DDC 629.22/93—dc23
LC record available at https://lccn.loc.gov/2018051291

BRITISH LIBRARY CATALOGUING DATA ARE AVAILABLE

ISBN (print) 978-1-4766-7289-2
ISBN (ebook) 978-1-4766-3466-1

© 2019 Kevin Desmond. All rights reserved

No part of this book may be reproduced or transmitted in any form or by any means, electronic or mechanical, including photocopying or recording, or by any information storage and retrieval system, without permission in writing from the publisher.

Front cover images: *top* The 1976 Yare e-tricycle prototype developed by Dr. Harold D. Kesling (La Porte County Historical Society Museum); *left* Fulton Gardner's 1892 patent for an electric bicycle; *right* Airbus APWorks' 3D-printed Light Rider motorcycle (APWorks)

Printed in the United States of America

McFarland & Company, Inc., Publishers
Box 611, Jefferson, North Carolina 28640
www.mcfarlandpub.com

To
Πήγασος (Pegasus)
Ἠλέκτρα (Elektra)

Acknowledgments

The author would like to thank the following people and organizations for their help in preparing this history: Florian Bailly; Ed Benjamin; Hervé Charpentier (Peugeot Adventure Museum, Sochaux); John Claes; Mike Corbin; Rob Cotter; Bill Dubé; Kate Elms (collections officer, Brighton Royal Pavilion & Museums); James Gilbert (Morgan); Tom Haas (McKinley Presidential Museum and Library, Canton, Ohio); Eva Håkansson; Frank Jamerson, PhD; Edward Kemp (IET); Richard Hatfield; Damien Kuntz (Electropolis); Cees Lengers; Ralf Luther; Cedric Lynch; BNF; National Motor Museum, Beaulieu; Hannes Neupert (*ExtraEnergy* magazine); Nathalie Postic (Institut pour l'histoire de l'aluminium); Lisa Sanchez (Center for Local & Global History, Cleveland Public Library, Ohio); Johan Schaeverbeke; Gordon Scott; Aad Steng; and Chip Yates III.

Thanks once again to the team at McFarland, to Alexandra Desmond (my long-supporting wife) and Kathryn Cooper (my indexer).

Table of Contents

Acknowledgments	vi
Foreword by Ed Benjamin	1
Preface	3
1. Pioneers	5
2. The Early 1900s	41
3. From Socovels to Spacelanders	53
4. 1950s–1980s	63
5. The 1990s	79
6. Urban E-Bikes Worldwide	96
7. EM Hotshots	112
8. China: Almost 300 Million E-Bike Riders	140
9. Marathons	148
10. Speed Records	157
11. Variations on a Theme	176
12. Return of the Electric Three-Wheeler	193
13. Secret Weapon?	203
14. Riding into the Future	206
Appendix: Electric Motorcycle and Battery Builders (Past and Present)	231
Chapter Notes	233
Selected Bibliography	237
Index	239

Foreword
by Ed Benjamin

My interest in electric-powered two-wheelers comes from these simple ideas:

- Humanity needs personal transportation that does not pollute, make noise, or require endless parking lots and roadways. Bicycles address this need, but electric bicycles do it for more people, a bit faster, and much more comfortably. Electric motorcycles/motor scooters will extend this solution further, especially in combination with metros, light rail, trains, and bus systems, serving as first- and last-mile transport to the station.
- Electric bicycles and other powered two-wheelers are improving, and they will further improve the lives of billions of people.
- Automobiles, of any type, are useful, but they are not the answer for billions of people—especially those who live in our ever larger, and ever more dense, big cities.

Reading this book, I have learned that inventors and businessmen have been working on solutions to transportation problems for more than a century. One of them, Dr. Frank Jamerson, brought some electric bikes to my bicycle shop in 1994, and I became fascinated by this vehicle category.

Success for the industry started in the 1990s, and today electric bikes/motorcycles are the fourth largest category of transportation vehicles—heading for the top by unit volume. At least 260 million people used an electric two-wheeler today. In the near future, that number will increase to 1.5 billion. This success has been created and furthered by a widely diverse international group of people, often collaborating across cultural, language, and national borders. To a large degree, they have been under the radar, little noticed by the media, government, or the auto/motorcycle industry. This anonymity has resulted in great ingenuity, novel ideas, and opportunities to change the paradigm of personal transportation. I am grateful to know or have known many of the people mentioned in this book. They are passionate, determined, and unrelenting. Their passions make them larger than life and multidimensional to me. They remind me of this line from George Bernard Shaw: "The *reasonable man* adapts himself to the world; the *unreasonable* one persists in trying to adapt the world to himself. Therefore *all progress* depends on the *unreasonable man*."[1]

Such persistence has been a major part of this story. The naysayers and "when will it happen?" commenters have been along for every moment of this story. At a time when humans badly need new ideas about personal transportation and its impact on the environment, the many unreasonably determined inventors and businesspeople included in this book have given us one of the most important tools for our future. Thank you, Kevin, for telling their story ... so far.

Edward Benjamin is senior managing director of eCycleElectric Consultants LLC and chairman of the Light Electric Vehicle Association. Benjamin's business has taken him to 29 countries, serving about 160 clients over the last 22 years.

Preface

The electric-powered two-wheeler is the only transportation device that has managed in the last 20 years to claim a significant part of the bicycle market share. With its simple design that closely mimics the traditional bicycle, small and efficient electric motor, lithium-ion battery and easy control methods, this vehicle has experienced rapid sales growth since 1998.

It is, however, necessary to clarify what is meant by an electric-powered two-wheeler. An **electric bicycle or e-bike** is a generic word that includes all types of electrically assisted bicycles. A **pedelec** is an electric bicycle or tricycle that one must pedal for the motor to run, while an **electric motorcycle** has enough power and speed to operate safely on the highway in the manner of a gasoline-powered motorcycle and is homologated the same as a gasoline motorcycle. An **electric motor scooter**, whether two or three wheeled, is equivalent in function and performance to a 50cc gasoline motor scooter; an **electric mini scooter** (e.g., T3) is a stand-up, small scooter that is usually not regulated; and a **human transporter** is a Segway-type vehicle, with two or more wheels.

Today, it is estimated that there are more than 250 million electric bicycles in China alone. The use of electric bicycles in Europe and North America is growing fast, with reported yearly sales of more than 1.5 million units. This book will trace the history of humanity's quest for the best way to fit a motor and battery to propel or assist in pedaling cycles with one, two or three wheels.

In the winter of 1991, as a freelance journalist, I was given the task of testing the Vessa Vision—an electric three-wheeler for disabled people. The vehicle was duly delivered and, together with my little son Andrew, I took it out onto the ice and snow of the roads of North London; afterward, I provided a write-up. At the time I was very involved in the promotion of electric boats, so this assignment was a pleasant change from afloat to ashore. Twenty years later, I purchased an electric scooter to take me around the lanes of the hilly wine-growing region just outside Bordeaux, France, where we were living. I soon realized that this yellow machine simply did not have enough autonomy to handle the steep gradients. Eventually I replaced it with a more powerful pedelec: a navy-blue Lafree Twist Lite, a mid-drive, nickel-metal hydride battery–powered electric bike. Manufactured by Giant (a Taiwanese company and one of the largest bicycle manufacturers in the world), its Panasonic crank-drive enabled me to pedal up those same hills with electrical assistance. At the time, I was conducting research for my biography of Gustave Trouvé, who had developed the world's first battery-electric tricycle as long ago as 1881. Now, ten years later, following my published histories of electric boats and airplanes, I present this history of the electric motorcycle, not merely as a researcher but also as someone who knows what it's like to use one prudently!

1

Pioneers

London in the 1830s: Among the fashions of the day was the pedestrian curricle, built in its hundreds by Denis Johnson of Long Acre, London. Otherwise known as the Dandy-Horse, this was a two-wheeled vehicle, with wheels in-line, propelled by the rider pushing along the ground with the feet as in regular walking or running. The front wheel and handlebar assembly was hinged to allow steering. There was also dropped-frame version for ladies to accommodate their long skirts! Ten minutes' walk away from Johnson's works, at King's College, John Daniell, a professor of chemistry, was working to improve the Voltaic battery, developing a primary cell that produced a constant reliable source of electrical current over a long period of time. As Professor Daniell walked through the streets of London, did he ever envisage that, one day, a battery would be used to propel a velocipede?[1]

In 1859 Belgian inventor Etienne Lenoir took his single cylinder two-stroke liquid hydrocarbon motor and installed it on a three-wheeler he called the *Hippomobile*. He made a trial run from Joinville-le-Pont to Paris and back, a distance of 6.83 miles (11 km), in one and half hours, at less than walking speed, though doubtless there were breakdowns. This succeeded in attracting the attention of Tsar Alexander II, and one was sent to Russia, where it vanished. Lenoir was not pleased; he sold his patent to the Paris Gas Lighting and Heating Company and turned to a motor boat project.

During the 1860s, attempts were made on both sides of the Atlantic to build and ride steam velocipedes. In the United States, it was Sylvester Howard Roper (born in New Hampshire on November 24, 1823) who led the way. At the early age of 12, Roper built a steam-powered engine without any help. Moving to Boston, he continued to invent, improving sewing machines and various rifle types. In 1863, Roper drove his "horseless" carriage featuring a steam engine around the city. Though his experiments were interrupted by the American Civil War, in 1869 Roper attached a twin-cylinder steam engine to a hickory-framed velocipede. Roper's bike, which rolled on iron-shod wooden wheels, had one cylinder on each side of the frame connected by rods to driving cranks on the rear-wheel axle. A firebox and boiler were spring mounted and suspended between the wheels, and a short chimney projected up from behind the saddle. A charcoal fire was built in the grate beneath the boiler. The fire's heat boiled the water in the boiler and produced steam to power the engine. Water was supplied from a reservoir in the seat. A cable attached to the handlebars operated the throttle valve. Tightening the cable activated the valve, and rotating in the opposite direction applied the spoon-type brake on the front wheel. Footrests were attached to the front axle ends.

While his steam-powered bike was popular at exhibitions, Roper's neighbors were less thrilled. His two-wheel steamer was described in local news reports as loud and emitting an acrid odor. When riding into town, Roper would spook horses and often annoy townspeople. He was once arrested on one of his rides, though quickly released when it was determined that he had broken no laws.

In 1895, with backing from the Pope Manufacturing Company, Roper built an improved version of his steamer bike. Pope foresaw the possibility of adding new business to its bicycle empire. By the end of the century, gas-powered motors were already beginning to prove viable, but Roper had more than 30 years of experience with steam power, so he continued in vain with this project. His latter steam-powered bicycle, weighing 150 pounds (68 kg), had a one-gallon water reservoir, which was good for a journey of 8 miles (12 km). On test rides into town, Roper would remove the burning coals on arrival and place them in a small covered bucket. When he was ready to leave, he would restoke the fire, get up steam, and return home.[2]

On June 1, 1896, Roper, 73, decided to test his latest prototype on the 1.3-mile Charles River wooden bicycle track, near Harvard Bridge, Cambridge, Massachusetts. He felt that his creation could serve as a great pacemaker for training racing cyclists. There he made several laps, pacing the bicyclists, including professional rider Tom Butler, who could not keep up with the puffing machine. For Roper, however, winning against a regular bike was not enough: he decided to test the maximum speed of his velocipede. He was clocked at 2 minutes, 1.4 seconds for the flying mile, and reached a speed of 30 miles per hour (64 kph). But this still was not enough for him, so he tried to beat his own record. On a straight road, Roper's velocipede started to wobble, and the inevitable happened: he fell from the vehicle and was thrown into the sand at the side of the track. Suffering a head wound, he died instantly. After the autopsy, the cause of death was found to be heart failure, although it is unknown whether the crash caused the stress on his heart or if his heart failed prior to the crash.[3]

Over in France, ever since 1869, Louis-Guillaume Perreaux of Paris had, like Roper, been developing his own steam velocipede, often modifying his original French patent, No. 83691. His purpose was addressing the well-known drawbacks of ordinary bicycles and, ideally, making a machine capable of seriously competing with the horse. At the age of sixteen, Perreaux had invented a cane-gun. Perreaux coupled one of his smaller alcohol-burning brass-plated steam engines, a single cylinder with a weight of 136 pounds (62 kg), onto an iron velocipede manufactured by Pierre Michaux. Drive was achieved by twin belts, and it was capable of about 9 miles per hour (14 kph). Perreaux exhibited this device at the Exposition Universelle of 1878, but he never met with commercial success. This failure may have been because it took too long to build up steam pressure, while climbing onto and pedaling a simple velocipede remained so much easier.

If Perreaux and Roper can lay claim to inventing the first motorcycles, the first engineer to propel a tricycle with a battery-electric motor was the ingenious Gustave Pierre Trouvé at his workshop at 14, rue Vivienne, in downtown Paris.

Until recently, the name of Gustave Trouvé, Chevalier de la Légion d'Honneur, and a prolific Parisian electrical instrument inventor, was absent from popular French encyclopedias. Yet when, at the end of the 19th century, Alexander Graham Bell, the world-famous inventor of the telephone, visited Paris, he insisted on visiting Trouvé's workshops. According to Bell:

> I wanted to surprise you amongst your works that I so much admire. In addition, I want to take away to America, a complete collection of all your inventions, because for me they make up the highest expression of the perfection and the ingenuity of the electric science in France.

Gustave Pierre Trouvé was born on January 2, 1839, at La Haye-Descartes, northeast of Poitiers. His father, Jacques Trouvé, was a gentleman-farmer who, with Gustave's mother Clarissa, brought up five children. From his earliest years, although Gustave did not show great passion for math, he was very keen on mechanical objects. He never played with children of his age. From morning to night, armed with a knife, a hammer and several nails, he amused himself by fashioning little chariots, telegraphs, rabbits and automatons fitted with wings moved by the wind. In 1846, the seven-year-old boy built a little fire pump from a sardine tin. Then, with nothing more than hairpins and bits of lead, this prodigy made a miniature working steam engine, using an old tinder box for the generator. Four years later, between October and December 1850, Trouvé began his studies alongside his brother Jules at Chinon College. But, as he wanted to specialize in math and mechanics, Gustave left his large family and his region to study at the Imperial School of Industrial Arts and Crafts at Angers. The marks obtained by the teenager (Control No. 264) for the first term of the 1854 school year were surprisingly lower than average, with his strongest point being drawing.

By 1859, only 20, young Trouvé had obtained a job in Paris with one of the principal French clockmakers. During his spare time, he studied architecture, math and precision work. Seven years later, he set up his own establishment for the creation and manufacture of precision and scientific instruments, of which he would conceive and construct some 75 in all, particularly in the field of electricity. Among these were forms of transportation, both ashore and afloat.

Werner Siemens and Johann Halske of Berlin-Kreuzberg in Germany had recently developed an electric motor to power both the world's first elevator and the streetcar. Trouvé improved the efficiency of this motor and built one weighing only 11 pounds (5 kg), which he subsequently patented (Patent No. 136,560, dated May 8, 1880). He began to consider how his little engine might be used for motive power, thinking that perhaps the most lightweight and stable vehicle to test it out on would be a pedal tricycle.

From the mid–1870s, James Starley of the Sewing Machine Co. of Coventry, England, had been building and improving tricycles—the Coventry Rotary and the Coventry Lever—for a world enamored with "wheeling." In the summer of 1881, Starley proudly delivered two of his stable "Salvo tricycles" to Osborne House on the Isle of Wight, for possible use by Her Majesty Queen Victoria and her daughters. The Salvo was renamed the "Royal Salvo," and before long there was not a crowned head in Europe or beyond who did not have a fleet of tricycles. A firm called P. Rousset & Ingold became the general agent for France.

For Trouvé, the Salvo seemed the ideal mount. On April 16, 1881, he reported his trials along a straight road near his workshop in the Tissandiers magazine *La Nature*:

> On a heavily built English tricycle, I fitted two of my little electric motors and 6 electric accumulators like the one in my polyscope. One of my friends climbed onto the tricycle, switched it on and accelerated it several times along the rue de Valois, certainly as rapidly as a good hackney cab. The experiment lasted an hour and a half. A speed of 12 km/h (7.4 mph) was recorded. The weight of the vehicle and of my friend amounted to 160 kg (352 lb.) and the force of the engines corresponded to 7 kilogrammètres ($1^1/_{10}$ hp). Encouraged by these results, I immediately began to build a motor which was alone more powerful than the two others, even up to 10 kilogrammeters, so as to get even greater speeds, that is from 20 to 30 km/h (12 to 18 mph.).

There were eyewitnesses:

> One of Trouvé's friends has tried the new velocipede on the bitumen of the rue de Valois. He went up and down the road several times at the speed of a good carriage.[4]

His friend and supporter, journalist Abbé Moigno, was also there:

> I had just crossed the Palais Royal and arrived on the Rue de Valois, when my attention was drawn by a man who was on a tricycle and was arriving at full speed. I would have left immediately if, upon the approach of the tricycle, I had not heard a

1. Pioneers

few exclamations uttered by passers-by who said "Of course it is steam or electricity which propels it!" Upon hearing the word "electricity," I paid closer attention to the vehicle which was going by me at that precise moment and it was easy for me to notice that, the "soul" of the movement was indeed electricity, because I immediately recognized the small motor which had been presented and demonstrated by its inventor during a social gathering given by Vice-Admiral Mouchez in the Paris Observatory. However, I did not recognize M. Gustave Trouvé, the famous electrical engineer, as being the person who was on the tricycle, but I soon heard he was standing apart and that from a window in the Hotel de Hollande, he had followed all phases of the experiment. Let me tell you about it.

The tricycle had two steering wheels and a simple, large propelling wheel, the latter being, I believe of English manufacture, and appearing quite heavy. Placed beneath the axle joining the two small wheels were two small, Trouvé motors, each the size of a fist. These motors were communicating movement by means of two link chains each of which engaged its respective sprocket gear on either side of the big propelling wheel.

Behind the seat and sitting on the axle, a rough, newly fashioned wooden box contained six secondary batteries. These accumulators were quite similar to those of Mr

In April 1881, Gustave Trouvé's electric tricycle was ridden down the rue Valois, downtown Paris, reaching a speed of 7.4 mph (12 kph). Using a converted English Starley Salvo, Trouvé believed that with a more powerful motor, he could have reached speeds of 12–18 mph (20–30 kph) (Musée EDF Electropolis, Mulhouse).

Gaston Planté and actuated the motors. To the left of the seat was a brake lever easily reached by the driver. On the lever was an electrical switch by which the driver could easily stop or start immediately.[5]

One man who saw the potential of Trouvé's electric tricycle was Jean-Baptiste Godin, an industrialist who had made his fortune from the manufacture of cast-iron stoves built by a cooperative at Guise in Picardy, where some 1,500 workers were employed to make 280,000 units annually. Godin was interested in commercializing some form of bicycle. In early 1881 the Harvard-educated dilettante Edward Howland, a protagonist of the model industrial village, had written about "rapid collective circulation" in his article "The Bicycle Era" in *Harper's Magazine*. A man after his own heart, Howland sent Godin a letter about an improved pedal bicycle. On May 29, 1881, Godin wrote back requesting plans and that Howland file a patent, sending an authorization for the Familistere de Guise Godin et Cie to manufacture the vehicle in France, specifying the duration of his patent and the royalty he would require for each unit sold. Then, on July 6, Godin wrote:

> On the other hand, the newspapers have recently announced the application of electricity to the bicycle. With such a machine, travelling would take place without the rider having anything else to do than to steer the vehicle. This would be an invention which could really render useless any kind of bicycle. In this state of things, I think it is necessary to wait. Accept, Sir, the assurance of my devotion. Jean-Baptiste Godin.

Production of the Trouvé electric tricycle never even started.[6] Jean-Baptiste Godin died seven years later; the annual output of Godin et Cie was valued at more than four million francs. Writing in 1895, journalist Georges Dary explained:

> It's true to say that its success at first did not respond to the attempts, even perfected, which took place in this order of ideas ... we are unable to believe that the pleasure of eating-up a kilometer without fatigue could ever completely satisfy the record men: they always prefer to peal their lightweight machines rather than adapt an instrument which would transform their beloved sport into an invalid's outing.[7]

Usually Trouvé would take out a patent on his latest invention, but not for his electric tricycle. At present, no documentary explanation has been found for this situation. But perhaps, for Trouvé, the answer was quite simply his electric motor, less heavy and quicker in response. Could it be that Perreaux's detailed patent, described above, prevented Trouvé from taking out his own patent? After all, the Perreaux patent covered *any* form of motor installed in a velocipede, including electricity.

In the autumn of 1881, Paris decided to organize an International Electrical Exhibition to display the advances in electrical technology since the small electrical display at the Universal Exposition only three years before. George Berger was the commissioner general. Aside from the provision of the building by the French government (the Palais de l'Industrie, in the Champs Elysées), the exhibition was privately financed. Organizers would donate profits to scientific works in the public interest. A total of 1,786 exhibitors came from the United Kingdom, the United States, Germany, Italy and Holland, as well as from France. The event caused a great stir.

Among those visiting were two English electrical engineers: William Edward Ayrton and his colleague John Perry. During the 1870s, having worked for the Indian Telegraph Service, Ayrton held the professorial chair of physics and telegraphy at the Imperial Engineering College in Tokyo, which at the time was the largest technical university in the world. With his colleague, Irish-born John Perry, Ayrton succeeded in electrifying the city of Tokyo, particularly with the first public electric lighting system at Tokyo's central telegraph station, as well as innovating various devices to measure current. In 1879, Ayrton and Perry returned to London, where the latter became professor at the newly founded City and Guilds Institute. From 1881 onward he was professor of applied physics at the institute's Finsbury Technical College, with John Perry working as associate professor. While visiting Paris, Ayrton and Perry may well have seen Trouvé's tricycle, although there is no evidence that it was on display at the exhibition.

The Planté batteries used by Trouvé were then being surpassed by the latest technology developed by his compatriot Camille Faure. This was a lead-acid couple in which the lead plates were coated with a paste of lead oxides, sulfuric acid and water, which was then cured by being gently warmed in a humid atmosphere. The curing process caused the paste to change to a mixture of lead sulfates that adhered to the lead plate. During charging, the cured paste was converted into electrochemically active material (the "active mass") and provided a substantial increase in capacity. In short, it meant that the battery could be regularly recharged. The use of paste allowed the plates to have much more active material on them than the plates of a Planté cell, in which the active material is formed on the surfaces of the lead plates by repeated charging and discharging.

As consulting engineers for the Faure Electric Accumulator Company, Ayrton and Perry decided that, once back across the English Channel, they, too, would make a few improvements based on the Trouvé prototype. They adapted a tricycle from Howe Machine Company from Glasgow; it had two large wheels on the front axle and a small rear wheel. The motor produced 0.5 horsepower (0.37 kW). The Faure accumulators had a capacity of 1.5 kilowatt-hours and a voltage of 20 volts. Cells from Sellon-Volckmar were also used. The batteries were placed on a board under the seat. The speed was controlled by individually switching the 10 accumulator cells on and off. The vehicle featured the scientists' own voltmeter and amp meter, along with a debut outing for a speed-controlling battery-regulating switch. They also fitted it with electrical lights. In October 1882, Ayrton and Perry drove with their electric vehicle for the first time on Queen Victoria Street in London. Subsequent trials showed that it had a range of up to 24.8 miles (40 km) and a top speed of approximately 8.69 miles per hour (14 kph).

Almost as soon as driven, Ayrton and Perry's electric tricycle was shown to be in violation of the so-called red flag laws of the island kingdom, as noted in a letter by "Chancery Lane":

> Sir. What is the use of an electric tricycle? The Locomotive (Roads) Act, Sec.3 enacts that "every locomotive propelled by steam, or any other than animal power, on any turnpike, road or public highway, shall be worked according to the following rules and regulations amongst other, namely: Firstly, at least three persons shall be employed to drive or conduct such locomotive; secondly, of such persons while any locomotive is in motion one shall proceed such locomotive in motion on foot by not less than 60 yards, and shall carry a red flag constantly displayed, and shall warn the riders and drivers of horses of the approach of such locomotives and shall signal the driver there of when it should be necessary to stop, and shall assist horses, and carriages drawn by horses, passing same." And by Section 4, the speed at which such locomotive shall be driven along a highway is limited to four miles per hour, and through a city, or village to two miles per hour. Is this how electric tricycles are proposed to be driven? That a tricycle is a locomotive within the meaning of the act of Parliament if driven by other than animal power has been recently decided by the Queen's Bench in the case of Parkyns v Preist 7 Q B D, 313.
>
> Yours etc. October 31, 1882 Chancery Lane.[8]

The year before, commissioned by Sir Thomas Parkyns, 6th baronet of

In October 1882, William Ayrton and John Perry drove with their electric tricycle along Queen Victoria Street in London. Subsequent trials showed that it had a range of up to 24.8 miles (40 km) and a top speed of approximately 8.7 mph (14 kph) (Musée EDF Electropolis, Mulhouse).

Bunney Park, Nottinghamshire, an engineer named A.E. Bateman had adapted a "Cheylesmore" front-driving tricycle as made by the Coventry Machinists Company in the Coventry district of Cheylesmore to carry a petroleum-fired steam boiler driving a double-acting two-cylinder steam engine. This made it one of the first petroleum-powered vehicles. In the law case in point, Parkyns' steam tricycle had been judged a locomotive, a precedent that in turn condemned Ayrton and Perry's tricycle. However, the two English engineers regarded their e-trike as a "mobile" billboard to advertise their new electrical inventions at trade shows throughout Europe.

In 2011, a team led by Horst Schultz at Autovision located in Altlußheim, a small town in Baden-Württemberg, Germany, spent a year creating a working replica of the Ayrton and Perry tricycle. They first had to source the rumored sole example of the Starley tricycle left in the world. Rather than adding an electric drivetrain to the priceless original, the team created an exact replica and set about re-creating the electric motor and batteries to match the original specifications. The 0.5-kilowatt motor sat underneath a wooden panel that forms the seat, and a battery-regulating switch was fitted to control the power from the 54-volt/7.5-amp-hour batteries. A large, fixed roller was also re-created by Autovision to transmit power from the motor to the huge front wheels. With Schultz at the controls, the replica proved capable of a speed of 8 miles per hour and a range of 25 miles.

Another who was inspired to make an electric tricycle was Antony Reckenzaun, chief engineer of the London-based Electric Power Storage Company. Reckenzaun was born in Graz, Austria. He served his apprenticeship at his father's ironworks, whose main client was the Hungarian Railways. In 1872, Reckenzaun, only 22, moved to England and obtained work at the marine engineering firm of Ravenhill & Miller, where he became involved in steam engine design and construction. After his first visit to the Paris Exhibition of 1879, he resolved to devote himself to the study of electrical engineering. In 1881, again at the Electrical Exhibition in Paris, Reckenzaun spent nearly every day for three months walking from stand to stand the Palais de l'Industrie, including a very careful examination of Trouvé's electric boat. (One wonders whether Reckenzaun met Trouvé and conversed with him.) The Austrian subsequently returned to England with unique knowledge. Once back, Reckenzaun built an electric tricycle with a speed of 8 miles per hour and an autonomy of one hour, which he exhibited in the Rotunda at the Vienna International Exhibition in 1883.[9]

Over in the United States in 1885, the aerial bicycle was devised by G.P. Hachenberger of Austin, Texas, to utilize the newly erected telephone poles and wires for transportation. However, this idea was soon abandoned.

News items often inspire fiction writers. In his novel *A Fortnight in Heaven: An Unconventional Romance* (1886), Harold Brydges (a.k.a. James

In 1885, G.P. Hachenberger of Austin, Texas, believed that cyclists might derive their power from overhead electric cables (Musée EDF Electropolis, Mulhouse).

Howard Bridge) describes the voyage to Jupiter of an English sea captain's "spiritual double." On Jupiter the double discovers gigantic humans living in an alternative futuristic America. Here the city of Chicago has become a city of crystal. The driving force behind this transformation is electricity, which powers "electric pedestrianism" (by means of an accelerated bicycle).

If anyone was equipped to make an electric tricycle, it was Charles F. Brush of Cleveland. Having obtained U.S. Patent No. 189,997 ("Improvements in Magneto-Electric Machines") in 1877, during the next decade, Brush developed a range of dynamo and arc lights, which first illuminated a Cincinnati physician's home in 1878, followed by Cleveland Public Square in 1879. Brush's generators were reliable and automatically increased voltage with greater load while keeping current constant. By 1881, New York, Boston, Philadelphia,

Baltimore, Montreal, Buffalo, San Francisco, Cleveland and other cities around the world had Brush arc light systems, producing public light well into the 20th century. These and more than 50 other patented innovations made Brush a wealthy man. Nathan S. Possons was superintendent of the Brush Electric Company while his brother W. J. Possons was assistant superintendent. In 1886, the Possons brothers built an electric tricycle, equipping it with a Swan incandescent electric headlight, which could be switched on and off at will. In 1890, when the Brush Company was sold to Thomson-Houston Electric Company, they resigned their positions.

On July 27, 1888, Philip W. Pratt of Boston, Massachusetts, demonstrated an electric tricycle built for him by the Fred M. Kimball Company. The vehicle's 10 lead-acid cells, provided by the Electrical Accumulator Company, sent 20 volts to a 0.5-horsepower DC motor. The driver sat above the battery assemblage. The whole setup weighed about 300 pounds and had a top speed of 8 miles per hour. In the August 2 issue of the Boston magazine *Modern Light and Heat*:

> We received an invitation last Friday from a gentleman who is giving much attention to electric vehicles—Mr. P.W. Pratt of Boston—to take a ride on an electric tricycle that had just been completed for him by a well-known electrical manufacturing firm.

That same year, over in northern England, John Kemp Starley (nephew of the successful bicycle manufacturer, James Starley) assembled an electric tricycle at his Meteor Works in Coventry. The motor and accumulators were supplied by Elwell Parker of Wolverhampton, and the carriage itself was built by a local coachbuilder Henry Hollick. Unfortunately, the Starley e-trike was built at a time when the Locomotive Act of 1865 (the red flag law) was in force. In the United Kingdom, this law set a speed limit of 4 miles per hour in open country and 2 miles per hour in towns. The act required three drivers for each vehicle: two to travel in the vehicle and one to walk ahead carrying a red flag. So, to give his prototype a good public trial, Starley shipped it across the English Channel to Deauville, France, where it averaged 8 miles per hour. Strange how seven years before the Parisian inventor Trouvé had used a British Starley for his electric prototype, and now the British inventor had to go to France to test out his own device. But because of the speed limit, Starley relegated his prototype to the back of his Coventry works.

Another way to approach the challenge was to take a vehicle normally pulled by a horse and electrify it, as did Magnus Volk of Brighton, on the southeast coast of England. The son of a German clockmaker, Volk was born at 35 Western Road, Brighton, on October 19, 1851. Educated in the town, he was eventually apprenticed to a scientific instrument maker, but on the death of his father in 1869 he returned home to help his mother run the family business. Around 1879 Volk established the first telephone link in Brighton, to his friend William Jago's house in nearby Springfield Road, and in 1880 he fitted his own house with electric lights. The following year he opened a larger workshop at 25 Ditchling Rise and demonstrated a fire alarm that was connected to the police fire station at the Town Hall. After moving to 17 Gloucester Place in 1883, Volk used the Hammond Company's electric supply to light his new house and conceived the idea of a seafront railway using his now redundant generator; he built only one other railway, a short-lived venture at Aston Hall near Birmingham. Volk also fitted the Royal Pavilion with electric lights in 1883, and the following year he completed the illumination of the Dome, the Corn Exchange, the museum, the art gallery, the library and Pavilion grounds. All this eminently qualified him to attempt an electric motorcycle.

What was needed was a small, light vehicle that still had room for the bulky electric battery required to power the motor. The answer was a dog-cart, so called because of the large boot under the seat in which hunting dogs were carried to meets. The two-wheeled model of the dog-cart was ideal for the conversion Magnus had in mind. He went to see Job Park and his sons at the Sussex Coach Works in George Street, whose adverts boasted "Carriages of Every Description for sale or hire of the Latest and Most Fashionable Designed Fitted with All Modern Improvements. The Most Improved Buggies, with or without movable hind seat, also the Celebrated 'Beaufort' Cart."[10]

Park, for a price, agreed to specially modify of one of his dog-carts, which was to have a tiller-steered front wheel added instead of shafts, making it a tricycle. Volk finally decided on a 1.5-horsepower Immisch motor weighing as little as 40 pounds to be powered by a 16 EPS battery. He stowed the battery snugly in the boot under the seat (on which two couples could sit back-to-back). From the motor, he took the drive by Renold chain to a countershaft under the front footboard, and thence again by chain to a 4-foot-diameter toothed ring bolted through distance-pieces to the inside of the offside wheel. The third wheel was mounted well out in front on a forked cantilevered framework. A switch gave two speeds, which on a good level surface were designed to be 3.5 and 7 miles per hour, and of course there was a powerful brake—brakes on the two hind wheels enabled the driver to stop the dog-cart instantaneously.

Trials showed that on an asphalt road a speed of nine miles per hour could be obtained, whereas on a soft macadam road only 4 miles per hour was possible:

> Mr Volk whose electric railway is known to all visitors to Brighton, has constructed and electrically driven dogcart, which attracts a good deal of attention among the leisured crowds which throng the gay Sussex watering place.... But this vision of a country where all roads are paved with asphalt, and everyone travels on his own electric carriage at 40 miles an hour is not likely soon to be realised.[11]

1. Pioneers

Magnus Volk, Anna Volk, center, and her sister Deborah in October 1887 in the converted electric dogcart in which the inventor motored up and down the Parade at Brighton, England (Royal Pavilion & Museums, Brighton & Hove).

The headline of the article published in *The Electrician* on January 6, 1888, reads "Volk's Electric Dog-Cart for Ordinary Roads." A photo taken in October 1887 shows Magnus Volk, top-hatted and unusually spruce, in the driving seat, with one of his wife Anna's sisters (seventeen-year-old Deborah) beside him and his small son Bert perched up behind them; the e-dog-cart is parked in front of Volk's Brighton Electric Railway building.

According to Volk's son Conrad:

> If Magnus did in fact believe it would be more than a nine days' wonder, he was sadly mistaken. From among the hundreds of people who must have seen the vehicle gliding along the Madeira Road, not a single order was forthcoming. Perhaps for the young it was much too slow, and for older folk too "new-fangled," even dangerous. Whatever else may be said, it was certainly far ahead of its time. For Magnus, the last few months of 1887 must have been as depressing a period as he had ever experienced. Belated accounts of the dog-cart appeared in the local press, but the interest these aroused was sporadic and led nowhere.[12]

As Magnus Volk would write in 1932, "In 1887 I made my first motor-car driven by electricity, and used it on the King's Road and Madeira Drive,

Brighton. On this account I have been made a member of the Circle of Nineteenth Century Motorists."[13]

Some did not believe in rechargeable secondary batteries. John Vaughan-Sherrin of Codrington Road, Ramsgate, England, thought that the future of electric carriages and boats still lay in a primary battery that should be replaced each time it was discharged. To promote his zinc-carbon primary battery, Vaughan-Sherrin formed the Electric Tricycle, Carriage, Boat, and Machinery Syndicate Ltd. in 1889 and invited *The Electrical Engineer* to visit the premises:

> We have been up this week to 48, Eaglewharf Road, Hoxton, the offices of the Henry Rifled Arms Company, to inspect an electric tricycle and an electric launch driven by a new primary battery and motor devised by Mr. Vaughan-Sherrin, electrical engineer, of Ramsgate. We propose to simply say what we saw and what Mr. Vaughan-Sherrin said. We have seen primary batteries in scores rise, glitter for a moment, and fall, not to be heard of again. All we can say of Mr. Vaughan-Sherrin's battery at the present is that it is compact, evidently powerful, constant, and handy, and it has received very flattering reports from Prof. Silvanus Thompson, and Mr. Kempe, of the Post Office, and has, besides, received considerable attention from would-be users.
>
> The electric tricycle shown, or Bath chair rather, is a wickerwork chair on three india-rubber-tired wheels, with front steering. A tray is fitted by springs behind, and on this are placed two narrow boxes of cells about 2 ft. long and 8 in. or 10in. high, each containing nine cells of the new battery. A specially constructed and neat little motor is geared by chains to the tricycle driving wheel. The whole arrangement in the trial Bath chair is yet rather crude and rough, but the Bath chair goes, and goes very well, and the electric part of the arrangement certainly does not seem excessively large; in fact, is much about the size that the purchaser of an electric tricycle might expect it to be. We had a ride in this extemporised electric chair, and found it went along the level road at a very smart walking pace "some five miles an hour" and mounted the slight hills that were tried at a slow walking pace; in fact, did what an electric Bath chair should do. The price of the electric tricycle is to be only £30 complete, with motor and battery; and the number of people who will buy these novelties, even if the maintenance should be twice or three times as much as the small sum mentioned, and in spite of the joltings about of chemicals, may quite conceivably be large enough to employ a tricycle-battery motor works as a specialty—to say nothing of larger game of launches and tramcars hinted at.[14]

In 1892, Fulton Gardner of Chicago patented his ingenious idea for a tricycle in which the batteries were placed at various points around one or more of the wheels of the vehicle or in the tire: "By means of this construction I distribute the load more uniformly and in such manner as to offer the least possible resistance to propelling the vehicle, a wheel so constructed being of substantial uniform weight and operating somewhat after the manner of a fly-wheel."

Over in Italy, Count Giuseppe Carli, a wealthy textile entrepreneur and

1. Pioneers

(No Model.)

F. GARDNER.
ELECTRICALLY PROPELLED VEHICLE.

No. 473,871. Patented Apr. 26, 1892.

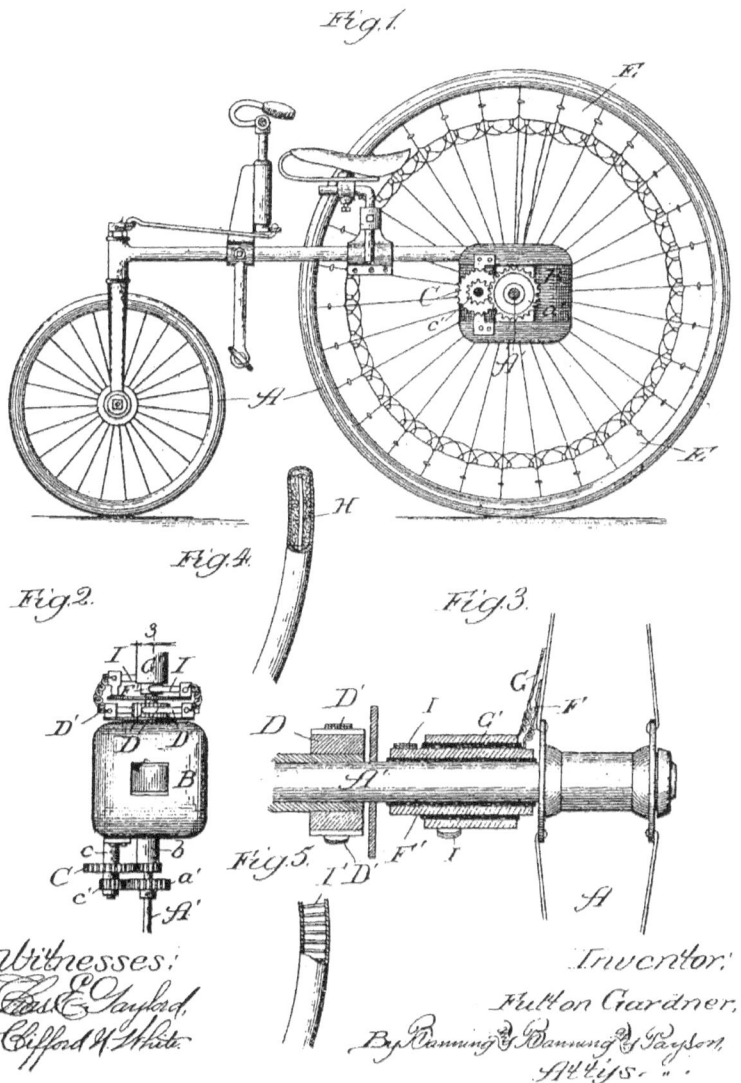

In 1892, Fulton Gardner of Chicago patented an electric tricycle, whereby the batteries were placed at various points around one or more of the wheels of the vehicle or in the tire.

philanthropist of Castelnuovo di Garfagnana, Tuscany, decided to assemble an electric tricycle. In this the count was helped by electrical engineer Francesco Boggio from Piedmont. With its 940-watt motor and ten small accumulators in rubber boxes, the converted 5.9-foot (1.8 m) two-seater dogcart weighed only 308 pounds (140 kg). Equipped with an impulsion box that held a system of rubber tension springs to produce an impetus on the axle for a run of 160 feet (49 m), Carli's tricycle was almost surely the first hybrid electric vehicle. Also equipped with electric lights, horn, brakes, safety fuses and inverter rotation, it was patented by the Ministry of Agriculture and Commerce in Rome.

On October 1, 1891, the local newspaper, *Corriere di Garfagnana*, reported, "With this new means of traction you drive the roads for up to ten hours at an extraordinary speed ... its future must be propitious. It is certainly a means to travel very cheaply."[15] The vehicle was also written up in the *Elettricità* journal in Milan and *Le Petit Journal* in Paris. In 1894, Count Carli and Boggio decided to enter their electric tricycle in the *Petit Journal* Horseless Carriages Contest from Paris to Rouen, held that July. Frustratingly, they were stopped at the border by over-patriotic French Customs officers. In 2009, a replica of this vehicle was built by students at the S. Simoni Superior Institute of Electricity and Electronics and the Francesco Vecchiacchi Technical College in Castelnuovo di Garfagnana.

During the spring of 1892, "Marquis Henri de Graffigny" (whose real name was Raoul Marquis, an amateur scientist and highly prolific journalist), searching for something new to write about, tested out his version of an electric tricycle around the city of Albert in the Somme. Staying close to the workshops where his tricycle had been built, de Graffigny used a 17.6-pound (8 kg) Trouvé motor switching between the lightweight primary battery or conventional pedaling to attain an average speed of 13.5 miles per hour on a level road and 6 miles per hour on steep ascents. He also made use of the chlorine-zinc flow battery design, invented by Charles Renard and Arthur Constantin Krebs, which was at the time propelling the famous dirigible airship *La France* above the skies of Paris. With this latter 44-pound battery, on a second trial (which lasted for five consecutive hours) the Graffigny tricycle covered almost 60 miles on the roads of the Somme Department.

The engineer Andrew Lawrence Riker was born at New York City on October 22, 1868, the son of William J. and Charlotte L. Riker. He was a descendant of Abraham Rycken, a native of Holland who settled in New Amsterdam in 1638. In 1884, at the age of sixteen, Riker began experimenting at home with electric vehicles. He continued his education and attended Columbia University for one year. In 1886, however, he dropped out so he could devote all his time to electrical and mechanical engineering. In 1888, he founded the Riker Electric Motor Company to build fans and industrial motors. Then, in 1894, he modified a Rudge Rotary tricycle with a 0.167-horsepower motor. Successful trials at 8 miles per hour and with a range of 30 miles encouraged Riker to set up a business, the Riker Electric Vehicle Company (based in Elizabethport, New Jersey), to make electric motors based on his patents, including his slotted armature and laminated field core designs. In 1895, he rigged two Remington bicycles together to create his four-wheeled "motor cycle," the battery of which weighed 135 pounds. Riker went on to make a full range of electric vehicles from 1895 to 1902, ranging from a light two-seat tricycle up to a five-ton truck.

In 1892, "Marquis Henri de Graffigny," whose real name was Raoul Marquis, was seen motoring this tricycle around the Somme region of France (Musée EDF Electropolis, Mulhouse).

Emil E. Keller, vice president and general manager of Westinghouse Machine Co., Pittsburgh, Pennsylvania, had already patented an electric railway trolley in 1891 (an electric perambulator with a hand-switch controller and speed-changing mechanism) when, with Fred Dagenhart, he proposed creating an entire fleet of electric tricycles for the World's Columbian Exhibition in Chicago during 1893. After all, George Westinghouse had won the contract to power the exhibition's lighting and electrical systems; more than two hundred thousand electric light bulbs were illuminated by Nikola Tesla's polyphase alternating current system. In the end, however, Keller only made two or three of the thousands of units that had been promised. Perhaps this was because the popular mode of transport for the Expo was electric boat. Managed by General C.H. Barney, a fleet of 55 launches made 66,975 trips during the six and a half months of the exhibition, carrying 1,026,346 passengers 200,925 miles (323,357 km) and earning $314,000 for the World's Fair organizers. Their greatest test came on Chicago Day, when 622 trips (with each trip being three miles) were made by fifty boats. Six of these boats averaged more than 40 miles (65 km), carrying on each trip about 40 people. There were no fewer than 25,000 passengers carried that day alone.[16]

The mid–1890s saw the publication of the world's first science-fiction periodicals, called dime novels, which enthralled millions of readers with tales of fantastic inventions and adventures. Among the heroes of these books was Jack Wright, created by "Noname" (the pseudonym of Luis Senarens, the so-called "American Jules Verne"). Among his adventures one finds *Jack Wright, the Boy Inventor and His Electric Tricycle Boat; Or, The Treasure of the Sun Worshipers* (1892). Then there was Electric Bob, a 10-year-old who lived near (but not in) New York City. He was brilliant, of course, and capable of creating the most advanced technology possible, but, unlike the other boy inventors, he did not build his own equipment and weaponry; instead, he drew up the blueprints in very detailed fashion and then sent them to the most efficient and skillful shops to construct for him. Among his adventures is *Electric Bob's Big Bicycle; Or, The Nerviest Boy in the World* (1893) by Robert T. Toombs. Here Bob's "Big Bicycle" is electrically operated with a canopy, storage space for food and equipment, and steel-covered tires; its only weapon is that it can be electrified, but Bob also carries his "electric pistol," which shoots lethal bullets at extremely high speeds. Last but not least, there was Frank Reade, Jr., who used a whole range of gadgetry, including electric airships, helicopters, one-person battery-powered electric flying suits (complete with wings), "electric cannon" (pneumatic machine guns), and an electric bicycle. One of these dime novels was titled *From Tropic to Tropic; or, Frank Reade, Jr.'s Latest Tour with His Bicycle Car*, published in 1895. Such stories were known as Edisonades (the term inspired by Thomas A. Edison of Menlo Park, the famous inventor of electrical equipment including a battery-electric car and designs for electric airliners). Good science-fiction is usually based on reality, and various real inventors continued to take on the challenge of constructing electric bicycles and tricycles.

In 1895 Charles A. Barrows of Willimatic, Connecticut, designed an electric tricycle with a combination of forward drive and steering wheel. Its primary batteries enabled it to travel more than 100 miles. Sufficient electrolytes could be stored, it was claimed, to run some 500 miles. Barrows set up a company to manufacture his tricycles, although it was short lived.

On September 19, 1895, 23-year-old Ogden Bolton, Jr., made a patent application for "an electrical bicycle." His novel idea involved the use of a custom rear wheel, with the motor serving as an integral part of its hub. The patent primarily covers construction details, but it does note that the motor would be wound to use high currents at a low voltage. Bolton's example of 100 amps at 10 volts would have resulted in more than 1 horsepower of output power, assuming a relatively efficient motor. This amount is adequate for most bicycle travel. However, since no pedals were provided for assisting with start-up and hill climbing, and since there was no reduction gearing, the motor must have been able to produce a very high torque. To control the motor, Bolton simply connected a single battery via a rheostat. By considering the types of batteries then available, as well as the amount of power dissipated by the rheostat, it is safe to conclude that the driving range before recharging was rather short.

At the time, Ogden Bolton, Jr., was working at his Liverpool-born father's Canton Steel Company, manufacturers of high-quality steel. Based on patents taken out in Pennsylvania by Ogden Bolton, Sr., the firm produced several grades of steel, tempered for special purposes and designated by colored labels. The "Canton" brand (yellow label) was best suited for the hardware trade, machinists and blacksmiths. The "Canton Soft" (blue label) was adapted for oil-well drilling and tools subject to constant concussions. The "Canton Hard" (dark red label) was used for taps, dies, reamers and lathe tools. The "Canton Extra Hard" and "Canton Choice" were designed for other specific uses. Bolton may therefore have seen his electric bicycle as a new outlet for the family's steel production.

The Canton Steel Company vice president was Englishman Reginald Bulley, the older Bolton's brother-in-law. Not only a talented metallurgist, Bulley also had an excellent tenor voice, with a love of Wagnerian music, and his high-wheeler bicycle was the first to appear in Canton's streets.

At the time he applied for his seminal patent, Ogden Bolton, Jr., lived with his brother Louis; the latter worked at the Gilliam Manufacturing Company, which, among other items, made bicycle seats. To make the electric tricycle, Bolton may well have gone to the local Monnot family firm, owned by Charles Monnot and his three sons, who had a bicycle shop in Canton that included "Developing Inventor's Mechanical Ideas made a Speciality (Communications in this branch Strictly Confidential) Wooden and Metallic Patterns Made to Order"[17] (these models would then be presented to the U.S. Patent Office). The Monnots themselves had obtained patents for several bicycles, including a convertible tricycle with pneumatic "sulky" wheels, and were active members of the Canton Bicycle Club, part of the League of American Wheelmen's Ohio Division. Bolton and the Monnots may well have contacted the Willard Storage Battery Company, recently established by Theodore A. Willard in Cleveland to produce small lightweight batteries for use by dentists and physicians, in Edison phonographs, and for lighting railroad cars. Alternatively, they may have gone for the Columbia dry cell just produced by the National Carbon Company. Unfortunately, detailed research has not revealed the outcome of the e-bike.

By 1899, Ogden Bolton, Jr., had married an opera singer called Esta Ellesworthy and moved to East Ninth Street. He continued to work for the Canton Steel Company, and in 1900 he patented a bread and biscuit crusher. When, in 1902, his uncle sold the family company to the Crucible Steel Company in Syracuse, New York, Bolton disappeared from Canton's historical record.[18]

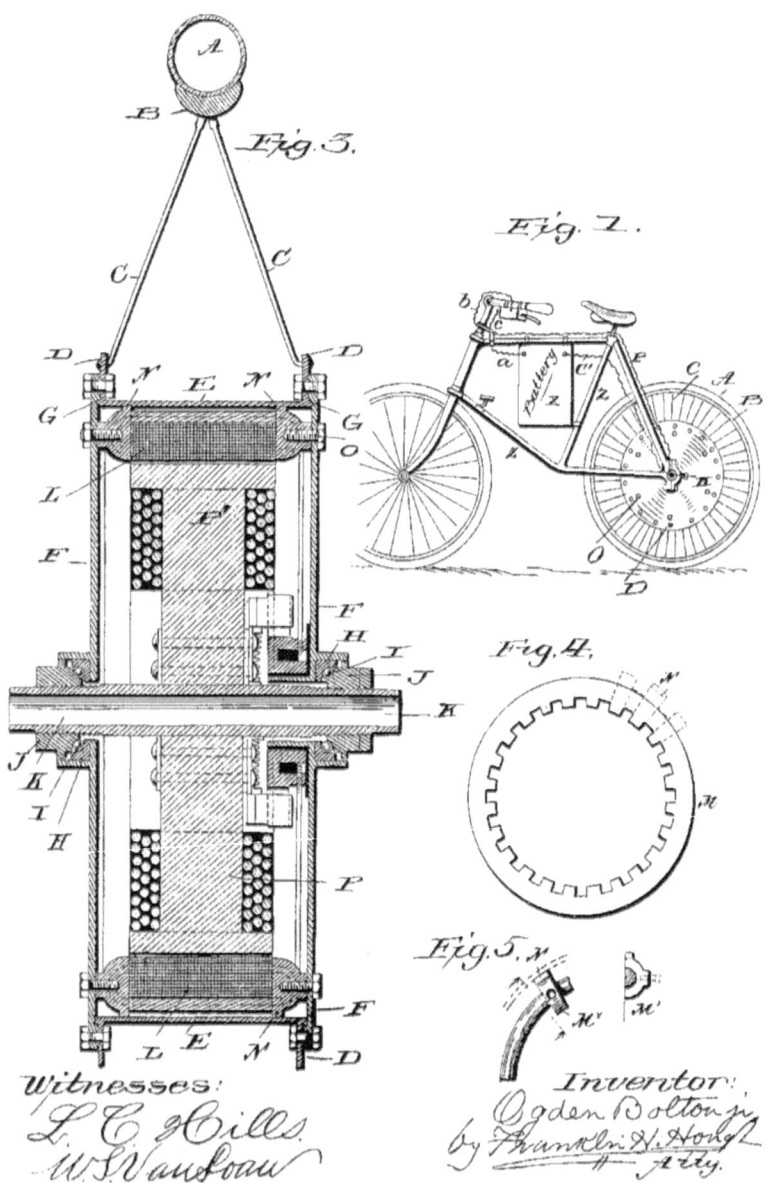

In 1895, Ogden Bolton, Jr., of Canton, Ohio, patented this electric bicycle with its hub motor and frame-slung battery.

Each and every pioneer of electric motorcycles has come from a different walk of life, and nothing could be more different than the life of Dr. Hosea Wait Libbey and his Velocipedrome. Libbey was born in Chichester, Merrimack, New Hampshire, in 1835 to Moses and Huldah Libbey. He claimed to have traced his ancestry back to the year 1574. Libbey was educated at Boston public schools and attended two courses of lectures, but he was too poor to go on and graduate. He then began to look into the herbal medicines used by North American Indian tribes such as the Shawnee: a wide variety of roots, barks, leaves, seeds, berries, flowers, and stalks. While some plants were used fresh, others were dried and powdered or prepared as liquids, salves, or poultices. At the age of nineteen, in 1854, Libbey went to Sandusky, Ohio, and tried to set up his unorthodox practice. Being refused advertisement by a newspaper in Oberlin, Ohio, he started his own paper there known as *The Oberlin New Era*, which destroyed the other newspaper in two years.

Before long Libbey had established "hygiene-tariums," or dispensaries, in Boston and Cleveland, 640 miles away from each other. He alternated his surgeries, working at his Cleveland dispensary for the first 18 days of each month and at his Boston dispensary for the rest of the month. Despite accusations that he was a quack, before long Dr. Libbey was mailing his remedies and seeds across the United States, performing cures without ever seeing his patients. In 1863, he published *The Indian Medical Infirmary and National Bath Rooms*, with a sequel titled *A Complete Guide to Invalids* released two years later. Among his products was an Indian hair restorative. This was during the American Civil War, during which Libbey served as a physician to the wounded soldiers of the Union. In 1866, he was charged with killing a woman, Lepha J. Houghton, while attempting to perform an abortion. Libbey was tried and convicted of manslaughter and sentenced to eight years of hard labor. While in prison he was visited by numerous female supporters, and after only six weeks he was released on a perjury petition signed by the trial judge. He subsequently resumed his successful practice. Though his name periodically resurfaced in newspaper accounts of lawsuits, arrests for theft, and even the auction of his home and goods to settle debts, the wealthy Dr. Libbey continued with what seem to have been profitable practices in Cleveland and Boston.

From the 1880s Libbey also entered into the new field of invention. His first patent, for a meat broiler, was obtained in 1881. By the time he died in Boston in 1900, he had accumulated 118 patents, with another 49 pending. These ranged from a cartridge shell (1886); a combined sleeper and railway car (1889); seats, heaters and life-saving apparatus for streetcars (1890); a waterproof blanket (1891); an attachment for operating telephone call-bells (1893); and an automatic aerial railroad (1893). Then came Libbey's electric bicycle, which he called a Velocipedrome. It employed a primary battery

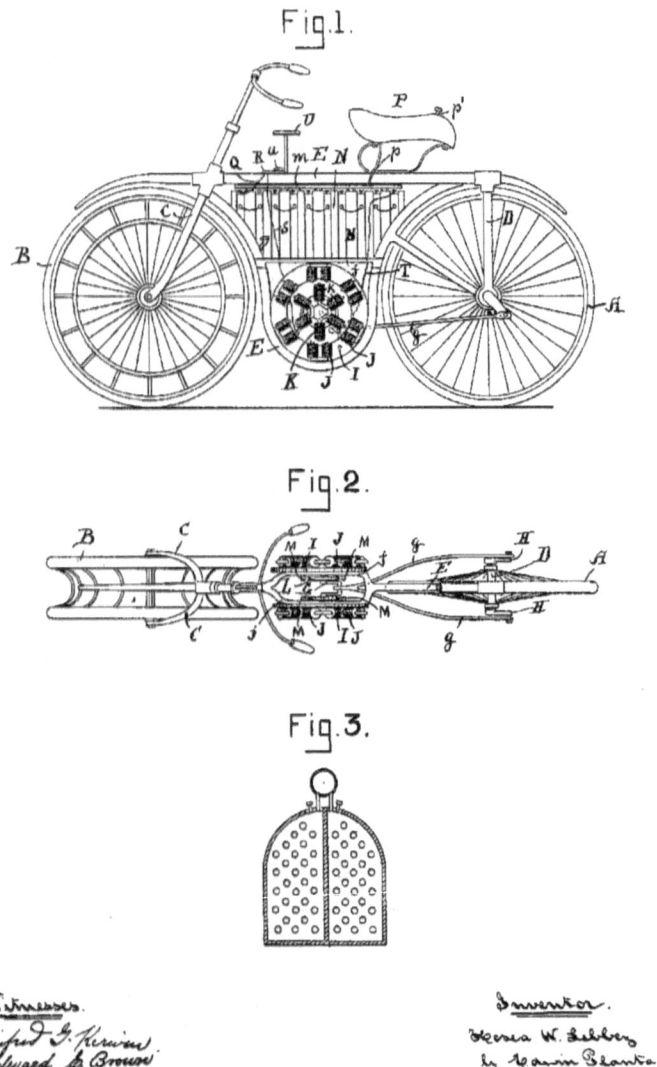

Above and opposite: In 1897, Dr. Hosea Wait Libbey of Boston was a naturalist doctor and inventor (from *The Libby Family in America, 1602–1881* [B. Thurston & Co: Portland, ME (1882)]). His Velocipedrome used two motors, either in place of the pedals or mounted over the rear wheel and connected by standard chain. It had a double wheel either on the front or at the rear, probably to help stabilize the extra weight. By using multiple motors, he hoped to provide a backup in case one motor failed.

placed in the tubes of the bike powering a hub-mounted double electric motor, which powered the rear axle via a twin-pushrod system. The battery fluid was controlled by a tap, using the same electricity for a front lamp. On May 3, 1896, the Cleveland *Plain Dealer* reported that sixty-year-old Libbey had publicly exhibited his bicycle at his home (particularly to a succession of ladies) and at the roller-skating rink; he was next planning to make a ride along Lake Erie from Cleveland to Conneaut, a distance of 71 miles, and maybe then on to Boston:

> Those who have formed an idea that the forthcoming trip to Boston is to be a feat of strength are mistaken as to the true intent of the inventor. The object is to demonstrate that one or more persons can propel a carriage of this kind without fatigue. The inventor and builder have tested every part of it thoroughly, and are sanguine in the belief that every emergency has been provided for. The first day will tell the tale. It will go to Conneaut or go to pieces.

History has lost the details of Libbey's pioneering ride. But in 1897 he received three consecutive patents for electric bicycles. The first used a motor in place of the pedals to drive a double rear wheel via cranks and connecting rods. The other versions used two motors, either in place of the pedals or mounted over the rear wheel and connected by standard chain. All three models had a double wheel either on the front or at the rear, probably to help stabilize the extra weight. By using multiple motors, he likely hoped to provide a back-up in case one motor failed. In all versions, Libbey used a split battery, so as to offer a two-speed control system. Interestingly, his U.S. Patent 596 2723 on December 28, 1897, was witnessed by two women: Laura E. Hayward and Winifred G. Kerwin. The ingenious doctor spent the last three years of his life inventing various devices, including an automobile or automobile truck to be propelled by compressed air, liquid air, or compressed or liquefied gases, as well as a street car wheel with an elastic tread that would run noiselessly upon the rail while at the same time having greater adhesion and less friction than wheels with metal treads.[19]

A bicycle railroad was developed by William Boynton of McMorris Park, New York, whereby a boat-shaped in-line two-wheeler deriving its power from an overhead electric cable had a potential speed of 100 miles per hour. In 1897, a prototype system was built to run from Bellport to the Sound across Long Island, but this project was short lived.

Over in France, in 1895, the Marquis Jules-Albert de Dion, Georges Bouton, and Bouton's brother-in-law Charles Trépardoux of Paris joined the electric tricycle craze, but not for long, as they were soon wooed away by the gas engine. However, in 1896, Charles Theryc and Alfred Oblasser of Paris made a further improvement by increasing the power and efficiency of a brushed planetary-geared hub motor so that it spun faster than the bicycle wheel. The sun-gear was a 10T, the single planet-gear was a 24T, and the ring-gear was a 56T, for a total revolutions-per-minute reduction of 5.6:1.

In Paris, Louis Antoine Kriéger had begun designing and building electric automobiles in 1894. By 1898, when interest in electric-powered vehicles increased in France, Kriéger organized the Kriéger Company of Electric Vehicles (Société des Voitures Electriques Systeme Kriéger). One spin-off was an electric tricycle for invalids—a world first.

While these pioneers were at work, large cities all around the world were "drowning in horse manure." In order for these cities to function, thousands of horses were necessary to transport both people and goods. In 1900, there were more than 11,000 hansom cabs on the streets of London alone. There were also several thousand horse-drawn buses, each needing 12 horses per day, resulting in a staggering total of more than 50,000 horses transporting people around the city each day. This problem came to a head when, in 1894, the *Times* predicted, "In 50 years, every street in London will be buried under nine feet of manure." This became known as the "Great Horse Manure Crisis of 1894."

In 1898 the first international inter-urban planning conference was held in New York, bringing together world leaders and problem solvers; its major theme was the problem of horse manure. Although the conference was meant to run for ten days, they closed the doors after only three days, as delegates could see no easy solution.

A major breakthrough came with the development of the cable car and the electric trolley car in the late 1880s. Traction companies were quick to substitute mechanical power for animal power on their streetcar lines. Writing in *Popular Science Monthly* in 1892, U.S. Commissioner of Labor Carroll D. Wright maintained that electric power was not only cheaper than horsepower but also far more beneficial to the city from the perspective of health and safety. But private transport—single riders on horses—presented another challenge. On average, a horse will produce between 15 and 35 pounds of manure per day. On Saturday, July 25, 1896, after months of organizing by cyclists and advocates for good roads, residents took to the streets in downtown San Francisco, inspired by the possibilities of the nation's wonderful new machine, the bicycle. The lone pioneers of battery-electric tricycles and bicycles must also have seen the potential—that of cities full of electric wheelers, reducing the manure problem to almost zero.

In 1892, Paul Decauville (whose Essonne-based company built narrow-track railway equipment and bicycles), always seeking other outlets for his new workshops, announced that he would be building bicycles and tricycles with electric propulsion. Among his products was the "Bertoux seat," invented by Jean Bertoux, chief gunsmith with the 46th Infantry Regiment in Fontainebleau: this was a seat mounted on a third wheel attached to the bicycle, which made it possible to transport a person or a parcel—in other words, *the sidecar*. Regrettably, Decauville stopped making electric cycles in 1900, due to a lack of interested customers.[20]

Over in the English Midlands, Thomas Hugh Parker, son of the founder of the Electric Construction Company, was, like his father, a brilliant innovator and inventor. He had shown an early interest in powered vehicles and claimed to have had a battery-powered car running as early as 1884. In 1896, Parker, based in Bushbury, near Wolverhampton, developed a two-seater electric tricycle: the Bushbury Electric Dog-Cart. Reins were used to steer the vehicle because A. B. Blackburn, the works manager, was very fond of horses, used to follow hounds, and preferred to ride to the works on horseback, so the vehicle had to be as similar as possible to a horse-drawn one! The motor controller was operated by means of a sliding seat. Walter "Wattie" Wall, employed at the works, who often drove the dog-cart, later stated that this arrangement worked quite well when the movement consisted of sliding the seat backward, but not so well when it was necessary to pull it forward. This difficulty was overcome by screwing a half-egg-shaped wooden block to the seat. It rested between the driver's legs and provided the necessary lock between him and the seat.

The Bushbury could travel up to 12 miles per hour on a level tarmac surface. The Faure-King–type accumulators, manufactured by the Electrical Power Storage Co. Ltd., would carry it no more than twenty miles without recharging. There were two driving wheels and one steering wheel in front. The two-pole motor was geared by means of a Renold chain to the driving axle; it was carried by a frame, articulated at one end to the road axle-bearing cases and at the other end slung by an elastic attachment to the underside of the foot board. In driving, the distance between the motor and road axles could be adjusted to compensate for wear in the chain. The driving wheels were 39 inches in diameter and the steering wheel 45 inches, made of steel with solid rubber tires. The switch gear consisted of a reversing and a controlling switch, placed under the driver's seat; the former was manipulated by a vertical lever on the right, while the controlling switch allowed several different arrangements of cell connection. The reversing facility could be used for checking the speed of the cart on long descents.

Having tested his Bushbury on trials up and down the steep hills between Newbridge House, his home in Tettenhall village and the Bushbury Works, Tom Parker brought it down to the Metropolis, where he motored it through London with Alexander Duff, 6th Earl Fife, as passenger. In 1896, the trike was entered in a race for self-propelled road vehicles, from the Crystal Palace, London, to Birmingham. This was organized by *The Engineer* magazine, and there was a 1,000-guinea prize for the winner. There were 72 entries, but on the appointed day only five runners were present, and so the race was cancelled, which resulted in a lot of bad publicity. The Bushbury, however, was highly commended, in horse-like terms:

> Thus three speeds are provided, practically corresponding to the paces of a horse, viz., walking, slow trot, and fast trot. An electric brake enables the speed to be checked when descending gradients, and in addition there is a hand brake actuated by the foot, capable of bringing the car to a standstill within a distance of a few feet. It will thus be seen that the cart will do about as much work in the day as one horse for every day in the year, but by having a spare set of accumulators it will do as much as two horses. A person using a car of this description, and living within a few miles of an electric supply station, could easily at small cost, say not more than 3d. per unit, arrange for charging his accumulators, which could be sent and returned by rail. Most electric lighting companies using continuous current would gladly entertain any chance of increasing their day load. We have no doubt that the Bushbury Car will be largely patronised by medical men and country residents of limited means, for whom it seems very suitable.[21]

With no orders received, Tom Parker's dog-cart was eventually broken up at the works, and the motor was used for many years to drive an ash-hoist in the company's boiler house.[22]

In 1894, Walter C. Bersey, a brilliant 20-year-old electrical engineer based in London, patented an "improvement in electrically operated common road vehicles" (UK231,523), allowing horse-drawn vehicles to be adapted for electric propulsion. Two years later, with another electrician, Desmond Gerald Fitzgerald, Bersey patented "improvements in voltaic batteries," which used dry materials to avoid the problem of electrolyte sloshing. In his book, *Electrically-propelled Carriages* (1898), there is an illustration of a vehicle made for Swedish-born chemical engineer John Gustaf Adolf Rhodin of Clifton Hall, Manchester, who had also patented improvements in plates for secondary voltaic batteries. This finely upholstered one-off was not an outrigger-stabilized bicycle, but rather a three-wheeler (probably converted

John Gustaf Adolf Rhodin of Clifton Hall, Manchester, asked Walter Bersey of London to build him this tricycle, with motive power from a fourth wheel (Institution of Engineering and Technology).

from a horse-drawn vehicle) with a motor-driven fourth wheel attached to the back to propel it. One can see the elliptical leaf springs on the axle. No braking system is apparent; presumably before conversion the vehicle relied on a horse to stop it. Bersey put most of his energies into building up the 77-strong fleet of the London Electrical Cab Company Ltd., nicknamed "Hummingbirds" due to the humming noise they made.

Another British firm that had entered the Crystal Palace race was New & Mayne Ltd. based in Woking, Surrey. To compensate for the battery weight, Andrew George New and Arthur James Mayne sought to make the vehicle lighter, so their rickshaw and dog-cart tricycles used aluminum where possible. The accumulators were suspended from a very strong under-framing between the front and the hind axles, thus keeping the center of gravity low and enabling the box containing the cells to be unshipped in a few minutes. But this enterprise was also short lived.

In 1897 Henry F. Eastman of Cleveland, Ohio, working for the Winton Bicycle Company, teamed up with Hector J. Hayes to build their first vehicle—a tricycle electric automobile with a body made entirely of sound-insulated lightweight sheet metal. It had three forward speeds and a reverse, with a lever for a motor brake. This model proved best for road conditions and was easier to steer out of ruts and vehicle tracks. Hayes and Eastman patented the design and formed the Eastman Automobile Company in 1898. The battery used in the Eastman Electro-Cycle was a prototype made by Cleveland's Willard Storage Battery Co., and it enabled the vehicle to travel about twelve miles per charge. Eastman and Hayes spent several weeks in Detroit, Michigan, visiting the Edison Electric Company to have their battery recharged under Thomas Edison's personal supervision. But when they realized the limitations on battery range, they reverted to steam power. Hayes ultimately became friends with Henry Ford, and various Hayes firms would later supply fenders for Ford's Model T gasoline automobile.

Gordon John Scott and William S. Janney of Philadelphia, Pennsylvania, having developed a single-phase omnibus electric motor combining DC and polyphase AC advantages, set up a company to exploit its applications from streetcars to office fans. Included in this enterprise was an electric "velocipede" in which, instead of a battery, the pedals spun a generator (dynamo), and the power from that dynamo drove a small motor (US598819). Here was a prototype of the pedal-electric bike.[23]

At this time, one way to train racing cyclists was to pace them using special bicycles built to accommodate two, four, or even more cyclists. One of these devices—the 23-foot-long, 305-pound "Oriten" built by Charles Metz of Waltham, Massachusetts—involved no less than ten cyclists on the same machine! But maybe there was a more economical way of doing this? So thought Pierre Alexandre Darracq. Darracq was born into a Basque family living in Bordeaux. From successfully designing a sewing machine that won a gold medal at the 1889 Paris Exhibition, Darracq progressed to manufacturing material for wine cellars; then, in 1891, he teamed up with Jean Aucoc to manufacture bicycles with the brand name *Gladiator*. Four years later, Darracq decided to convert a tandem (a bicycle built for two riders) to electric power, believing this would be cheaper than paying for teams of pacers on multi-seat tandems. He was assisted by Adolphe G. Pingault, a French electrical engineer, and Clovis Clerc, former administrator of the Vélodrome d'Hiver, an indoor bicycle racing track and stadium (velodrome) on the rue Nélaton, not far from the Eiffel Tower. Working with Darracq, Pingault first designed and tested an electric bicycle during the winter of 1894/1895 before tackling a tandem.

The latter was powered by two men, using a command chain and pedals developing approximately 23 feet, and by two electric motors mounted on the same shaft, on each side of the rear wheel, commanding a wooden pulley that acted directly on the tire. The 2.8-kilowatt motors were powered by four batteries enclosed in ebonite boxes placed between the legs of cyclists and

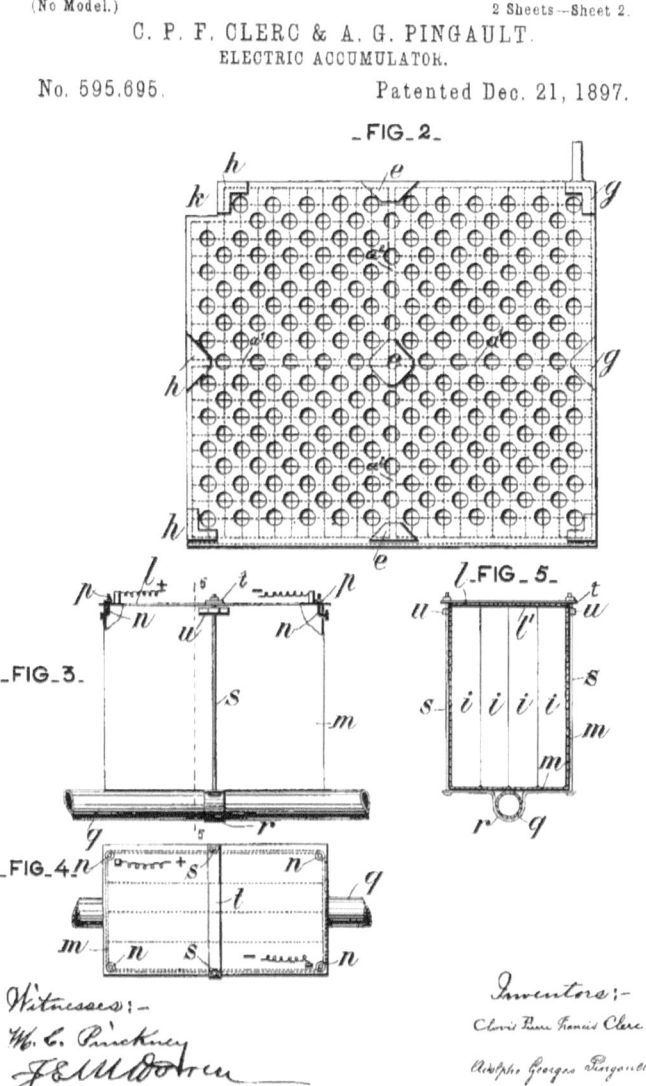

1899: **The lightweight battery developed by French engineer Adolphe G. Pingault, which provided the energy for his electric pacer tandem.**

coupled at will, depending on the speed to be achieved, by means of a switch mounted on the right handle grips, easily turning around its axis in order to get the contacts corresponding to each combination. The lightweight battery provided up to 25 watts per kilogram of weight and one hour's riding.

The appearance of this remarkable machine in the middle of triplets and quintuplets (bicycles built for three and four riders), hitherto regarded as the *ne plus ultro* of training, was initially frowned upon by the coaches, who did not hesitate to question the three boxes of airtight energy and did not spare their expressions of contempt: "A simple tandem proposes to eliminate the quintuplet? Nonsense!" But once the humming machine had left the others far behind, opinions rapidly changed, as the cycle industry realized the advantage offered by an electric tandem whose speed could be regulated. The Pingault electric tandem, equipped with Michelin tires, was demonstrated at the Buffalo velodrome at Neuilly-sur-Seine, Paris, in July 1896, and later, in November, on the British track at Wood Green Cycle Track in north London. The strength of the tires was a major problem for the manufacturers because the speeds reached were becoming higher and the tires suffered a lot on the bends, and more particularly on the shorter tracks where they were, in fact, tighter. This was a very simple machine: a mixed device driven by both the force of the pedals and electricity as a complementary force.

At the Stanley Cycle Show in 1896 in London, England, bicycle manufacturer Humber, which had merged with La Société des Vélocipedes Clément and La Société des Cycles Gladiator, also exhibited a Pingault-style electric tandem bicycle whose speed control was achieved by a resistance placed across the handlebars (the prototype twistgrip?). The number of battery boxes had been increased to four, and the motor was placed further back. The machines were fragile and their transport from one velodrome to another required a lot of attention. A machine that had been damaged during the trip would be unable to race upon arrival.

On Good Friday, 1897, the Pingault electric tandem was again demonstrated at the Catford Cycle Track in southeast London, stunning an overcrowded grandstand of spectators, beating all world records up to 100 miles. The machine was fitted with a small lever to adjust the electric power to suit the speed required by the riders. The riders pedaled an exceptionally high gear aided by the electric motor. However, the weight of the accumulators made steering tricky and increased the danger in the event of a crash.

On May 22, 1897, when new trials of the Pingault e-tandem were conducted at the woodblock-paved Vélodrome de la Seine, with the Jallu brothers in the saddles, the brother behind was no longer seated as on a classic tandem; instead, he occupied a much more rear position in order to better shelter the stayer. This design proved worthwhile because the Jallus completed the kilometer in 57.8 seconds and 10 kilometers in 10 minutes, 0.6 seconds—both new world records. The reporter of the daily newspaper *Le Journal* commented, "In spite of all their efforts neither Linton nor Champion can follow this train."[24]

One ace cyclist who benefited from the electric tandems was Albert Champion of France, who was paced around the velodromes of Berlin, Dresden,

In 1899, electric tandems were capable of moving at 37.3 mph (60 kph) around the velodromes of Europe and the United States (National Motor Museum, Beaulieu).

Hannover, Leipzig, Cologne, Hamburg, Frankfurt and Antwerp. Champion was accompanied by three electric tandems ridden by Dacier, Jalabert, Hunter and/or Lefranc. Everywhere he went, the crowds were dazzled.[25] In 1898, paced by an electric tandem, Champion covered the 1,000 meters of the Parc des Princes in 56 seconds (the previous record was set by the Englishman John Platt-Betts in 58.6 seconds). "On level ground we know no other automobile system apart from the Bollée which is faster. It represents a speed of more than 64 kph."[26] During the 1900 season Champion raced behind motor-powered tandems on outdoor board velodromes in cities from Boston to New York and down the Eastern Seaboard to Atlanta.

It is very likely that at one of these velodromes, at least two electric tandems would have had an unofficial head-to-head race, just to see whose was faster. If so, it would have been the birth of circuit motor racing.

Patents for the Pingault tandem had been bought by the British Motor Syndicate, as Gladiator had already become part of Harry Lawson's empire. Alexandre Darracq, who had now created a firm to build automobiles, felt he could go even faster and built an electric triplet, known as *la triplette Darracq-Gladiator*. It was tested around the Seine Velodrome with three riders on board: Demester, Déneau and Vonin (Ninov), who was also the mechanic. The prototype covered 6.2 miles in 9 minutes and 45 seconds.

1899: In the photographer's studio ace cyclist Jimmy Walters behind an electric tandem. The two photos differ in the extension of the rear framework, most likely for stability reasons. Photographer Jules Beau was one of the world's first sports photographers (Bibliothèque nationale de France).

Although it reached an impressive top speed of 37 miles per hour, the Darracq triplette was only able to improve the record by a fraction of a second. Frustrated, like so many of his contemporaries, Darracq turned to the gasoline engine and went on to build a stable of victorious racing automobiles. On the cycle tracks as well, the Dion gasoline-engine tricycle soon became the standard pacer machine. Albert Champion went on to incorporate the Albert Champion Company in Boston to make porcelain spark plugs for gas automobiles. Three years later he founded the Champion Ignition Company in Flint, Michigan.

Meantime, other inventors had continued to innovate. In 1898, a rear-wheel-drive electric bicycle, which used a driving belt along the outside edge of the wheel, was patented by Commodore Mathew Joseph Steffens of Chicago, Illinois. Steffens, of German origin, was a highly successful society photographer, using an improved daguerreotype system, with an electrically equipped studio and darkroom. He had also applied for a patent for a "photographist"—an automatic photo machine that would take a photo and process it in 20 seconds. But Steffens regarded his electric bicycle, like his private steam yacht, as a hobby.

Another inventor was John Schnepf of New York. Schnepf had already conceived of an improved pneumatic door-lock opener and a machine for cleaning ships when, in February 1899, he obtained U.S. Patent 627,066 for a rear-wheel friction "roller-wheel"–style drive electric bicycle. In 1898, Albert Hänsel of Zeitz, in Saxony-Anhalt, Germany, created a lady's e-bike, the battery of which could be recharged during downhill pedaling or regenerative pedaling.

In 1899 in Russia, Hippolyte Vladimirovich Romanov (no close relation to the imperial family) designed and exhibited the first domestic electric car along the streets of Saint Petersburg. During the next fifteen years, Romanov built eight different electric vehicles, including a tricycle van. The Douma (parliament), with its vested interest in horse power, refused him money to go into production.

Eduardo Vedovelli's firm at 160 rue Saint Charles, Paris 15ème, was the first to manufacture components for electric streetcars: insulators, tensioners, switches, circuit breakers, surge arresters and other specific parts for trolleys. For example, the company made insulators measuring from 1 or 2 inches to 3.5 inches. In 1899, with Charles Marie Edouard Priestley, Vedovelli electrified an elegant dog-cart. Designed for two people, comfortably installed, it could accommodate two others by deploying the front apron that turns into a seat. The batteries gave the Vedovelli model a range of up to 50 miles (80 km). To recharge, a small 1.75-horsepower (about 1,300 watts) Dion-Bouton petrol engine, carried in a trunk at the back of the dog-cart, powered a dynamo to provide a current of 10 amps at 110 volts. This unit weighed 308 pounds (140 kg). Vedovelli exhibited the electric dog-cart at the 1900 Universal Exhibition while also supplying the electrical equipment and lighting for the Palace of Electricity.

Enter Charles Mildé. In 1878, Mildé and his father had presented an ingenious electric bell and clock at the Paris Universal Exposition and were

In 1899, Charles Marie Edouard Priestley assisted Eduardo Vedovelli in electrifying an elegant dogcart. Inside were two small crystal flower vases to take the latest fragrant blooms (Musée EDF Electropolis, Mulhouse).

awarded a silver medal. They had earned another silver medal at the 1881 Paris International Electrical Exhibition. In 1882, Mildé created "Charles Mildé, Fils et Cie" in the rue Laugier, Paris 17ème, manufacturing and installing electrical equipment. In 1897, Mildé installed a 3-horsepower electric motor on a horseless carriage. It weighed more than a ton, with a range of 31 miles for a speed of 9 miles per hour. Mildé took part in various competitions, including one organized by the newborn French Automobile Club. In 1900, taking advantage of the sudden enthusiasm for electric vehicles caused by the 65.792-miles-per-hour (105.882 kph) record of Camille Jénatzy in his electric automobile called *La Jamais Contente*, Charles Mildé launched his new model: a tricycle whose single front wheel supported a circular plate on which were mounted a 65-pound Greffe series-wound motor and three batteries of 5 cells each. Nicknamed "the electric pony" because of its power (equivalent to that of the animal) and steering handle (which resembled reins), the Mildé tricycle was not really an aesthetic success and its stability seemed very precarious. In the 1900 catalog, the 2.50m tiller-steered tricycle car, with its pneumatic-tired, wire-spoked wheels "Type 5," could be purchased for a price of 4,500 francs, including a light, removable canopy in rubberized canvas; a surrey; a leather hood; a 40-cell, 65-amp-hour replacement battery; and even a box of tools: "It is the most economical vehicle for a businessman going about in big cities, alone or accompanied."[27] With a 6-speed gearbox (4 for forward and 2 for reverse) hand-controlled at the side, the maximum speed of this machine was 18 miles per hour, but the 30-mile range at a reduced 12 miles per hour proved a disappointment to the clientele, even if it cost less than a pony!

The early 1900s saw the introduction of the electric delivery truck by many businesses, mostly four-wheeled versions. However, there were exceptions. In 1903, Schuckertwerke in Nuremburg, Germany, which was run by electrical engineer Johann Schuckert, a friend of Edison, produced several

In 1900 Charles Mildé, Jr., of Paris electrified this tricycle with its horizontal steering wheel. It came with a light removable canopy in rubberized canvas; a surrey; a leather hood; a 40-cell 65-amp-hour replacement battery; and even a box of tools (Musée EDF Electropolis, Mulhouse).

electric delivery tricycles for the Bavarian postal authorities. They were equipped with both a foot and an electric brake. Because of their greater speed, they were used for "Eilsendüngen" (express delivery); later Schuckert became part of Siemens. An electric cargo three-wheeler was developed by William G. Wagenhals of Detroit, Michigan. Wagenhals, a railway engineer by profession, had not only designed a three-rail system for the New York Central but also invented the first working electric headlight for automobiles in the Motor City. Some 200 Wagenhals three-wheeler horseless trucks, with their 800-pound capacity, were built between 1910 and 1914, when the firm switched to gasoline engines.

In 1901, in Germany, a Reichspost delivery e-tricycle was used on a route of roughly 4 miles (6.4 km) in the city of Munich that included 27 mailboxes, which all had to be emptied 15 times a day. Therefore the vehicle, with a weight of 948 pounds (430 kg), could be equipped with a battery-vehicle ratio of only 30 percent. But the batteries could not cope with continually accelerating from a standstill position: their life span was only a quarter of what had been promised, so the economical operation did not seem possible. When, however, the three-wheeler was transferred to Stadtverbindungsdienst (bulk mail transport service) in 1903, where the stopping-and-starting operations were not necessary, it was perfectly satisfactory.[28]

2

The Early 1900s

The lightweight, swiftly refillable gas engine posed a major threat to electrically powered cycles and tricycles. Interestingly, several early motorcycles slung their gas tanks exactly where the electric-assisted tandems had placed their batteries, particularly Cyklon, Bayliss, Minerva, Werner and Triumph. By 1903 Triumph was producing and selling more than 500 units. Other British firms were Royal Enfield, Norton and Birmingham Small Arms Company, which began motorbike production in 1899, 1902 and 1910, respectively. Indian of Springfield, Massachusetts, began production in 1901, and Harley-Davidson of Milwaukee, Wisconsin, was established two years later. By the outbreak of the First World War, the largest motorcycle manufacturer in the world was Indian, producing more than 20,000 bikes per year.

Yet, in spite of the move to gasoline, electric motorcycles never quite died out. Between 1901 and 1903 Ajax Motor Vehicle Co. of New York City, run by brothers Alfred L. and Walter Simpson, produced a limited number of electric scooters.

Over in Canada, Warren Y. Soper, the partner of Thomas Ahearn in Ottawa's electricity business (which owned the Ottawa Electric Company and Ottawa's tram system, among other things), was an early automobile investor. He was part of a group that bought out Canada's leading bicycle companies in 1899 to create the Canadian Cycle and Motor Company (CCM) in Toronto. Though primarily a bicycle company, the new firm under President Walter Massey did produce an electric automobile called the "Ivanhoe," as well as an electric bicycle, before following the trend and converting to gasoline engines. An electric tricycle was also exhibited at the 1908 Berlin Industrial Motor Show.

In these times, few electric vehicle makers, whether using four wheels or two, paid attention to streamlining. Between 1902 and 1903, Walter C. Baker of Cleveland, Ohio, was determined to become the fastest man in the world; he had his team, accustomed to building surreys, phaetons or landaus, create a unique prototype that he called the Road Torpedo. They mounted a torpedo-shaped frame of wood and angle iron on four 36-inch wire wheels with wooden rims and three-inch pneumatic tires. The body was covered with oilcloth and painted black, as were the wheel disks. The Torpedo was the first car to have an aerodynamic body that enclosed both driver and platform. Under the torpedo-shaped body was tandem seating for a driver in the front and an electrician behind; the electrician switched the battery as the car gained speed. The vehicle had a 12-horsepower Elwell-Parker motor. The 3,100-pound vehicle marked the world's first use of a safety belt. Before it crashed, Torpedo proved capable of operating at more than 75 miles per hour (121 kph). Many of its features would only be revived a century later.

The 1900s were an interesting time for fairground carousels as they switched to electric power. In England, Sir Hiram Maxim, keen to win people over to the idea of flying, had built a ride that he called "Captive Flying Machines." A series of cars ("flying machines"), attached by arms to a central rotating upright, flew through the air. At the bottom of the central column, in the machine room, was a large-toothed horizontal gear wheel driven by beveled pinions. Two identical 50-horsepower *electric* motors made by Lister Ltd. of Dursley, with 39-inch (990 mm) diameter drive wheels, delivered drive via six ropes to the main, 12-foot (3.6 m) diameter flywheels. These gave rides at London's Crystal Palace, Brighton, Southport and Blackpool, as well as Pennsylvania in the United States. Since the 1870s carousels had offered bicycles as one of the mounts, and before long electrically powered carousels were offering "motorcycles," built of wood.

If only somebody could come up with a better battery! Researchers at the Primary Battery Division of the Edison Manufacturing Company had spent twenty years struggling to make a lighter-weight copper-coated nickel-iron

This electric scooter was photographed in 1915 (author's collection).

battery outperform the lead-acid unit. In 1910, "Maud," a Bailey electric automobile equipped with the new Edison battery and driven by Captain George W. Langdon, completed a thousand-mile endurance run from New England to New Hampshire. We do not know whether an Edison battery ever powered an electric motorcycle prototype—although they were certainly used for ignition and lights for the Indian gas-powered motorcycle.

In 1910 Victor Harhorn designed an open electric three-wheeler for use around Berlin. Built by Elektromobilfabrik Gebhardt & Harhorn, it sold as the "Geha." Its 3-horsepower motor was located in the front-wheel axle. The Geha had a top speed of 15.5 miles per hour and a range of almost 50 miles. After World War I, the company was bought by Elitewerke AG, and the Geha trike was sold under the name of "Das elektrische Pferd" (the electric horse)![1]

The October 1911 issue of *Popular Mechanics* mentioned the introduction of an electric motorcycle. Called the "Electra," and made by the Electra Cycle Co. of Chicago, it was said to have a range of 75–100 miles (121–160 km) per charge. The motorcycle had a three-speed controller, with speeds of 4 miles (6.4 km), 15 miles (24 km) and 35 miles (56 km) per hour. With an Edison storage battery, the range was doubled.

World War I was the first time the motorcycle had been adopted for military issue, starting with the British Model H, produced by British Triumph Motorcycles Ltd. in 1915. After the U.S. entry into the war, the American military purchased more than 20,000 gas motorcycles from Harley-Davidson. The front cover of the February 1916 edition of *Electrical Experimenter* shows the "Electric-Gyro-Cruiser," a 200-foot-high two-wheeler designed by Eric R. Lyon, associate professor of physics at the Kansas State Agricultural College. It was never actually built, although the following year gas-engine ironclads or tanks took part in the battle on the Western Front. America's version, the hybrid-electric Holt tank, never saw action.

Following the loss of life from the war and the Spanish Flu pandemic, after the armistice in 1919 only three electric automobile makers survived: Detroit Electric, Milburn, and Rauch & Lang. While production slowed to a trickle, other electric innovations continued.

The first electric headlamps were introduced in 1898 on the Columbia Electric automobile. This company built only electric cars and offered the low-powered headlamps as an optional accessory. In 1912, the Cadillac division of General Motors integrated its electrical ignition and lighting systems into gas automobiles. In 1915, the Delta Electric Company of Marion, Indiana, began to manufacture and sell its electric bicycle lamp, which used a single 1.5-volt #6 dry cell battery (6" tall × 2.5" diameter). But, for the most part, lighting was achieved by acetylene generated by a chemical reaction between calcium carbide and water.

Despite this, some still believed in the electric option. Johannes Bjorge

An Electric Motor Cycle.
DETAILS OF AN INTERESTING NORWEGIAN EXPERIMENT.

FROM a Norwegian source comes a description of a motor cycle driven by electricity, which has been invented by Johannes Bjorge, of Christiania, Norway.

We are in some doubt as to whether it is a completely designed electric cycle or an ordinary American motor cycle converted for the purpose. It appears to be the usual type of frame for a four-cylinder engine with accumulators in place of the engine unit, and an electric motor mounted in place of the usual countershaft gear box driving the back wheel direct by a chain. The elliptical box in place of the tank contains the controllers and regulating devices.

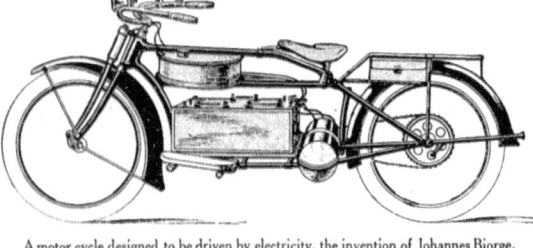
A motor cycle designed to be driven by electricity, the invention of Johannes Bjorge, of Christiania, Norway.

A trial demonstration was recently given before a number of Norwegian motor cycle representatives, and their reports are favourable.

The weight is about the same as that of an ordinary motor cycle. There is said to be sufficient power in the storage battery fitted for about forty-five miles riding, but the inventor is at work on a specially constructed battery which he hopes will give a range of seventy-five miles without recharging. The maximum speed is about forty miles per hour on the level. The running cost of the machine is said to be about four miles for one penny. A further development upon which the inventor is working is a permanent addition to the machine to facilitate recharging wherever electric current is available. We are not convinced that there is anything particularly new or novel in this attempt to produce an electrically driven machine, but it certainly affords possibilities in the way of converting a motor cycle to avoid the use of petrol or coal gas. Whether a storage battery of any efficiency could be temporarily accommodated in place of an ordinary engine unit, single or twin, and whether a lightweight motor of sufficient power could be driven therefrom, are points in doubt. We imagine that many English riders and makers have considered the *pros* and *cons* of this method of driving a motor cycle, and possibly have arrived at the decision that the probable result is not worth the expense. The electric motor cycle is still some way ahead in the future.

There is no reason why it should not come, but steam may turn out to be a serious opponent.

By 1918, when Johannes Bjorge of Christiania, Norway, developed this electric motorcycle, he retrofitted a gas-engine version (Mortons Media Group Ltd.).

of Christiana, Norway, made a conversion from an American motorcycle. It had a range of more than 45 miles (70 km), plus a specially constructed battery for a range of 75 miles (120 km) without recharging.

In England, in 1919, Ransomes, Sims & Jefferies, a major British agricultural machinery maker based in Ipswich, Suffolk, having built 350 Royal Aircraft Factory F.E.2 fighter planes, planned to diversify. Since the war, the company had also been building electric trucks and mobile cranes according to the ingenious designs of a brilliant Belgian-born engineer, Paul Alphonse Hubert Mossay. From 1902 to 1906, Mossay had designed the first induction motors built by the British Thomson-Houston Company in Rugby, going on to innovate larger induction motors for the British Westinghouse Electric and Manufacturing Company in Manchester. He then spent four years as chief engineer at Hansa Lloyd Works in Bremen, Germany, designing engines and battery-driven vehicles. Returning to his native Belgium, Mossay was responsible for the design and manufacture of gasoline-engine pleasure and

2. The Early 1900s

commercial vehicles at the Germain Workshops in Monceau-sur-Sambre. Back in London, he had started up his own consulting company in London when Ransomes, Sims & Jefferies asked him to design a truck.

Following the success of the Orwell truck and mobile crane, Mossay designed an electric motorcycle and sidecar in which the batteries were fitted under the seat of the sidecar. The nickel-iron NIFE batteries battery used was called Ironclad-Exide IMV8s (the Ironclad was another name for the wartime tank), and it had been developed by the Swedish battery company Svenska Ackumulator AB Jungner; Waldmar Jungner had developed a battery couple very similar to that of Edison (and was in fact in fierce competition with the American). Even though the vehicle, with a top speed of 16 miles per hour, was registered for road use (Registration DX-1834) and ran at a third of the cost of gasoline, it never went into the manufacturing stage; instead, it was used by Mossay to commute to the plant. From 1926, Ransomes, Sims and Jefferies' plug-in electric motor mower met with reasonable sales. In the years that followed, Paul Mossay remained inventive, patenting, among other things, pneumatic tools, a multiphase AC transformer and a flameproof electric motor; his telegraph address was appropriately "Asynchrone."

In 1919, Ransomes, Sims & Jefferies of Ipswich built this one-off as designed by P.A.G. Mossay. The nickel-iron batteries were fitted under the seat of the sidecar (Ransomes, Sims & Jefferies, Ipswich, England).

Also in 1919, two engineers, Stanley O. Needham (formerly of Rolls-Royce) and Arnold R. Garrett (an invalid without the use of his legs), set up the Stanley Engineering Co. Ltd. in Egham, Surrey, England. They produced an invalid carriage tricycle initially powered by a Villiers gas motorcycle engine called the "Argson." Then, in 1923, they developed a quieter electric version called the "Runnymede," powered by an electric motor rated at 370 watts. It was equipped with a pram hood, an armchair-type seat with tiller steering and speed control as developed by Dennis Murphy.

In 1920, Heinzmann GmbH (based at Schönau, in the Black Forest), which had been making electric motors for diesel engines for more than twenty years, started to manufacture electric motors for tandem bikes, some of which were used by the German Post Office for deliveries. It would be another seventy years before Heinzmann developed a motorized bicycle, but during that period the company continued to produce electric motors for other vehicles and tools. In 1923, Bosch GmbH launched its dynamic (magneto) lighting system for pedal bicycles; more than 20 million units had been produced by the 1960s.

In 1923, the Societé des Applications Electro-Mécaniques of Lyon, France, produced an electric automobile. Five years later the company brought out its "Electrocyclette." With a single wheel at the rear and two in front, the Electrocyclette was almost 6 feet (1.8 meters) long, and it had a 0.5-horsepower motor for a maximum speed of 15 miles per hour (25 kph). A battery of 150 amp-hours guaranteed a range of 20 miles (30 km). Its weak point was the weight: 165 pounds (75 kg). But the Electrocyclette remained second fiddle to AEM's electric delivery vans, with their top speed of around 15–19 miles per hour (25–30 kph). In 1929, Engelbert Zaschka, observing the parking problems in his home town of Freiburg-im-Breisgau, Germany, produced a three-wheel folding electric car, which could be taken apart within 20 minutes. It was capable of going 25–30 miles per hour (40–50 kph).

In 1925, Rambola, a manufacturer in Munich, produced an electric motorcycle, with its special framework housing the battery, motor, voltmeter, ammeter and various sub-switches, junction boxes and lines. The 12-cell battery, with a voltage of 24 volts and a capacity of 80 amps, had been specially designed to give energy to a 24-volt motor. The performance of the same on the brake was constantly 1.5/3 hp, according to the tax formula for the operation charged 0.7 hp, making the "Rambola" two-wheeler tax-free. Switching on was done by a lever attached to the right outside and easy to use. The regulation of the 3 speeds was also effected by a lever. The braking was done by means of two brake hubs (namely, hand and foot brake); the foot brake was connected to a breaker, whereby braking with the motor was not possible. The charge was achieved by clipping wires to the three terminals on the circuit board and could be made by means of a charging device to each lamp

2. The Early 1900s

and each plug contact. Of the Rambola, the city's newspaper *München-Augsburger Abendzeitung* had this to say: "So we have a new means of transport in the Rambola. The rattling, hissing and stinking of the petrol wheels will soon (hopefully) disappear from the city traffic. For large tours it's still the petrol engine, but for city traffic 'Rambola,' that would be in a sense the most ideal solution.... I hope you can soon greet a 'Rambola' bike in Berlin."[2]

There were very few who foresaw the coming of the electric motorcycle. Hugo Gernsback, the son of a Luxembourg wine merchant, was an American inventor, writer, editor, and magazine publisher, best known for publications that included the first science-fiction magazine. He began as an entrepreneur in the electronics industry, importing radio parts from Europe to the United States and helping to popularize amateur "wireless." Then, in 1908, he published the first issue of *Modern Electrics*, a magazine aimed at the scientific hobbyist, but in 1913 he sold his interest in the magazine to his partner and launched a new magazine, *Electrical Experimenter*, which soon began to publish scientific fiction. Among Gernsback's 80 patents were radio-controlled cars, an electric dog that followed a magnetic walking cane in any direction, and a combined electric hair brush and comb. Writing in the 1920s, Gernsback envisaged that rocket transport as well as electric ships and *electric tricycles* would be commonplace by the 1980s.

The 1930s were the years of the Great Depression in the United States, and anything that could help the American middle class save money was more than welcome. Do-it-yourself projects answered two specific needs: saving money and feeding the entrepreneurial and independent spirit of the American people. To answer this need, Lawrence D. Leach of the LeJay Manufacturing Company in Minneapolis, Minnesota, began publishing a cheap manual or handbook where readers could find a number of DIY projects, most of which focused on the electrification of common objects, such as bicycles. LeJay also sold wind turbines to farmers. As new editions of his manual came out, more and more plans were added. The 1941 catalog had 1,000 electrical bargains; by 1945, there were 50 separate "chapters." The LeJay GoBike was described as an amazing product: copywriters told potential customers that the bike had a range of 70–75 miles (110 km) for every recharge, even without pedaling. The e-motor was mounted laterally on the back wheel, pushing the bike through a smaller wheel.

At the fairgrounds in 1933, the New Dodgem Cycle, as developed by Max and Harold Stoehrer of Methuen, Massachusetts, was described as a full-sized motorcycle redesigned and rebuilt for amusement park service. Like dodgem cars and boats (a.k.a. bumper cars), the motorcycles, sitting on a platform surrounded by a resilient bumper, operated on a tram-type power system, with a pole at the back of the motorcycle connected with an overhead electrified network driven by a DC generator. Dodgem's competitors, Joseph and Robert "Ray" Lusse of Philadelphia, followed with their Auto-Skooter.

During this decade, electric bikes started to become something more than some bizarre creation of a visionary inventor. Many big European companies started producing proper electric bikes. Technology at the time did not allow for light vehicles with a long range, so electric bikes were the link between traditional bikes and the more reliable motorbikes with a combustion engine.

For several decades, Philips of Eindhoven had its Natuurkundig Laboratorium (or Naturlab), where technicians were given freedom to develop anything that might be interesting. The focus was on innovation with light bulbs. From the incandescent lamp, Philips developed vacuum tubes and laid the foundation for X-ray tubes and later TV. One challenge, taken up in the late 1920s, was to make the power transmission to electrify a bicycle; the team leader was engineer Gilles Holst. The motor was built specially for Philips by E.M.I. (N.V. Elektrotechnische Mechanische Industrie) in Utrecht, a manufacturer of electromotors. The somewhat heavy 12-volt KY aircraft batteries came from Varta. Philips presented its motor and battery solution in June 1932. Thus assembled and running on a flat road, the Philips e-bike could reach a maximum speed of 14 miles per hour (22 kph) with a moderate range of 5 hours. Philips staff could buy the bike at a special trade price. Philips then presented the technology to five Dutch bicycle companies: Gazelle, Burgers-ENR, Simplex, Juncker and R.S. Stokvis, all of which produced their own versions with much publicity.

Gazelle only made 117 bikes, but none of them was successful. It did not help that owners had to pay a motorcycle tax. The Gazelle had balloon tubes, 26 × 2", back-pedaling brakes and a rim brake. Price inclusive of lighting and an adapter for the battery was 243,00 guilders (about 115 euros).[3] However, Philips remained interested in small motors, going on to develop bicycle dynamos in the 1930s and the electromotor for the iconic Philishave shaver.

Otto Kynast of Badbergen in Quakenbrück, Germany, also electrified a batch of his bicycles. Although some of these were exhibited at the RAI exhibition in January 1933, once again, the electric bicycle did not win people over.

With the outbreak of World War II and the consequent shortage and rationing of gasoline across Europe, engineers again turned to electric propulsion. One of the most innovative projects was the brainchild of Paul Arzens, a French painter, sculptor and industrial designer of streamlined railway locomotives and automobiles. In 1938, Arzens designed and built an electric automobile transformed from a very curvaceous American Buick; its 2,425 pounds (1100 kg) of Fulmen batteries gave it a speed of 84 miles per hour (135 kph) and a range of 60 miles (100 km). In 1941, Arzens progressed to a three-seater electric city car. He chose a three-wheeler model—two wheels for steering at the front and a rear wheel linked to the rear-mounted motor and low-down batteries. Searching for a moving sculpture shape, he went for lightness: over a Duralinox tubular chassis measuring 4 inches (100 mm) in diameter and 0.1 inches (3 mm) thick, Arzens created a highly curvaceous egg shape made of aluminum and alloys and Plexiglass, closely resembling an airplane cabin. Empty, L'Œuf Electrique (The Electric Egg) weighed 130 pounds (60 kg); with 53 pounds (40 kg) of batteries, a 65-pound (30 kg), 6-kilowatt motor, and 45 pounds (20 kg) of accessories, the total weight was about 296 pounds (136 kg). Its 5-foot (1.5 m) width allowed for 2–3 people, with the driver using a conventional steering wheel and a pedal; by pushing down the pedal, he braked, and by lifting up, he accelerated. Seen around the gasoline-deprived streets of Paris, Arzens was able to achieve an unheard-of range of 60 miles (100 km) and a single-driver top speed of 40 miles per hour (100 kph); with three passengers, he had a reduced speed of 35 miles per hour (60 kph). It cost Arzens just 10 francs per nightly recharge.[4]

Over in the United States, in 1938, Thomas M. McDonald of Saint Ignatius, Montana, applied for a patent for an electric bicycle that had the innovation of a front-wheel electric hubmotor. Though the patent was granted in 1939, the war precluded any production.

Elsewhere, the aircraft industry building warplanes had fitted itself out with giant factories. In September 1935, Consolidated Aircraft Corporation opened its new "Building 1," a 247,000-square-foot (22,900 m2) continuous-flow factory in San Diego, California, while Douglas Aircraft Company's largest facility was its Long Beach plant, totaling 1,422,350 square feet. How executives and technicians could get around these hangars silently and safely was solved by Consolidated's chief test pilot, William B. Wheatley. Bill Wheatley as much an innovator as a pilot, having patented an "Apparatus for arresting launching devices for airplanes"; "Launching airplanes from water" (flying boats); "Device for handling aircraft," etc. His solution to mobility was the "Electricycle," a standard bicycle with a battery and single-speed motor mounted on the front fork. Wheatley's Electricycle was as streamlined as the airplanes he was test-flying, with production advantages secured through utilizing standard parts, foot-controlled throttle and brakes, and easy-to-exchange batteries. For manufacture, in April 1941, Wheatley joined forces with Newton C. Blood and O. L. Weaver of Blood Sales Co. Inc., which had a plant in Long Beach, California. At the time, Consolidated was developing the XB-24 Pratt and Whitney-engine bomber. In June 1941, Wheatley and his crew of four were killed undertaking the final test of the B-24 before the aircraft was to be delivered to the Royal Air Force in England. The crash into San Diego Bay was initially thought to be sabotage, but it was later discovered to have been caused by a mechanical anomaly in which the elevator locked

French industrial designer Paul Arzens created this unique *Oeuf Electrique* (Electric Egg) for silent transportation around a fuel-rationed Nazi-occupied Paris (Institut pour l'histoire de l'aluminium).

in the "up" position, rendering the crash unavoidable. While more than 18,000 B-24s Liberators were built in just over five years, making it the largest military production in U.S. history, nothing else was heard of the Electricycle.

During the 1930s, Great Britain already had a flourishing industry in the manufacture of four-wheeled electric milk floats. Despite the serious damage caused by the Nazi Luftwaffe bombers in most major British cities, milk deliveries continued (potholes permitting). Milkmen used three-wheeler battery-assisted prams and barrows (today's PCVs). These were built by Nelson & Collin Ltd. of Shalford, Surrey, with their Nelco Type MP3, combining two-handled tiller which embodied Murphy speed control. Other vehicles included A.E. Morrison Ltd. of Leicester's Trilec, which suffered from a lack of weather protection for the operator, who sat over the rear wheel (this also restricted forward visibility); the Murphy Servitor; the Lewis Pram; the Graisley Barrow;

In 1940, William B. Wheatley, Consolidated Aircraft Corporation's test pilot, invented this Electricycle for moving around the huge factory buildings (San Diego Air & Space Museum).

The Electricycle would have been built by Newton C. Blood and O. L. Weaver of Blood Sales Co. Inc. at their plant in Long Beach, California (San Diego Air & Space Museum).

and the Manulectric, made by Sidney Holes Electric Vehicles Ltd. of Brighton. All had a 10-mile range, enough for a door-to-door milk round.

The only example of the series production of electric motorcycles was found in occupied Belgium. The name: Socovel.

3

From Socovels to Spacelanders

The German occupation of Belgium began on May 28, 1940, when the Belgian army surrendered to German forces. It lasted until Belgium's liberation by the Western Allies between September 1944 and February 1945. On March 13, 1942, the basic civilian ration was abolished. After that, vehicle fuel was only available to official users, such as the emergency services, bus companies and farmers. The priority users of fuel were always, of course, the armed forces.

Enter the de Limelette brothers of Belgium: Maurice, an Arts et Metiers–trained engineer, and Albert, a businessman. A serious auto accident in autumn 1940 caused Maurice de Limelette to be hospitalized. During this forced rest, he sketched out his ideas for an electric motorcycle, one that could bypass the rationing problem. As Maurice still lived in Le Condroz and Albert was in Brussels, 5 miles (8 km) away, there was a lively correspondence between them regarding the design of the electric motorcycle. Maurice drew up the blueprints and subcontracted the necessary parts to small suppliers and producers, financed by Albert. They tried out their first prototype in January 1941. Of course there were obstacles, one of which was that the vehicle did not have enough power, suffering the embarrassment of being overtaken by cyclists. Improvements were made until the machine was deemed viable by the brothers. Three 6-volt, 45-amp-hour batteries (either Prest-O-Lite or Tudor), weighing 220 pounds (100 kg), rechargeable in 10 hours and mounted crossways on a conventional lightweight frame, powered a rear-mounted ACEC or Moës 1-horsepower motor controlled by a twist-grip. This gave the Socovel a range of 31 miles (50 km), at a speed of 15 miles per hour (25 kph).

Socovel (**SO**ciété pour l'étude et la **CO**nstruction de Vehicules Electriques) was established on March 1, 1941, with its registered office at Louizalaan 359, Brussels (residence and offices of Albert de Limelette). The motorcycles were assembled at 16 rue du Magistrat, Maurice's home, a large property with courtyard, cellars, and annexes. As Belgium was now occupied territory, the brothers also had to ask permission from the German Financial Office in Clovis Avenue. Their request to build 500 engines was forwarded to Berlin and granted. By June 1941, some 15 units had been assembled by the brothers, aided by their mechanic Julien and accountant Cappuyns: they sold immediately.

In spite of the vehicle's high selling price, during 1942 the de Limelettes succeeded in selling 400 Socovels, with some of them sent over to the Netherlands. For the sidecar version, 12-volt batteries supplied energy to a 26-horsepower, 48-volt motor. Starting in 1943, the Germans themselves showed interest in the Socovel and wanted to submit a large order for their airfields to be equipped with these scooters. But the de Limelettes did not like the Germans and tried to gain time. In the end, not a single unit was sold to the Third Reich.

The Germans had authorized the production of only 500 Socovel units. When the de Limelettes reached that number, their demand for renewal was rejected. So in 1943 and 1944, the Belgian firm cheated by renumbering subsequent units (i.e., Serial No. 450 was used twice). But with materials to build automobiles being sparse, not many more were built. The brothers also built a version for a friend who enjoyed playing golf, as well as electric trolleys for use in factories.

At the end of the war, the de Limelette brothers planned a more powerful scooter, but, anticipating the end of gasoline rationing, they gradually phased out the electric motorcycle, with the last one being built in 1948. Later production consisted of motorcycles with third-party engines (125cc Villiers 2-stroke engines, among others) or even rebadged Maico mopeds with a 98cc engine. Production ceased entirely in 1956, but Maurice's son later built some Socovel go-karts around 1960.[1] It was the same for Paul Arzens, who converted his "Oeuf Electrique" to a gas engine and continued to use it around Paris until his death in 1990 at the age of 87.

The de Limelette brothers were not alone. In 1940, Hispano-Suiza, evacuated from Bois-Colombes to Tarbes in the Unoccupied Zone, made a type 351 electric tricycle truck with a 1,763.7-pound (800 kg) payload whose unique front-wheel drive had a 12.8-foot (3.9 m) turning circle, with its batteries housed on either side of the car and mounted on a sliding trolley. However, it never went into production.

In early 1941, Pierre Faure of Paris, formerly a collaborator of airplane manufacturer Louis C. Breguet, presented his 1,212.5-pound (550 kg) Electra PFA three-wheeler. While Breguet was producing a four-wheeler called the A2, Faure concentrated on the three-wheeler, equipping it with a tubular chassis, an electric motor, hydraulic brakes in the front, and a chain on the

"The Motor Cycle" Introduces — AN ELECTRIC

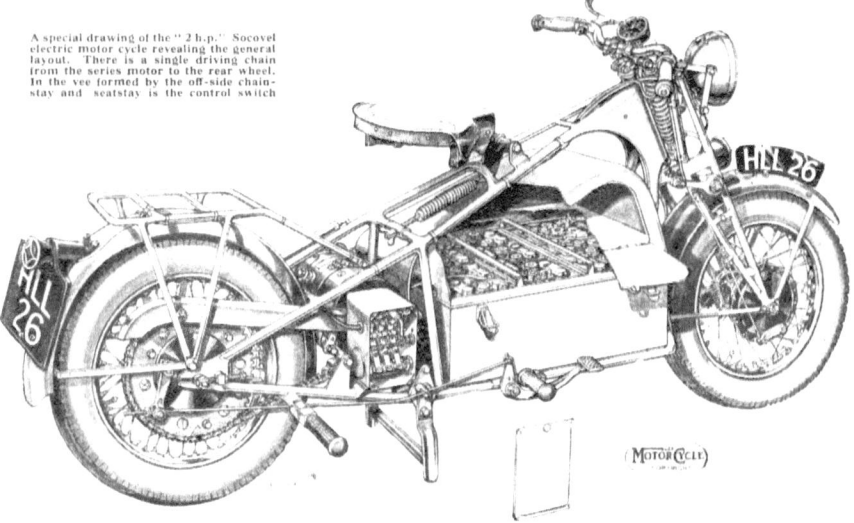

A special drawing of the "2 h.p." Socovel electric motor cycle revealing the general layout. There is a single driving chain from the series motor to the rear wheel. In the vee formed by the off-side chain-stay and seatstay is the control switch.

Production=model Belgian Machine Tried on the Road : Its Appeal and Its Limitations

HAS the electric motor cycle a future? What are its advantages and disadvantages? On the Continent the electric motor cycle has made considerable headway. Was that solely owing to lack of petrol during the war or has the machine an appeal of its own? In Britain electric motor cycles have been made—not many, but a sufficient number to cause the Chancellor of the Exchequer to regularize the position over their taxation in the interim Budget last October, when it was laid down that electric motor cycles should be taxed at 17s 6d a year, the same as autocycles and motor cycles up to 150 c.c. These machines, however, were nearly all of a home-made variety, with car batteries and car starter motors fitted in lightweight motor cycle or even bicycle frames. What of true production model electric motor cycles?

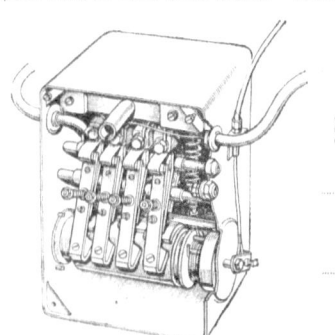

(Left) Detail layout of the control switch. Operation of the drum carrying the contact strips is by twistgrip

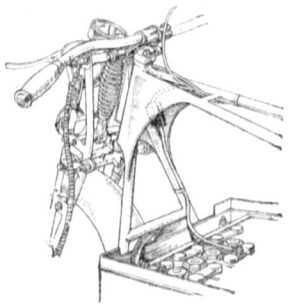

(Right) How the steering head is built up by welding

Above and following page: During 1942, the de Limelette brothers of Brussels, Belgium, built more than 500 Socovel electric motorcycles. Three 6-volt 45-amp-hour batteries (either Prest-O-Lite or Tudor), weighing 220 pounds, rechargeable in 10 hours and mounted crossways on a conventional lightweight frame (made in Liege), powered a rear-mounted ACEC or Moës 1-horsepower motor controlled by a twist-grip. This gave the Socovel a range of 27.5 miles (50 km), at a speed of 15.5 mph (25 kph) (Mortons Media Group Ltd.).

MOTOR CYCLE

A Belgian manufacturer, Socovel, has made over 1,000 electric motor cycles. *The Motor Cycle* decided to import one—to examine it, test it, use it and learn all it could about such a machine. Mr. Geoffrey Smith, Editorial Director of *The Motor Cycle* and its associated papers, had already seen the Socovel on the streets of Brussels—had done so in the course of an official mission to Germany and the (previously) occupied countries. He was so impressed by its silence, simplicity and convenience that he ordered a specimen for trial and examination by interested parties in the trade.

Last month the latest Socovel arrived. It is an interesting machine with appealing characteristics. In no way, however, is such a machine a rival to the motor cycle. Its speed and its range per charge are too limited. On the other hand, an electric motor cycle might attract many whose needs or desires are not met by motor cycles and autocycles. Doctors, priests and owners of large estates, for example, might well find the silent, ever-ready electric motor cycle of value, as the elderly for, say, shopping and short journeys into the country or for visiting friends. There are no gears, no clutch, no starting difficulties—merely a twist-grip on the right handlebar and the brakes. To start the machine the grip is turned and the machine gently and silently glides away, picking up speed in the manner of a trolley-bus. To stop the machine the grip is moved backwards, whereupon the machine free-wheels and is halted by applying the brakes. Could anything be more simple?

Construction of the Machine

The Socovel is a machine built on motor cycle lines, and usually has a pillion seat. No doubt the makers felt that with their wartime market, and the conditions under which they were labouring, such were the best—perhaps, the only—lines on which they were to work. In this country a firm that has also expended much thought on the subject, Small Electric Motors, has experimented with an electric light-weight. In the case of the Socovel, as the special drawings and the photographs reveal, there is a heavy type of duplex cradle frame of welded construction,

central spring front forks and, generally, a heavyweight motor cycle specification that includes large-section tyres on small-diameter rims—3.25×14 Englebert tyres—a spring top saddle with a single, adjustable tension spring as the suspension and a normal rear carrier of tubular construction.

In the earlier models the electric motor was of 18 volts and rated at 1 h.p. With the very latest model which has been imported there is a 48 volt series motor rated at "2.6/1.2 h.p." This is

On the road with the Socovel. A picture taken during the course of the first duration tests

mounted between the rear mudguard and the twin seatstays, while the three 12-volt batteries—a total of 36 volts for the 48v motor—are carried in the neat pressed-steel box in the middle of the frame. The batteries are arranged crosswise and, with their low position in the frame, the machine affords a feeling of great stability. In the cover there is a locker for tools and small parcels.

On the off-side of the motor is the switch box. The switch is of very simple type. Movement of the twistgrip on the

Arrangement of the three 12-volt batteries. A 6v. tapping provides current for the lamps and horn. Note the adjustable saddle suspension

A7

axis of the rear wheels. With a capacity of 100 amps at a voltage of 72 volts, six batteries ensured power to the motor. The trike could reach almost 25 miles per hour (40 kph), and its autonomy was estimated to be around 30–45 miles, depending on the number of starts, load and road conditions. The body's contoured shape, aeronautically inspired, was designed by the architect-decorator Michel Dufet and could accommodate two people. Total production of the PFA was about twenty units.

Also in 1941, the design team at Peugeot developed their *Voiture Legère de Ville* (Light City Car), its four 12-volt batteries giving it a speed of 20 mph and a range of 50 miles. With two wheels at the front, the third wheel at the rear was made up of two wheels at a distance of only thirty centimeters which eliminated the need for a differential. Officially, between 1941 and 1945, only 377 VLVs were manufactured at the Peugeot factory in Sochaux, in the Doubs, held back by the Germans. This is sharp contrast with the 3.8 million Peugeot 2CV lightweight gas automobiles manufactured in France between 1948 and 1988 (and in Portugal from 1988 to 1990).

The occupying Germans being no respecter of national borders, in the Netherlands an auto company called Story also began producing an electric tricycle with Pennock bodywork and powered by a 24/30-volt series motor and five lead-acid batteries, which gave it a range of 35 miles (56 km) and a speed of 20 miles per hour (30 kph). More than 75 units were built, some of them making up a fleet of taxis used in The Hague. In occupied France, Roger Paupe, working for New Map in Lyon, patented an electric scooter powered by two Paris-Rhone motors, type TA 11, powered by 24 volts and each developing 0.5-horsepower at 1,800 revolutions per minute. The battery was a traction type, with a capacity of 90 amperes. A single motor ran at first speed, then both operated in second, controlled by a lamellar contactor actuated by a lever on the handlebars. The e-New Map claimed a range of roughly 35–45 miles at 15.5 miles per hour and a top speed of 25 miles per hour.[2] While limited numbers were being built, Roger Paupe was one of those courageous Frenchmen who fought in the French Resistance, smuggling USAF pilots and crew into the Zone Libre.

On page 176 of his book *La Voiture Electrique à Accumulateurs* (1943), author Henri Petit describes an auxiliary electric motor, invented by les Etablissements R.B of Lyon, which could be attached to the rear wheel of a bicycle to enable it to go up hills. It was made up of a two-wheel trailer, which carried a 12-volt battery and motor controlled by a Bowden cable.

In 1943, William-Viktor-George Baudin, Hubert Autrand, and Etienne Avezard took out a French patent for rider-propelled cycles with auxiliary electric motor power driven at axles. The fashionable Lafayette Department store in Paris exhibited an e-bike that, once the batteries had been discharged, could be pedaled, although with difficulty. In Sweden, Birger Vigerstroem made an electric bicycle that weighed 200 pounds (90 kg), half of which was the battery; recharging took eight hours for a 25-mile (40 km) range at just under 20 miles per hour (32 kph).

In the United States, Earle Williams of Long Beach, California, invented

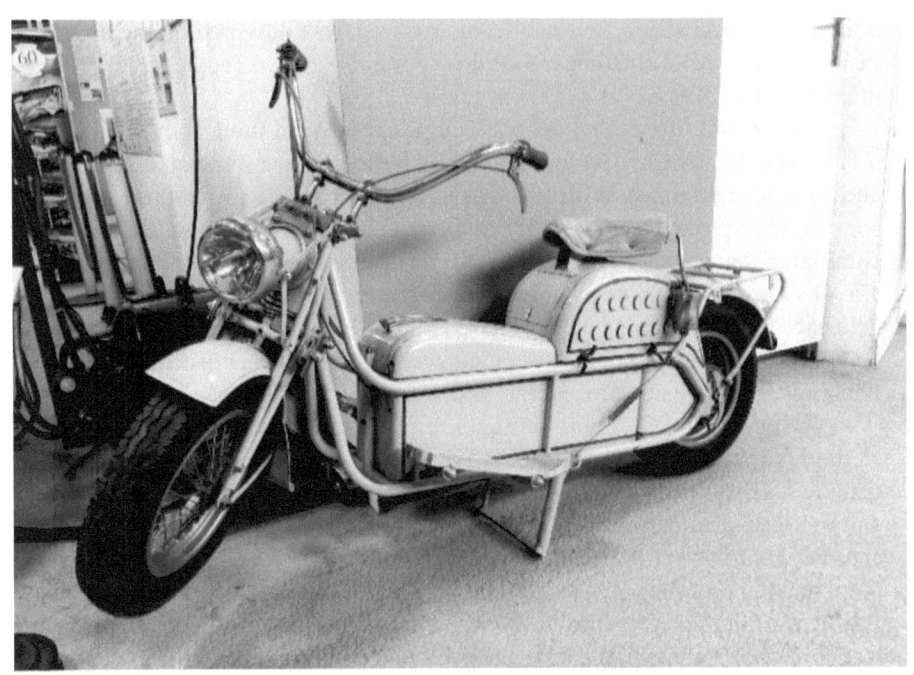

a two-wheeled electric motorcycle that towed a single-wheeled trailer. Due to demand for the product, Williams started making more such vehicles in his garage. In 1946, this development led to the formation of the Marketeer Company (current-day ParCar Corp.).

Over in England during 1943, fuel rationing caused a number of individual motorcycle engineers to think electric. Thomas Larmuth & Company Ltd. of Todleben Iron Works, Salford, Manchester (makers of air compressors, cranes, travelers, winches and associated machinery and rock drills), offered an adaptation of a motorbike for £5 that would cover 100 miles (160 km) using 6-volt, 75-amp Lucas car–type batteries supplying current to a 10-volt Dyno-motor of the type fitted to the 1932 Morris-Cowley automobiles and 1932 Morris Commercial vehicles. Control was achieved by twist grip, which operated a simple switch gear, subject to a provisional patent. J. Pidcock of Peterborough used his electric motorcycle daily—adapting his 1922 350cc Douglas with a Morris starter motor with direct chain drive to the rear wheel, lead-acid batteries and some BSA parts; the range was only 5 miles, but that was enough to get Pidcock to work and back at a modest 18 miles per hour. In Belfast, a Mr. Emerson, a wholesaler, and Mr. Murphy, an electrical engineer, converted a Hercules cycle powered by two six-volt, 100-amp-hour batteries mounted pannier-wise on the top tube of the frame supplying current to a Lucas A.900.R dynamo. It also enabled normal pedaling action and gave Emerson a range of 30–40 miles at a speed of 12–15 miles per hour. J.W. Barrs, electrical manager at Messr. Thomas Dryden and Sons Ltd. of Preston, used a Smith of Cricklewood constant-voltage-type IDA three-brush dynamo to convert his 150cc Coventry Eagle. We know of these engineers because they appeared in the pages of *The Motor Cycle*, but there were certainly more.

Following the armistice, with rationing still in force, electric motorcycles were still a solution—not many were available, but there were sufficient to cause the Chancellor of the Exchequer to regularize the position over their taxation in the interim budget of October 1945, when it was laid down that electric motorcycles should be taxed at 17 shillings and 6 pence (87.5p) a year, the same as autocycles and motorcycles up to 150cc.

Word had crossed the English Channel about the Belgian Socovel. *The Motor Cycle* magazine decided to import one—to examine it, test it, use it and learn all it could about such a machine. Geoffrey Smith, editorial director of *The Motor Cycle* and its associated papers, had already seen the Socovel

Opposite, top: Roger Paupe, engineer for New Map motorcycles of Lyon, France, since 1930, converted a scooter to electric propulsion with a range similar to that of the Belgian Socovel (Collections Malartre). *Bottom:* Another French approach was this electric-assist developed in 1943 by Les Etablissements R.B., also of Lyon (Musée EDF Electropolis, Mulhouse).

on the streets of Brussels, having done so in the course of an official mission to Germany and the (previously) occupied countries. He was so impressed by its silence, simplicity and convenience that he ordered a specimen for trial and examination by interested parties in the trade. But with the easing of restrictions on gasoline provision, even the electric Socovel fell out of favor.[3]

Perhaps what was needed was a revolutionary approach like Paul Arzens' Electric Egg. Enter Benjamin George Bowden, a forty-year-old British industrial designer, popular in the automobile design field. In 1946, Bowden created the "Bicycle of the Future"—an electrically assisted bike. Bowden's design was on display in September of that year during the "Britain Can Make It" fair at the Victoria and Albert Museum in London. It was one of a handful of creations selected from hundreds of entries in 1946 by the British Council of Industrial Design. Bowden was even awarded U.S. Patent 2,537,325.

Instead of a framework of welded tubes, Bowden's model consisted of two, mirror-image pressed-aluminum halves joined together to form a hollow "body," with a fully enclosed front mudguard. Its sculpted curves recalled the 1930s American streamlining craze, but the bike contained innovations such as drive from pedals to rear wheel achieved by means of a steel shaft instead of a chain; this meant the rear wheel could be removed simply by pulling out its spindle. There was suspension for the front fork and batteries hidden inside the bike's frame-powered lights, along with a horn and even a built-in radio. A locker under the seat concealed a pump and tools.

The original model included an electric motor that gathered energy on downhill and flat terrain and helped the rider reach 5 miles per hour (8 kph) on a 10 percent uphill slope. The bicycle's unusual appearance generated substantial public interest, and King Farouk of Egypt ordered 6 of them. The bike was meant to be produced in Wales in a factory that employed former miners; British bicycle makers in a financially crippled nation were reluctant to invest in the high degree of retooling needed to manufacture the bicycle. In 1949, Bowden moved to South Africa, where the government seemed to be interested in funding his project. They gave him enough money to order the material he needed from the United Kingdom. Unfortunately, they blocked the import of goods shortly afterward, making the production of the Bicycle of the Future impossible. The South African government leaders even confiscated the only working prototype Bowden owned. Undeterred, in the early or mid–1950s, Bowden moved to the United States. While in Muskegon, Michigan, in 1959, he met with Joe Kaskie, of the George Morrell Corporation, a custom-molding company. Kaskie suggested molding the bicycle in the new technology of fiberglass instead of aluminum. Although he retained the futuristic appearance of the Classic, Bowden abandoned the hub dynamo and replaced the drivetrain with a more common sprocket-chain assembly. The

3. From Socovels to Spacelanders

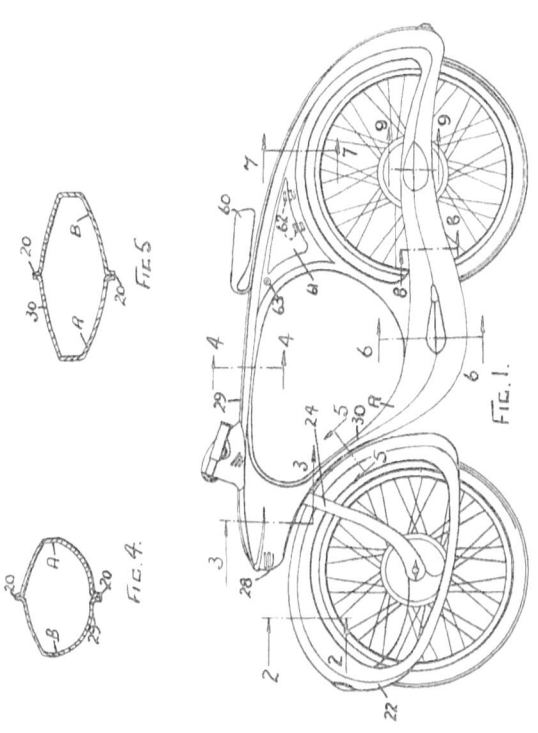

Jan. 9, 1951   B. G. BOWDEN   2,537,325
CYCLE FRAME
Filed Nov. 5, 1948   3 Sheets-Sheet 1

Ben Bowden's 1946 patent for his e-bicycle. The original model included an electric motor that gathered energy on downhill and flat terrain and helped the rider reach 5 mph (8 kph) on a 10 percent uphill slope. There was suspension for the front fork, batteries hidden inside the bike's frame powered lights, a horn, and even a built-in radio. A locker under the seat concealed a pump and tools.

Ben Bowden and his his e-bicycle (Design Council).

new name, Spacelander, was chosen to capitalize on interest in the U.S./USSR Space Race. Advertised as a plaything for "youthful persons of all ages," the Bowden model now looked somewhat dated. Bowden never returned to electric propulsion.

4

1950s–1980s

Electrically powered motorcycles remained the laughingstock of the automobile world. In September 1959, Nitor, the pseudonymed columnist of *The Motor Cycle*, writing at a time when men liked nothing more than tinkering with their tappets on a Sunday morning, was not convinced either:

> It will be a long time yet, before we are robbed of all the fun provided by poppet valves, sparking plugs and chains—and reduced to whiling away maintenance time merely by topping-up some very clever but dull and uninteresting looking fuel cell.

In postwar posterity Britain, Messrs. Nelson and Collin of Shalford, Surrey, developed an electric three-wheeler for invalids called the Solocar, recommended by the British Medical Association and approved of by His Majesty, King George VI.

Very much resembling the Runnymede electric invalid tricycle made in nearby Maidenhead some twenty years before, and equipped with the Murphy speed control tiller, it had a range of 35 miles and could climb hills. This vehicle was seen but not heard during this author's childhood.

In 1951, R.D. Taylor, a chicken farmer in Anaheim, Los Angeles, built his first electric truck to haul around chicken feed and other goods. With demands from neighboring farmers and ranchers, production began soon after. That year, Fred A. Dunn joined the business, and four years later it became the Taylor-Dunn Manufacturing Company. The first model, the three-wheel PG, designed for getting around the neighborhood while shopping, was introduced in 1955. It came with headlights, taillights, and tiller steering. The second model, Series R, called the Trident, with additional turn signals, was built from 1959 through 1963 and could be ordered with either tiller or wheel steering; it was also available with either foot or hand controls for the brake and accelerator. Snap-in side curtains were provided for use in bad weather. The Trident was one of a considerable number of such vehicles built in Greater Los Angeles, most of which were favored by residents of mobile home parks and other small communities where their severely limited

In postwar Britain, Nelson & Collin Ltd. of Shalford, Surrey, developed an electric three-wheeler for invalids called the Solocar, recommended by the British Medical Association. It had a range of 35 miles and could climb hills. It was seen (though not heard) during the 1950s (Stilltime Collection).

performance was not an issue. In 1961, Taylor-Dunn introduced the Tee-Bird line, its first golf cart. This was a 36-volt cart. It came in the model 2336G (three-wheeler) and 2347G (four-wheeler). One single-seater version, named Canary, was only available in canary yellow, the predecessor of later single-passenger industrial carts. Taylor-Dunn also made a fiberglass model 2333G Eagle III model with a distinctive classic styling. These were made until 1975, when the company introduced the angular-nosed model GT370 and GT371, which ran until 1985, when Taylor-Dunn built its last golf cart. In December 1991, the 100,000th vehicle made by Taylor-Dunn Manufacturing Co. in Anaheim was officially put into service for one of its most dedicated customers, Knott's Berry Farm, which has been buying carts since the 1950s.

In August 1967, the UK Electric Vehicle Association put out a press release stating that Britain had more battery-electric vehicles on its roads than the rest of the world put together. It is not clear what research the association had undertaken regarding the quantity of electric vehicles in other countries, but closer inspection disclosed that almost all of the battery-driven vehicles licensed for UK road use were milk floats.[1] For example, Harbilt of Leicester built electric trucks, tow tugs and milk floats that would account for 80 percent of the 50,000 electric vehicles on the UK roads. The fiberglass-body Harbilt 789, front-wheel drive prototype, commissioned by the South Western Electricity Board and designed by Berkely S. Hender, was built and tested in 1964. With its diamond-shaped chassis, its forward front wheel gave it the appearance of a three-wheeler, though an additional rear wheel made it a four-wheeler, similar to the Bersey-Rhodin vehicle of 1898 (almost seventy years earlier). Indeed, in an article published on March 19 in *The New Scientist*, titled "A Prototype for Tomorrow's Electric Runabout," Harbilt's J.M Warrington concluded:

> We are looking to the future with the Harbilt car. City and town centres are filled with obnixous fumes and the hurley-burly of noisy traffic. Common sense dictates that one day this must stop. Electric cars being noisless and fumeless, could be the answer—especially so if the intensive research currently underway on batteries and fuel cells meets with its expected success in the next few years.

In 1967, Sir Alec Issigonis, designer of the world-famous Austin-Mini automobile at the British Motor Corporation in Longbridge, appeared in a Pathé news film sketching out a two-seater electric three-wheeler on the back on a menu (this drawing has also survived). A motor would be in each of the rear wheels, with the battery in the middle. However, the Mini-E would have to wait another forty years before it would be constructed. Indeed, apart from railway tow tugs and golf carts, virtually all the UK BEVs were four-wheelers.

In 1969 Toyota exhibited the EX-II Type A, a glass egg with an electric motor for shopping and commuting; the EX-II Type B for carrying luggage within private premises; and the EX-II Type C for leisure use. Contact with the outside world took place through bull's eyes, and the headlights were situated behind the glass cabin that enveloped the entire vehicle. It was an attempt to lend a new shape to a microcar, but it never went beyond the concept stage.

Certain innovators believed in two-wheelers. From 1955 to 1977, Austrian-born Karl V. Kordesch worked for Union Carbide Corporation. He went from being a scientist to a group leader, then department head and finally corporate research fellow in the fields of batteries and fuel cells. Working with two other Austrians, he led two research groups: one concerned with the development of manganese dioxide batteries, and the other devoted to fuel cells. During this time Kordesch filed 22 patents. For example, in 1957, Kordesch (along with Paul A. Marsal and Lewis Urry) filed U.S. Patent 2,960,558 for the alkaline dry cell battery, which eventually became the D-sized Eveready Energizer battery; it was granted in 1960.

Another fundamental contribution that changed the battery world was Kordesch's creation of the thin carbon fuel cell electrode. He presented a fuel cell demonstration at the Brussels World Fair in 1958, using a suitcase with

In 1967, Karl V. Kordesch and Carl A. Grulke made a fuel-cell/nickel-cadmium-battery hybrid electric motorcycle. The motorcycle was featured in television commercials for the program *The 21st Century*, hosted by Walter Cronkite. Kordesch later relished telling people how he had to join the actors' union to ride in the commercials (Karl and Erna Kordesch Papers, Oregon State University, Special Collections and Archives).

a hydrogen-oxygen fuel cell. His development of thin electrodes for fuel cells came soon thereafter. He was awarded the Wilhelm Exner Medal from the Austrian Association of Small and Middle-Sized Enterprises.

In 1967, Kordesch and Carl A. Grulke made a fuel-cell/nickel-cadmium-battery hybrid electric motorcycle. The battery was later replaced with a hydrazine fuel cell, giving it a range of 200 miles (320 km) per gallon and a top speed of 25 miles per hour (40 kph). To prove his point, Kordesch drove his homemade electric motorcycle in circles on a plaza in Manhattan. The motorcycle was featured in television commercials for the program *The 21st Century*, hosted by Walter Cronkite. Kordesch later relished telling people how he had to join the actors' union to ride in the commercials. Kordesch accumulated more than 300 miles on the motorbike.

The late 1960s were a time of reawakening. In Newport Beach, Marshall "Duffy" Duffield began to make electric-powered dayboats—of which he has since built and sold more than 14,000. In 1968, 31-year-old Allan R. Thieme (pronounced "tee-mee") was working as a plumber and heating consultant in Bridgeport, Michigan, when a family member began to lose her mobility due to multiple sclerosis. Working evenings in his garage, Thieme built a front-wheel-drive electric scooter, capable of going 3–4 miles per hour, which he painted yellow and called the Amigo or "friendly wheelchair." The Amigo proved to be a great success with his relative, so Thieme decided to begin mass producing his invention.

In his patent (applied for in 1969 and granted in 1971), Thieme gave the Amigo its generic name: "Powered Operated Vehicle," or POV. He met with many organizations, such as the MS Society, to explain the Amigo's benefits and functionality. Consequently, Amigo Mobility International, Inc., was founded on November 12, 1968, and an entire industry was born. Although sales were initially slow, within a few years Amigo sales began to skyrocket as more people became accustomed to driving them. In 1981, the 10,000th Amigo was built. Thieme soon became involved with a variety of community groups. From 1972 to 1974 he served as chairman of the Saginaw Valley chapter of the National Multiple Sclerosis Society, and from 1974 to 1976 he was a board member for the Michigan state chapter. From 1995 to 1998, he served on Northwest Airlines Disability Awareness Advisory Board. Today Thieme is CEO of Amigo Mobility, a private company that is completed family-owned, with all its electric mobility devices constructed in the United States.

Some projects were not so fortunate. In 1967, Garfield A. Wood Jr. was the son of a famous powerboat racing champion. Wood, who had already invented a powerboat-based electrically powered fishing system, applied for a patent for an electric drive system for bicycles. U.S. Patent 4,406,630 was granted to the Woodstream Corporation but never realized. At the same time, sixty-five-year-old Floyd Clymer, a racer, motorcycle dealer and distributor of the Indian Motorcycle Company, built a prototype electric motorcycle, colored it yellow and called the Papoose. This vehicle is on display at the Starklite Museum in Perris, California. Unfortunately, Floyd's untimely death in January 1970 ended his attempt to revive the Indian marque. It would not be the last time that a well-known motorcycle brand would go electric.

Europe was also progressing slowly. At the time, of 17.6 million registered vehicles on Britain's roads, only 45,000 were electric vehicles in day-to-day use; of those, 90 percent were milk floats.

Between 1973 and 1977 Hans and Heinz Emmerich of Sindelfingen, Germany, built the Solo Electra moped, fitted with a Bosch 24-volt, 750-watt motor and two 12-volt auto batteries; they had both home sales and successful exportation to Luxembourg, Belgium, the Netherlands and even Australia. The vehicle was sold through mail order catalogs and the price was 1,100 marks. Its weight was absolutely tremendous: 150 pounds (67 kg) (the batteries alone weighed 66 pounds [30 kg]). Moving the Solo Electra with the pedals only must have been quite hard: best not to find oneself with empty batteries! The maximum speed was 15 miles per hour (24 kph); this put the Solo Electra in direct competition with all the other German mopeds that had the same speed.

In 1972, Eric Jaulmes, inventor and director of Motobécane, France's largest manufacturer of motorcycles, thought up the idea of an electric Mobylette. The motor on the front wheel would kick into action once the pedaling rider had reached 2.5–3 miles per hour. Lighter batteries and a flat motor with permanent magnets of 1 kilowatt under 24 volts would then propel the machine at 28 miles per hour (45 kph) with a range of 37 miles (60 km). However, the sixty-year-old Jaulmes' idea was not approved by the company's management, who were afraid to see the sales of Mobylette gas 2-strokes cannibalized, and the idea was shelved.

In 1973, the Auranthetic Charger "All Electric Motorcycle," built in California, was a 200-pound small electric bike using an automotive lead-acid battery and low-voltage PMDC motor. Apparently, a three-wheeler was produced in addition to the more common two-wheeler. The Charger was converted from imported Taiwanese Gemini Mini Scramblers and SSTs without motors. Auranthetic Corp. cut the frames, welded in battery boxes and motor loops, and installed the electrical components. Only a few thousand units were produced in two- and three-wheeled versions. The machines appear to have come in any color the customer wanted, as long as it was orange! There were distributors across North America and at least one in British Columbia.

Elsewhere, Mike Corbin, a 27-year-old ex–U.S. Navy electrician Somerville, Connecticut, built a street-legal commuter electric bike called the Corbin Electric. Its 3 Exide 36-volt lead-acid batteries gave it a speed of around 30 miles per hour (48 kph) for 40 miles (64 km). One hundred Corbin bikes were manufactured between 1972 and 1973. Corbin was the first company to be a licensed vehicle manufacturer for street-legal electric motorcycles. Provoked by frequent comments that electric vehicles were too slow, in 1973, Corbin built a motorcycle known as "Lightning" (see chapter 10 for details).

In 1975, Konuske Matsushita, founder of Panasonic (the largest Japanese consumer electronics company), revered as "the god of management," created a personal electrically assisted bike that used 24 volts of lead-acid car batteries. It was never built in series, but all its characteristics were similar to the pedal-assisted e-bicycle launched by the same company twenty years later.

Over in Honolulu, Hawaii, in 1978, Steve Fehr and Brooks Stevens, an American industrial designer, took a 1971 Harley-Davidson XLH Sportster and re-engineered the entire drivetrain by replacing the 900-cubic-centimeter OHV internal-combustion engine with a variable-speed Baldor electric motor

In this photo from 1972, Mike Corbin rides his Corbin Electric; its 3 Exide 36-volt lead-acid batteries gave it a speed of about 30 mph (48 kph) for 40 miles (64 km). One hundred Corbin bikes were manufactured between 1972 and 1973 (collection Mike Corbin).

and a series of deep-cycle batteries. Power was sent to the rear wheel through an automatic four-speed transmission with chain-drive. Use of a proprietary control system with an integrated-circuit mini-controller allowed the machine to accelerate from zero to 30 miles per hour (50 kph) in 5–6 seconds and reach a top speed of 50 miles per hour (80 kph). The machine's instrument panel was mounted to the handlebars, which featured an electric speedometer, a tachometer, and dual ammeters. Brooks Stevens himself allegedly racked up some 360 miles (580 km) of on-track testing of the red Transitron Mark II electric prototype around Allenton, Wisconsin, which eventually ended up in Stevens' own transportation museum in Mequon. It was not, however, the last time that a Harley-Davidson would go electric.

During the 1970s, Hisashi Suzuki produced a highly successful range of radio-control model cars at the Kyosho Kraft factory in Chiyoda, Tokyo. In 1978, they made an exception to the rule by producing the $\frac{1}{6}$th-scale Eleck Rider RC Motorcycle, complete with a 600-milliamp-hour nickel-cadmium battery. Another company, Royal, produced the RC Motorcycle FZR750, measuring 12" high 16.5" long and also using a nickel-cadmium battery. The Royal had fully proportional speed control with electronic braking and

In 1973, spurred by the oil crisis, Solo, Kynast (as pictured), Hercules and several other companies released similar electric motorized bicycles. The technology used was a 750-watt Bosch DC engine with brushes. For starting, two PD 12-volt batteries were in parallel; for higher speed, in series, the brushed motor was operated with 12 volts and later with 24 volts. The acceleration was quite powerful since between the motor and the chain ring there was a clutch that opened and closed via centrifugal force. Many of these robust bikes remained in operation for more than 20 years (ExtraEnergy.org/Hannes Neupert).

removable anti-roll training extensions with skid wheels. Its 380 Mabuchi Motor gave it a speed of 12–20 miles per hour, and it could run for 30 minutes on one charge.

Cedric Lynch

One engineer whose motor design was to have a major influence on the progress of electric transportation is Cedric Lynch, born in 1955. His story is worth recounting in full. During World War II, Cedric's father, Arnold Lynch, worked on an optical tape reader used in the construction of the code-breaking "Colossus," the first electronic computer that was built at the Post Office Research Station in Dollis Hill. After the war, Arnold worked on the dielectric properties of various materials. Cedric's mother, Edith had been a teacher of deaf children. When he was very young, Cedric's parents bought him a Ladybird book called *Magnets, Bulbs and Batteries*, which explained how a child could make an electric magnet, as well as an electric motor; it even detailed how to take an old battery to pieces and examine what was in it!

Although he attended the local Sunny Bank Primary School in Potters Bar, Cedric was not at all happy at the secondary school: "I really hated the maths teacher, he hated me. I used to skive off on the day when it was double maths, pretending to be ill." Leaving school at the age of 12, Cedric continued to study his favorite subjects at home in Heath Drive, Potters Bar, and he learned quickly, while his parents fended off attempts by the council to force him back to school. His mother Edith had taught deaf children to speak, which perhaps accounts for Cedric's distinctive way of talking. Working in the cluttered garden shed, the teenager was making a modest living repairing motorbikes, mowing lawns and working in a shop when he began to take an interest in electric vehicles.

In 1975, Peter Watson Leighton, Charles Patrick and Duncan Davidson of Lucas Industries PLC, a large manufacturer of electrical components for vehicles, had applied for a patent for "an electrically assisted pedal cycle including a frame rotatably mounting a ground engaging wheel. A pedal shaft is supported by the frame with its axis extending transverse to the plane of the frame, the shaft being supported for rotational movement and limited axial movement relative to the frame" This invention relates to an electrically assisted pedal cycle, particularly (but not exclusively) a bicycle.

Young Cedric was particularly intrigued to see how far electric vehicles could be made to go on a single battery charge. In 1979, Lucas Electrics Ltd. and the Institution of Mechanical Engineers organized a competition to find out how far it was possible to go in two hours in a vehicle run on two of Lucas' lead-acid car batteries, along a circuit that consisted of the pit lane and the start-finish straight of the Donington Park race track.

> At the time there was no reasonably priced DC motor with decent efficiency so I hand-made my first motor at home with an armature made from unrolled tin soup cans spread out flat to use as the laminations of the magnetic circuit wound with enamelled copper wire. My three-wheeled vehicle came second out of 52 competitors which success encouraged me to join the Battery Vehicle Society which organised a similar event some weeks later at Rushmoor Arena in Aldershot (hired from the Army) and then for the next twelve years regularly sponsored six or seven races a year.[2]

Just before the 1980 Lucas Electrathon, which was similar to the 1979 event but attracted about 200 competitors, Cedric appeared on BBC TV's highly popular program *Tomorrow's World*, showing the world that his vehicle was a soapbox with a sophisticated propulsion system. Viewers also noted how Cedric had (and still has) long hair: "It saved me the expense of getting it cut."

From 1983, and for the next ten years, Cedric won a considerable number of Battery Vehicle Society contests around England and Wales. During this time, he developed his own motor, which was to revolutionize electric transport:

> I wanted to use the proper material, but machining was very expensive so I thought of this design in which all the laminations are rectangular which meant that it could be guillotined from the right material by a firm that does transformer laminates—it gave higher efficiency because it is possible to use grain-oriented lamination material that has better properties in a particular direction at the expense of its properties in other directions. By designing the motor in the form of a disc, with an armature consisting of radial copper strips with wedge-shaped groups or iron laminations in the spaces between them and stationary magnets at both ends of the armature, I obtained a much greater efficiency, a lot less friction and much more compact shape. It worked surprisingly well. I was even able to beat the entries from universities and the like.

In the 1980s, this author was attending and reporting on human-powered vehicle contests ashore and afloat. In "The First Thamesmead Festival of Human Power," published in 1984, I wrote, "Never had these two and three-wheelers been given the option of a battery-assisted class known as 'pedal-electrics.'" It was a rather lengthy word invented by myself and approved by race organizer Peter Selby; perhaps somebody would shorten it one day.

The Greater London Council had set up a series of Technology Networks to support new ideas for socially useful production. One of these was London Innovation Network, set up by Richard Fletcher. In 1986, Cedric Lynch asked LIN to help him commercialize his new design of motor. Many manufacturers of conventional motors were offered licenses to the worldwide patent but found that they could not use their conventional production methods. With further development work, Cedric came up with LIN 1, a streamlined motor bicycle that, powered by two 48-amp-hour batteries, not only won races but also was said to have a range of about 60 miles (100 km) at 20–25 miles per hour (30–35 kph). With this vehicle he won the long race at the Electrathon86, organized by the Battery Vehicle Society at Mallory Park near Leicester, a competition to determine who could go the farthest in one hour powered only by commercial rechargeable batteries.

At this time Cedric was working at a general store in Finchley, north London, when he met India-born Arvind Rabadia, who was doing a morning newspaper delivery round. Arvind was a little disturbed by Cedric's long hair and very distinct way of speaking, but he started accompanying Cedric when he raced his recumbent wooden three-wheeler. Arvind, then 13, rode a small version of Cedric's streamlined three-wheeler in the Electrathon 86 Junior division (in which the power had to come from one 12-volt lead-acid battery weighing 44 pounds [20 kg] or less) and won the race. Arvind also rode in the race for electrically assisted pedal cycles, using the cycle that he usually used on his newspaper round but fitted with a modified SIBA motor (which came from a lawn mower) mounted below the handlebars and driving the front wheel through a chain and a Sturmey-Archer 3-speed hub gear. He came third in this race, ahead of some riders who were professional racing cyclists. Cedric and Arvind then built a two-wheeler that Cedric raced at Malory Park. Eventually they raced abroad. In 1991, they took two streamlined e-bikes to a competition in Alsace, northeastern France, where, with Arvind Rabadia at the wheel, they won all the events, in Mulhouse, Colmar, Turckheim-Trois-Epis and Strasbourg, in the 330-pound (150 kg) category. Arvind and Cedric were both riding, with similar (but not identical) bikes. Arvind won all events except the hill-climb from Turckheim to Trois-Epis, in which his bike's electronic controller cut out due to triggering its overheat protection, though he was the overall winner. His vehicle had a 24-volt system with

Arvind Rabadia, left, and Cedric Lynch testing their vehicles built for the Grand Prix du Soleil held in October 1991 in Strasbourg, Mulhouse, Turckheim–Trois-Epis and Colmar, sponsored by the regional council of Alsace. They took first and second places in the lightweight vehicles category. Arvind won all the individual races except the hill climb (courtesy Cedric Lynch).

electronic controller, while Cedric's had 12-volt with a resistor start and a mechanical gear change.

Cedric Lynch was not alone. In 1982, a German inventor, Egon Gelhard of Zulpich in North Rhine–Westphalia, Germany, patented his "bicycle, in particular with an electromotor." A bicycle was provided with a pedal drive and an electrodrive with an electromotor. Both were mounted on the boss of the rear wheel of the bicycle and could operate together or separately due to using individual freewheeling devices. Gelhard also patented an apparatus for measuring distance using ultrasonic echo signals, particularly for use on a motor vehicle.

Enter Dr. Paul MacCready of AeroVironment in Monrovia, California, whose team had built and flown Solar Challenger across the English Channel in 1980, using an AstroFlight motor unit. For an International Human-Powered Vehicle Association Championship, MacCready arranged for the Boucher twins of AstroFlight, pioneers of the Sunrise I (the world's first solar-powered drone), to give partial sponsorship to electrify streamlined recumbent bicycles using their model aircraft motors and controllers with car batteries. The Bouchers had already built a solar/battery bike in the late 1970s but had been unsuccessful in marketing it; they had also supplied special electric motors that allowed motorcyclists to maintain wheelies indefinitely for movie stunts, though it was not the primary power for the motorcycles.

In 1983, the diminutive Gino Tsai, 44-year-old mechanical engineer and president of the JD Corporation in Taiwan, needed to move faster around his factory in Chang Hua. So he had Johnson Ko design and build him a human-powered scooter he called the "Razor." From Tsai's personal transport, Johnson Ko gradually developed two electric models: a longer, more stable version and a shorter one for daredevils. In the summer of 1998, Tsai took the scooter to a convention in Chicago. Sharper Image Corp. ordered 4,000 of them. By August 1999, JD could not keep up with demand. The following year, Dan Green's landing of the first backflip with a Razor boosted output to 1 million in November. By 2016, Razor USA, based in Cerritos, California, had more than doubled its 1999 revenue of $40 million. Johnson went on to develop the substantial electrical bike and scooter business of TransX.

In 1984, Masao Ono, a racing car designer and head of Tokyo R&D, and Dr. Hiroshi Shimazu discussed the development of an electric trial bike with direct-drive hub motors. This lead to the development of electric scooters and a whole range of light electric vehicles (LEVs). In 1999, Tokyo R&D founded PUES Corporation to develop and manufacture electric motor, inverter, controller, and battery management systems for hybrid and electric vehicles.

The first solar "cars" were actually tricycles or quadricycles built with bicycle technology. Initiated by Josef Jenni and a group of the SSES (Swiss

Association for Solar Energy), the first Tour de Sol took place in 1985, a rally with solar-powered lightweight vehicles (solar vehicles). The critics had predicted in advance that riders would not be able to cross Switzerland in such a short time with solar cars. The rally started on June 25 in Romanshorn beside Lake of Constance, and it finished on June 30 in Geneva. 72 vehicles started in two classes; more than 50 finished. The vehicles mostly had three or four wheels, but from the beginning a few true solar bicycles were built, featuring large solar roofs, small rear panels or trailers with solar panels. More practical solar bicycles were built with solar panels to be set up only during parking. This event later led to the development of Swiss production electric bicycles and motorcycles. It was the same with the race across Australia from Darwin to Adelaide.

Science-fiction continued its flirtation with electric motorcycles. The film *Akida* (1988) was based on the comic book series by Japanese artist Katsuhiro Otomo. The electric bike ridden by the character of Kaneda was memorable. Created by Katsuhiro Otomo, it is stated in the film that the bike features "ceramic, double-rotor two-wheel drive, computer-controlled anti-lock brakes, and 12,000 rpms," and that you can "lower the rev below 5000 while changing gears." Eventually science-fiction becomes fact.

In 1989 the Sanyo "Enacle" was the first electric bike to use nickel-cadmium batteries size 26, 3-speed, Nexus Dynamo Hub, but with Japanese owners requiring an insurance number and helmet, response was weak.

The Story of the Sinclair C5

In the early 1980s this author was involved with a society called the Human Power Vehicle Association, whose members designed recumbent bicycles and tricycles with special gear wheels that enabled them to achieve higher-than-ordinary speeds. In 1984, these vehicles could also be fitted with a 250-watt permanent magnet motors weighing less than 10 pounds with a 12-volt battery no heavier than 29 pounds (13 kg). That year, at the Thamesmead Festival of Human Power, there was a round-the-houses race part-sponsored with £600 prize money by the Sinclair Vehicle Project; this event included power-assisted competitors using lead-acid or nickel-cadmium 12-volt batteries between 20 and 29 pounds (9 and 13 kg). The race was won by Peter Ross of Buckinghamshire with his "Trice."

Among those watching the HPVA contests was computer entrepreneur Sir Clive Sinclair of St. Ives in Cambridgeshire. Fascinated by electric cars since his childhood, Sinclair had asked one of his employees, Chris Curry, to carry out some preliminary research into electric vehicle design. Together they developed a wafer-thin motor that was mounted on a child's scooter, with a button on the handlebars to activate it. The research went no further, however, as Sinclair's development of the first "slimline" pocket calculator—the Sinclair Executive and its successors—took precedence. Then, in 1979, Sinclair and a colleague resumed development of what he called the C1 (Clive One), a personal electric vehicle with pedals.

A specification of the C1 emerged by the end of the year. It would address short-distance transportation needs, with a minimum range of 30 miles (48 km) on a fully charged battery. This goal reflected official figures showing that the average daily car journey was only 13 miles (21 km), while the average moped or pedal cycle journey was just 6 miles (9.7 km). The users were envisaged as being housewives, urban commuters, and young people, who might otherwise use bicycles or mopeds to travel. The electric vehicle would be safer, more weather-proof, and it would offer space to carry items. It would be easy to drive and park, and for the driver to enter or exit, and it would require minimum maintenance. The vehicle would be engineered for simplicity using injection-molded plastic components and a polypropylene body. It would also be much cheaper than a car, costing £500 (now £1,400) at the most.

The development program moved to the University of Exeter in 1982, where the C1 chassis was fitted with fiberglass shells and tested in a wind tunnel. By March 1982 the basic design had been established.

To meet the steadily escalating development costs of the vehicle, Sinclair decided to raise capital by selling some of his own shares in Sinclair Research. In 1983, he set up Sinclair Vehicles in Warwick in the West Midlands, an area with a long-established link to the motor industry. The project's prospects were boosted when, in 1983, the British Department of Transport introduced the category of "electrically assisted pedal cycle," exempt from insurance and vehicle tax, so that the user would not need a driving license or a helmet, all of which were required for mopeds. However, the maximum legal speed of the vehicle would be limited to 15 miles per hour (24 kph); it could not weigh any more than 130 pounds (60 kg), including the battery; and its motor could not be rated at any more than 250 watts. Just as Clive Sinclair had found with home computers like his hugely successful ZX81 and ZX Spectrum, an affordable electric vehicle might unleash pent-up demand for a market that did not previously exist.

Work now began in great secrecy at the Motor Industry Research Association's proving ground in Leicestershire on the C5, a three-wheeled design with handlebar steering; Lotus Cars would finish the vehicle's detailing, build prototypes and test rigs, carry out testing and take the program into production. The model was restyled by Gus Desbarats, with wheel trims and a small luggage compartment being added. Its motor, as produced in Italy by Polymotor (a subsidiary of the Dutch company Philips), derived its energy from

4. 1950s–1980s

In 1984, the Sinclair C5 was developed by Sir Clive Sinclair, a British microcomputer millionaire who was full of innovative ideas, such as the use of injection-molded parts for most of the structure and body. But the vehicle did ride not very well, and people criticized the low rider position and the feeling that they might not be visible to others on the road. After 17,000 units were produced, the company went bankrupt and the vehicles ended up as kids' toys or collector's items in the category "good idea but maybe too early and not exactly right" (ExtraEnergy.org/Hannes Neupert).

Oldham Batteries while the C5's electronics were produced by MetaLab, a Sinclair spin-off. The bodywork was injection-molded polypropylene. Assembly would take place at Hoover's washing machine factory in Merthyr Tydfil, South Wales, with an ambitious projection of 200,000 C5 units a year, increasing to 500,000. Full production began in November 1984, and by early January 1985 more than 2,500 C5s had been manufactured. Each production line could produce 50 vehicles an hour, and Hoover was capable of producing up to 8,000 units per week.

The C5 was shown to the public and the critics for the first time at the Alexandra Palace in London on January 10, 1985. It was a "spectacular disaster," as some of the journalists termed it. Some of the vehicles stopped working after they went around the building a couple of times. The press was unimpressed: Sinclair's trike had awful electronic components, low-quality gears made entirely out of plastic, and a motor that was too small and unable to go uphill without using the pedals. It also had poor protection from bad weather, and the position of the driver was too low to allow him to see properly while driving in the city's traffic. The vehicles were nicknamed "hedgehogs" because of the risk of running over the small animals.

Sinclair tried to fix the two latter points, but it was too late: on the day of the inauguration, only 200 models were sold, and sales never really improved after that. After less than one year, Hoover declared that it had stopped the Sinclair C5 production; in eight months only 8,000 models had been sold. Sinclair ultimately closed Sinclair Vehicles, having invested 12 million pounds in making his dream come. There was one race for a dozen C5s held around the roads of Milton Keynes, at which this author was a course marshal. Thousands of unsold C5s were purchased by investors and sold for hugely inflated prices—as much as £5,000 (compared to the original retail value of £399). Enthusiasts have established owners' clubs, and some have modified their vehicles substantially, adding monster wheels, jet engines, and high-powered electric motors to courageously propel their C5s at speeds of up to 150 miles per hour (240 kph). Chris Gavin-Egan, founder of C5 Alive, owned no less than fourteen of them.

Five years later, the irrepressible Sir Clive would go on to develop the Zike, a lightweight electrically assisted bicycle, using a 100-watt motor and nickel-cadmium batteries. It was also a commercial failure, selling only 2,000 units despite the original intention of producing them at the rate of 10,000 a month. The model was ended six months after introduction.

The Sinclair C5 and the Zike were ahead of their time, and, as we shall see in the next chapter, the idea behind them would return thirty years later.

Meanwhile, Cedric Lynch had been quietly working for Felice Campopiano of Stellmar in London. Financed by the Great London Council Enterprise Board, in 1984 Campopiano had designed and patented an electrically assisted bicycle he called the Pedelec, considerably smaller than the C5 and boasting a powered range of 25 miles.[3] The Stellmar Pedelec was a bicycle with small wheels and sprung suspension. It had a Bosch IPL 12-volt, 200-watt motor (intended to drive the radiator fan of a large car engine) and a 30-amp-hour lead-acid battery. The motor and pedals drove the rear wheel through two separate chains and freewheels (the motor chain being the tiny ANSI 25 size, one-quarter-inch pitch) that both drove through a Sturmey-Archer 3-speed hub gear; this arrangement gave the Pedelec good hill-climbing performance. Although the bike would not succeed, its name would eventually become a generic word.

5

The 1990s

Entering the final decade of the 20th century, certain innovative elements would play a key part in the long-awaited commercial success of the electric motorcycle.

In 1989, Dr. Walter Toriser of Vienna's Technical University, whose main research was in puvatherapy (or the use of light pulses to irradiate skin diseases), took time off to develop the E-Moped with a hub center motor.

In Basel, Switzerland, Michael Kutter, a long-haired philosophy student, reexamined the pedaling action that would enable the electric motor to start and assist the rider, rather than the rider using a direct throttle control. He took Cannondale mountain bike and installed the electric assist. His actual innovation was the gearbox, a stepless transmission and a sensor that measured how quickly the rider got into the pedals and regulated the motor. Kutter's first production model, the Dolphin, for the Velocity Company went on sale 1992. He sold licenses to Germany and to the United States, where the Los Angeles police used Dolphins for a while.

The Dolphin's transmission was in effect a differential with one output to the wheel and two inputs, one from the pedals and one from the electric motor. This means that the rider felt through the pedals the torque he or she was applying to the wheel, but the speed of the motor was added to the speed contributed by the pedals, so the rider went much faster for a given effort than they would on a normal bicycle. The rider could also use the motor without pedaling; in this situation, a free wheel prevented the motor from driving the pedals backward. This arrangement violates the regulations applying to electrically assisted bicycles in the European Union (which forbid any motor assistance above 25 kilometers per hour), but Switzerland is not a member and has adjusted its regulations to cater to this type of assistance. In EU countries the Dolphin is classed as a moped rather than an assisted bicycle.

Also in Switzerland, a toolmaker named Philippe Kohlbrenner was averse to commuting by car and felt that he was spending too much time on

Top: In 1990, Michael Kutter developed what some people feel was the first pedelec. The first production models were sold in 1992 under the Dolphin name for the Swiss company Velocity, but they did not survive. This photo shows Kutter in 1995 with his second and third pedelec prototypes. *Bottom:* Susanne Brüsch rides one of the first-generation Velocity drive systems from Switzerland, which later were the heart of the Velocity Dolphin bikes by Michael Kutter. It was part of the ExtraEnergy product field test in the late 1990s. The picture is taken from the *aktiv Radfahren* magazine that published the test results (both ExtraEnergy.org/Hannes Neupert).

his bike (his wife cooked so well that he always came home at noon). So he unceremoniously screwed a wiper motor with a car battery to his red Coronado bike. Work colleague and electrical engineer Reto Böhlen took care of the electronics. The first ride with "Roter Büffel" (Red Buffalo) pleased the two men so much that they marketed the BK Tech, promoted as BikeTech by Kurt Schär of Huttwil and launched as the Flyer, manufactured in series between 1995 and 1999 and later promoted by Movelo to Germany and Austria. BK Tech's patent on torque sensors was used by Panasonic to develop its industry-leading system.

In 1991 Hercules of Nuremberg, Germany, presented the "Electra" electric bicycle. A 0.36-kilowatt (0.5 PS) DC motor, switched on via a twist grip on the handlebars, accelerated the Electra to a top speed of 12.5 miles per hour. Under purely electric power, it had a stated range of around 15 miles

The Electra was introduced to the market by Hercules in 1991 after a three-year initial trial for this new category, the Leichtmofa, which was developed for this product. The Leichtmofa was allowed to run up to 12.4 mph (20 kph) with pure electric motor power but was restricted from its design features to be something like a bicycle—it was allowed to be operated without a helmet. However, it required an insurance plate and an entry-level driver certificate that could be granted from the age of 16 years onward. There were 1,000–3,000 bikes sold in the first years, the most successful electric bicycle at that time. The vehicles were extremely robust; many of them have been in use for up to 20 years, sometimes with the first nickel-cadmium battery, which very long lasting (ExtraEnergy.org/Hannes Neupert).

(25 km). Hercules advertised the Electra as making riders the "cyclists of the next millennium." The company failed to reach the production target of 20,000 per year, however, and had sold only around 20,000 Electras by 2001—but this was still better than earlier attempts at electrifying bicycles. The low range and legal classification of the Electra hindered its commercial success. Unlike the pedelecs of today, the Electra was considered a low-powered moped for which riders needed a license, third-party insurance and an insurance plate.

In 1991, Jim McGreen of Sebastopol, California, having enjoyed Electrathon racing, founded Zero Air Pollution (ZAP) to design, build and sell innovative electric vehicles. The company was incorporated on September 23, 1994, as ZAP Power Systems. Working with Mort Lashman for the friction drive system and joined by Gary Starr, McGreen developed the Zappy microscooter, which sold 2,000 units in 1998 and eventually totaled more than 30,000 units. Other products such as ZAP DX and SX, ElectriCruiser, PowerBike, S&W Patrol Bike, and ZAPTRIKE followed.

In Austria, a young mechanic, Franz Schachner of Seitenstretten in Austria, had been tuning gas engines but always went home feeling nauseous. So, in 1980, helped by his brother Thomas, Franz took a tractor battery and an industrial motor and built an electric bicycle (without pedals). They continued to improve the vehicle, and nine years later they took part in the Austro Solar electric rally 93 miles (150 km) across Austria. In 1990, the Schachners began to series build the first electric retrofit kit for existing bicycles (a friction roller drive), with a lead-acid battery. Further developments included a drive with chain and gear motor above the shift system in the rear wheel (1992) and a wheel hub motor (1993). In the years that followed, continuous improvements would be made.[1]

In 1992 Hannes Neupert, an industrial designer, set up *ExtraEnergy* in Tanna, a city in Thuringia, East Germany, and began to collect pedelec bikes, vintage and new. This would grow into an LEV museum with no less than 600 e-wheelers and a nationwide standardized and certified pedelec test track that can represent almost all the conditions that a pedelec has to cope with.

In the 1993, the World Solarcar Rally was held in Akita Prefecture Ogatamura Japan, which also included solar bicycles; the following year the World Solar Bicycle Race was part of the rally, which became known as the World Green Challenge.

Over in the United States, AeroVironment was part of the team that built the General Motors Sunraycer, which won the first Australian cross-country race; then, with the Impact battery-electric prototype for GM automobiles, Paul MacCready set up an electromechanical center in Monrovia, separate from the airplane operation in Simi Valley, with the objective of creating an electric-powered bicycle. At the time, putting electric power on a bicycle made it a motorcycle under Californian law, unless the rider still had to pedal. AeroVironment developed a bike that sensed the load on the chain from the pedals and then augmented it with electric motor power from a battery. This arrangement made the bike complex and expensive. Called the AV Charger, about 2,500 units were built, almost half of which were supplied to law enforcement agencies; the rest were never sold. After the Monrovia Police Department instituted its police bicycle patrol, AeroVironment approached the department with a proposal to test a special version of the Charger (called the Patroller) in 1994. It proved a great success, improving response times for bicycle officers and extending their patrol range. However, the system that sensed the bicycle tension was unreliable, required frequent maintenance, and did not appeal to bike enthusiasts who wanted a fast bike or exercise, nor did it appeal to seniors, who wanted something more stable like a three-wheeler. Ray Morgan of AeroVironment recalls, "I had two of them. Most of us who bought one either removed the battery (which was very heavy) and the motor or straight-wired it so you didn't have to pedal. Bottom line, it filled no niche."[2]

In 1993, Benno Bänziger and Jeano Erforth of Vista, California, started the Electra Bicycle Company. The Electra was designed by Bänziger and built by Taioku Bicycle Manufacturing in Taiwan. At first, they met with resistance from the bike shops, which told them that people did not need a cruiser bike to go to the grocery store. However, when those shops tried stocking the Electras, they began to sell, and word of mouth convinced more dealers to sign on. In fact, the fledging company's cruiser sales were so good that larger firms were spurred to start offering their own cruiser models. Paradoxically, Electras were not all electric bikes. Some of them were modified into electric bikes by Don DiCostanzo, who would later found Pedego. The first pure Electra electric bicycle would be sold as late as 2010.

Like its counterparts ashore and in the air, the electric motorcycle industry (including the pedelec) was discovering a technical breakthrough in energy. The quest for a lightweight battery with high energy density went back a long way.

In 1992, Stan Ovshinsky of the Ovonic Battery Company at Auburn Hills, Michigan, won the race to secure the first contract to develop nickel-metal hydride (NiMH) batteries for electric vehicles from the U.S. Advanced Battery Consortium, a group that included the automobile manufacturers Chrysler, Ford and General Motors. The patented battery was lighter, smaller and longer lasting than conventional batteries. It consisted of special alloys and specific multi-component alloy compositions, whose disordered structure enabled the storage of much larger quantities of electricity. Ovonic licensed these batteries to more than 50 companies worldwide, which used them in millions of devices such as laptop computers, digital cameras and mobile phones—and electric bicycles. Mercedes-Benz used the NiMH battery to launch a Sanyo-engine belt-driven electric bike. The battery pack was built into the down tube, but it proved too heavy, had a very limited range and handled sluggishly. Although Mercedes-Benz used its considerable marketing network to promote the product, it failed to make a mark. Giant of Taiwan, the world's largest bicycle manufacturer, led by King Liu with Tony Lo, produced a deluxe pedelec called the Lafree, first with NiMH. In 2003, Hans Goes, in charge of Giant in Holland, attempted to develop a semi recumbent—the Giant Revive, which did not prove a commercial success. This author acquired a Lafree and only gave up riding it twelve years later when he acquired a Renault Twizy LEV.

The major discovery for all forms of electric transport, including bicycles, came in the form of the lithium battery. In the fall of 1972, M. Stanley Whittingham, an English-born chemist working with a team at the Exxon Research & Engineering Company, announced that they had come up with a new battery, and patents were filed within a year. Within a couple of years,

King Liu, working with Tony Lo, produced a deluxe pedelec called the Lafree, initially using a nickel-metal hydride battery, which this author used for ten years until he acquired a Renault Twizy LEV (author's collection).

the parent company, Exxon Enterprises, wheeled out a 3-watt, 45-amp-hour prototype lithium cell and, linking it to a diesel engine, started work on hybrid vehicles. When solid-state physicist John Goodenough became head of inorganic chemistry at Oxford University in 1976, his research group included Dr. Phil Wiseman, Dr. Koichi Mizushima and Dr. Phil Jones. They set themselves the task of looking at the potential of rechargeable batteries, which began by simply "kicking around ideas on a blackboard." "We looked at it in a different way using lithium cobalt oxide at the positive terminal and pulling the lithium out; this produced a huge cell voltage, twice that of the Exxon battery," Dr. Wiseman explained. "It was this spare voltage that allowed alternatives at the other terminal where Exxon had been forced to use lithium metal which was fraught with problems. Instead lithium-ion material could compose both electrodes." The group's research was published in the *Materials Research Bulletin* in 1980. In 1977, Whittingham teamed up with Goodenough to publish a book titled *Solid State Chemistry of Energy Conversion and Storage*.

In 1985, Akiro Yoshino of the Asahi Kasei Corporation in Japan created the commercial prototype lithium-ion battery. Two years later, Sony of Japan entered an agreement with Eveready USA to develop mass-market rechargeable lithium batteries. Many alternative cathode and anode chemistries have been discovered since those first

In the 1970s, British-born chemist M. Stanley Whittingham (left) and a team at Exxon Research & Engineering Company, followed by American-born solid-state physicist John B. Goodenough (right) and a team at Inorganic Chemistry Faculty at Oxford University, laid the groundwork that led to today's universal lithium-ion battery. This photo of the two pioneers was taken in July 2018 (courtesy M. Stanley Whittingham).

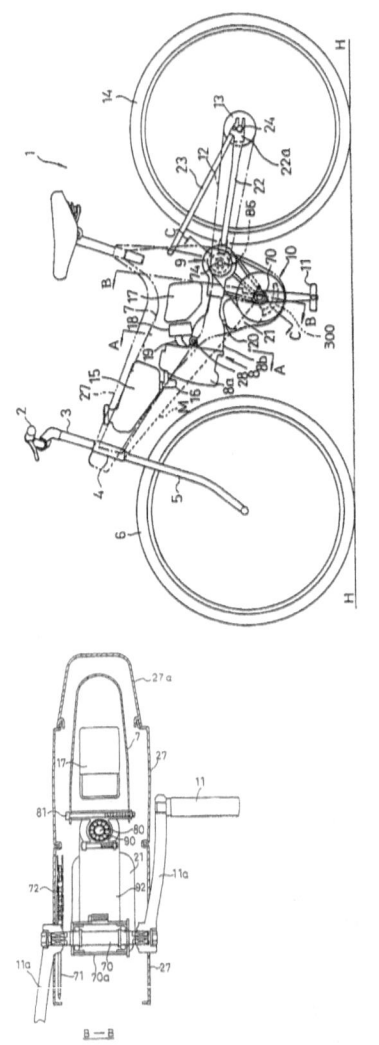

FIG. 5

The first Yamaha PAS, introduced onto the Japanese market in late 1992 and delivered in 1993, was a legal breakthrough. The bike had an electric-assist motor that was attached to the bottom brake and supported the rider in proportion to the owner's muscle power input. Yamaha managed to turn this idea, which was first described 10 years earlier by the German Egon Gerhard, into production reality. Yamaha managed to convince the Japanese government to accept this electric bicycle as fitting the legal definition of a bicycle with no exceptions: no specific insurance and no age restrictions. Later Yamaha also managed to convince European states to follow this legal consideration: a real breakthrough (ExtraEnergy.org/Hannes Neupert).

commercial batteries hit the market in 1991. The original cobalt oxide cathode's vulnerability to overheating, producing oxygen, and possibly catching on fire led to the 2006 "era of flaming laptops." Meanwhile, other cathode types, such as lithium manganese oxide (LMO) and lithium iron phosphate (LPO), were developed, offering greater resistance to overheating but having less energy density (measured in kilowatt-hours per kilogram, or kWh/kg). These types have become the principal players in the electric vehicle field.

Development continued. By the late 1990s, Japanese companies (particularly SONY) had made great strides in the commercialization of lithium rechargeable batteries. In 1997, Tsuyonobu Hatazawa, R&D manager at the Sony Corporation, Kanagawa, invented the polymer gel electrolyte and lithium-ion polymer battery. In 1997, Nissan Motors produced its Altra, an electric car, equipped with a neodymium magnet 62-kilowatt electric motor and run on lithium-ion batteries manufactured by Sony. The following year, Ji Joon Kong in South Korea founded Kokam to manufacture polymer processing equipment, including polyester film and polarized film manufacturing systems, and breathable (porous) film-casting systems. In the late 1990s, Kokam expanded its business to designing and manufacturing lithium-ion/polymer secondary batteries and succeeded in developing the world's first high-capacity lithium-ion polymer batteries.

It is therefore not surprising that it was a Japanese motorcycle manufacturer, Yamaha, that first made use of lithium battery technology for an electric bike. On April 1, 1994, using its power assistance system (PAS; Patent EP 0822136 A2) developed by Izumi Yamashita, Yoshiharu Yokoyama and Takeshi Nagase, Yamaha launched its first electric bike worldwide. While the cycle frame and wheels and finished unit were supplied by Bridgestone, the prismatic lithium-ion batteries and charger were made by the Japan Storage Battery Co. Ltd., which was already supplying this battery to PHS (Personal "Handy" System) phones.[3] Yamaha would go on to manufacture more than 300,000 electric bike systems a year, and, to date, its system is implemented on more than 2.7 million electrically assisted bicycles worldwide. Over in Europe, Yamaha MD, Maxime de la Morandière, successfully lobbied for the laws to be changed to allow for e-assisted bicycles, first in Germany and later at the European level. Since convincing consumers with a unique product was difficult, Yamaha soon persuaded its competitors Sanyo, Panasonic, Mitsubishi, National Bicycle Industrial, Honda, Suzuki and many others to position themselves in this new market. In 1998, manufacturers' total shipments reached 216,000 units.

Using a lead-acid battery, lone British engineer Cedric Lynch had continued to use his bike daily. Then, in 2000, he heard about the improved energy density of lithium batteries:

> I first contacted a firm called AEA Technologies the former Atomic Energy Authority which had been privatized in the 1990s. It was manufacturing lithium batteries. They wouldn't sell me cells, only a complete custom system and for 5 kwH they quoted about £30,000! I didn't go for it but then a couple of years' later I became aware of the Chinese ThunderSky cells which were available on the market. 5 kWh at £1,500. I had to develop my own management system so all the cells were kept within their specified voltage range.

Founded by Winston Chung, Shenzen Battery Ltd. (based in Shenzhen, Guangdong Province, China) had produced its first batch of white Thunder Sky lithium-ion batteries in August 1998. From 2005, this company's annual output would be more than 100,000,000 amp-hours. Although not all Thunder Sky batteries lived up to their advertised performance, with Thunder Sky products installed in his bike, Cedric was able to motor for 200 miles (320 km) at 50 miles per hour with a top speed of just over 60 miles per hour (80 kph).

> The original Thunder Sky cells were of the lithium-manganese type. In about 2004 the company introduced lithium-cobalt cells, which are a vast improvement because their internal resistance is lower by a factor of about 10. In 2006 Thunder Sky discontinued the lithium-manganese and lithium-cobalt cells and replaced them with lithium-iron-phosphate, with slightly lower energy density but longer claimed life. These cells also have low internal resistance and a very uniform voltage over almost the whole of the discharge, and they can be charged very fast. Some importers in other countries initially would not handle Thunder Sky lithium-iron-phosphate cells, because there was a patent dispute about them and the importers were worried that the cells could be seized by Customs. This dispute appears to have been resolved.

In 1993, Dr. Malcolm R. Currie, 64, after retiring from Hughes Aircraft and spearheading such projects as stealth aircraft, cruise missiles and satellite navigation in the U.S. Gulf War effort, teamed up with Malcolm N. Bricklin, a car importer, to establish the Electric Bicycle Company in Addison, Texas, to make the EV Warrior electric bicycle. It would be produced by Giant, a major bicycle company, and its electrical components produced by Sanyo. Bricklin briefed 140 dealers to sell the product. The Warrior, which came in seven colors and was three years in development, resembled a mountain bike with a steel box behind the seat that straddled the rear wheel. Inside the box were two 24-volt electric motors powered by two disadvantageous, rechargeable 12-volt lead-acid batteries. In the view of Bricklin and Currie, the electric bike promised a first step to winning people over to the idea of electric cars.

Jon Geffen and Ron Tonkins set up one of the first retail auto dealerships selling EV Warrior e-bikes in Portland, Oregon. Geffen recalls:

> I also spent many hours campaigning and lobbying Portland city officials at the Oregon Legislature to get e-bikes classified as bicycles rather than motor vehicles. I wore out a lot of shoe soles walking up and down the aisles of the Capital and sore fingers from dialling the phone, and in its final stages I accomplished that very goal. I also joined the Clean Cities Coalition where we educated the public about this cleaner form of transport.[4]

The EV Warrior eventually fell apart over cost, dissatisfaction with the supply relationships, and lack of sales, with the various partners going their separate ways.

While working at General Motors, Frank E. Jamerson, PhD, had started fuel-cell and lithium-ion research programs. Ready to retire in early 1990s, Jamerson gave his last presentations on behalf of the U.S. Advanced Battery Consortium, of which he was then the assistance program manager for electric vehicles, at a conference in Austria. It was here that he saw his first electric bicycle and was hooked, deciding to focus his retirement years on electric bicycles (and batteries specifically). In 1993, Jamerson tried to import a German Diamant "Citiblitz" to sell in shops to introduce the public to electrified transportation. His last assignment at GM had been the EV1 automobile, and he felt the electric bicycles would be a way to introduce the American public to electric transportation. He sold none, as dealers were not interested in anything other than pedal bikes. In 1995, he wrote a report for Malcolm Currie, of the newly established Electric Bicycle Company, titled "Electric Bikes Worldwide." This became an annual publication, *Electric Bikes Worldwide Reports*, with co-author Ed Benjamin, who with Susanne Bruesch and Hannes Neupert founded a global consulting business, eCycleElectric LLC, in 1996. This publication has had a major impact on the promotion of pedelecs worldwide.

In 1995, Joseph P. LaStella, who had worked for the Consolidated Edison Company in New York City for more than 20 years in various engineering and management systems, set up Battery Automated Transportation International (BAAT) to produce electric cars and bicycles in an old Lockheed factory in Burbank, California. According to BAAT, its zinc-air batteries would enable the vehicles to run for more than 400 miles without recharging. The first rechargeable zinc air batteries were manufactured in 1996 by Slovenian innovator Miro Zorič. Although prototypes were made, production never began. In addition, Diane Salutare, LaStella's girlfriend and the company's bookkeeper, was found to have run a lingerie business out of BAAT's office. She advertised in area newspapers for models to wear lingerie samples at parties she organized to sell the clothing.

In 1996, Dennis N. Sauve set up EV Rider Inc. in Sarasota, Florida. He not only became the first to import Japanese e-bikes but also designed and sold electric mobility scooters. With its lightweight aluminum alloy frame, the Citbug was chain-driven by a 24-volt 200-watt DC motor, with energy from two 12-volt SLA. In 2002, Sauve later designed and patented a lightweight, compact collapsible four-wheel folding electric scooter.

Over in Santa Rosa, California, Scott Cronk and Rick Whisman had plans to make an electric motorcycle. While Whisman left after a few months to focus on a new family, Cronk was joined by Tom Healey and David Lloyd to develop the first prototype, affectionately called Thunderchild (after H.G. Wells's *War of the Worlds*). Thunderchild was based off on a Mustang Stallion running chassis (12-inch wheels and hard-tail frame with a sprung seat), coupled with a series-wound DC motor and a helical gear box (the "Rock Box"). For energy, they chose VRLA units. Lithium was not the only option. Recently, a Gates team led by electrochemist John Devitt had innovated small, cylindrical lead-acid X cells containing spirally wound electrodes that had twice the capacity of a normal lead-acid battery. These were called valve-regulated lead-acid (VRLA) batteries. The small single cells made by Gates were trademarked as Cyclon cells. The Optima is a similarly constructed large car battery of 6 cells; the original weighs 37.5 pounds (17 kg), and there is also a version for deep-cycle use (as opposed to just engine starting) that weighs 44 pounds (20 kg). The Optima battery was originally sold by the Norwegian firm Gylling Energi; now it is offered by American firm Johnson Controls, though it has always been made in the United States. This type of battery has similar capacity to a normal battery at low discharge rates, but at high rates it delivers a much higher proportion of its nominal capacity than a normal battery does; in addition, it is possible to make a full recharge in about half an hour, which is not possible with a normal lead-acid battery.

Scott Cronk used Optima cells in a 48-volt DC, 38-amp-hour configuration. All lights and the horn ran directly off the 24-volt DC battery power. An innovative fabric body, styled by Roger Gutierrez of San Francisco, covered Thunderchild. This custom fabric body was stretched over tensioned fiberglass rods, mounted to the frame. The "e-meter" was mounted in the headlight and kept track of power and energy levels to provide basic engineering data. Lectra had a top speed of about 45 miles per hour (72 kph) and a range of 35 miles (56 km). In 1996, Che Voight, Volker Scholze, and Ralf Wohl joined Scott to develop the VR24 drive system. The VR24 was a "variable reluctance" motor and controller—a technology desired for its high efficiency, robustness, good power density, and low manufactured cost (in volume). The VR24 offered regenerative, anti-lock braking, and a unique "growling" sound. Until 1999, Electric Motorbike Inc. (EMB) built one hundred Lectra units, marketed as street legal. Each original Lectra had a 17-digit vehicle identification number (VIN) that began with "4ZMRAE" and ended with a serial number between 00001 and 00101.

In 1999, Lee Iacocca, 75-year-old former director of the Ford Motor Company and then Chrysler, started EV Global Motors to build electric bicycles, using sales staff from the former EV Warrior to set up dealerships in California, Arizona and Florida. EVG had already selected its supply partner: Fairly Bike Manufacturing Company (FBM), run by the Chien family and headquartered in Taipei, Taiwan, since 1977. EMB was also chosen by Iacocca to engineer drive systems. The power unit chosen was made by Fritz Heinzmann GmbH of Schonau, Germany. Heinzmann had been making a reliable, high-torque motor to operate the engine controls that came along in the 1980s and started to make its own disc motors because the company could not find a source for the motors it needed. In the early 1990s it started a project to offer electric bike hub motors, using the disc motor inside a hub with a gear reduction set. In 1995 Heinzmann launched its first e-bike motor following the launch of the Estelle e-bike.

Despite this expertise, the disadvantage of the Heinzmann-powered EV Global SX was its heavy lead-acid battery with a low autonomy. It is rumored

Heinzmann's Estelle pedelec proved very successful (Heinzmann GmbH & Co. KG).

that the final straw came when the company started offering the electric bikes with not-ready-for-prime-time lithium batteries that burned down a few garages. One of these incidents was in a hanger that housed some private jets, and the cost of cleaning the jets of the soot from the fire created by two EVG bikes burning was rumored to be more than a million dollars. EVG never recovered from such disasters.

Simultaneously, Peugeot PSA in France had been working on an electric scooter as part of the company's slogan, "Tomorrow's Town." This model was based on Peugeot's Zenith gas scooter, with which it shared body panels and suspension parts. It was powered by a 3.8-horsepower (2.8 kW) DC motor fed from three SAFT nickel-cadmium monoblocs giving an 18-volt, 100-amp-hour battery that took 2 hours to charge to 95 percent but 5 hours to recharge fully. Built around a "double cradle," the frame held the batteries low down between and behind the rider's feet, providing a very low center of gravity. The electronic controller and onboard charger were housed under the seat. The scooter weighed 254 pounds (115 kg). It had a nominal range of 25 miles (40 km) at 28 miles per hour (45 kph), but this distance could be extended by using economy mode, which limited the speed to 19 miles per hour (30

1993: The Peugeot Scoot'Elec was powered by a 3.8-horsepower (2.8 kW) DC motor fed from three Saft nickel-cadmium monoblocs giving an 18-volt, 100-amp-hour battery that took five hours to recharge fully (Fonds de Dotation Peugeot pour la Mémoire de l'Histoire Industrielle).

kph). Peugeot launched its Scoot'Elec product in 1995 at the Mondial du deux-roues in Paris. Buyers would be aided by l'ADEAME (Agence de l'Environnement et de la Maîtrise de l'Energie). Estimated sales for the 2003 season were 1,500 units, usually through motorcycle and other stores. The Peugeot Scoot'Elec continued to sell until 2006, with the company projecting an updated version by 2011.

In 1997, Sir Clive Sinclair, former creator of the C5 and Zike, continued to present innovations with the Zero-Emission Transport Accessory (ZETA), a motor that sat on the rear wheel of an ordinary pedal bike. Although more than 15,000 were said to be sold worldwide, this model was soon replaced by the ZETA II, a small lead-acid battery strapped to the bicycles crossbar a motor with a belt held above the front wheel by two metal poles, a couple of brackets and a piece of string with a lever. Lack of sales eventually led to the Excalibur ZETA III in 2000, comprising a single unit (containing motor, battery and charger) that fit over the front wheel and clipped on to the handlebar of the bicycle, for simple and easy assembly.

In the United Kingdom, Raleigh Bicycle Company had been manufacturing bicycles since 1885. In 1997, the company launched the Select, incorporating a proportional power-control system that automatically monitored and matched the rider's energy input, switching in electric assistance only when required. Unfortunately, Select was too early and too expensive to have much impact on sales, and it was dropped.

In 1998, for their graduation work at the Design University of Berlin, students Norbert Haller, Johannes Cremer and Heinz Redlich, inspired by the motorcycle designs of the 1920s and 1930s, came up with a retro pedelec: the A2B. It was presented at Eurobike by Hawk Bikes. Some years later, Hawk Bikes brought a variety of electric and non-electric models to the market, while Haller has continued to design LEVs.

The e-bike returned to the Netherlands after a half a century. In 1998, Sparta, a bicycle manufacturer from Apeldoorn famous for its mopeds, reintroduced the e-bicycle in 1998 through the nickel-cadmium Pharos. The company saw that the market for mopeds was going down and wanted to try a new road. It made use of the PAS system developed by Yamaha. A big advantage was that the batteries were stored in the tubes of the frame. Sparta opened the Dutch market for e-bikes, and a couple of years later other manufacturers in Holland followed this trend.

The early torque sensors for Sparta were designed by ID Bike. This was a strain gauge on the hub motor sold as a TMM-1. Sparta bought a license to this patent. Johnny Dube, of BionX, and Gijs Roovers, his partner at ID Bike, filed for patents on nearly identical systems in the same week, both regarding the use of strain gauge on a hub motor. BionX's application was filed a couple of days earlier than ID Bike, and the two companies would ultimately agree that BionX would benefit from the patent and sell it worldwide, while ID Bike would do so in Europe. ID Bike would later develop the TMM 4 Torque sensor, which would become the primary sensor for use on EU market pedelecs for several years. Alongside the BionX, ID Bike, and Panasonic/BK Tech sensors, there were some very clumsy sensors created in China to avoid the patents.

Folding pedal bikes had been around on both sides of the Atlantic since the first patent filed in 1887 by Emmit G. Latta of Friendship, New York, working for the Pope Manufacturing Company. Danish-born Mikael Pedersen of Dursley, England, developed a folding version of his cantilever bicycle that included a rifle rack and was used in the Second Boer War in 1900. Ninety-seven years, later Honda of Japan presented its Racoon Compo, a folding nickel-cadmium-battery e-bike, at the 32nd Tokyo Motor Show, where its dual potential for shopping around town and storage in a car for use with travel or leisure pursuits made it a popular attraction. There were three color options: Surf Blue Metallic, Matte Gray Metallic, and Fighting Red. But neither the Racoon Compo nor its successor the 44-pound (20 kg) Step Compo proved successful, and they soon went out of production.

In June 1997 Cedric Lynch went to Innsbruck, Austria, to take part in the Austro Solar event in the province of Tirol, organized by the automobile club ÖAMTC and the electricity industry VEÖ, as well as one of the EVN Cup events in Teesdorf, south of Vienna. Motorcycle adaptations used valve-regulated lead-acid batteries such as the Optima. Cedric was the overall winner in the Solar Cup Denmark rally from Esbjerg to Copenhagen. "I missed the ceremony at the end because my front wheel collapsed at the end of the last special test which was on a horse racing track (Travbane) with rough gravel surface (in Danish horse racing the horses pull light cycle-wheeled carts with the riders in)," he said. Cedric returned for the 1998 competition in and around Aalborg, winning the lightweight category, and he would have won overall if the scoring system had not been changed so that penalty points for energy consumption were now divided by the weight category of the vehicle (weight of the vehicle itself, not of the people or load it was carrying). The winning vehicle was a Toyota RAV4 that was in weight category 8, the highest.

At this time, Susanne Brüsch was studying languages at the University of Heidelberg. As part of her coursework, she tasked herself with creating a word in English and seeing that word in common use by the people involved. She was also working with Hannes Neupert at *ExtraEnergy* on various

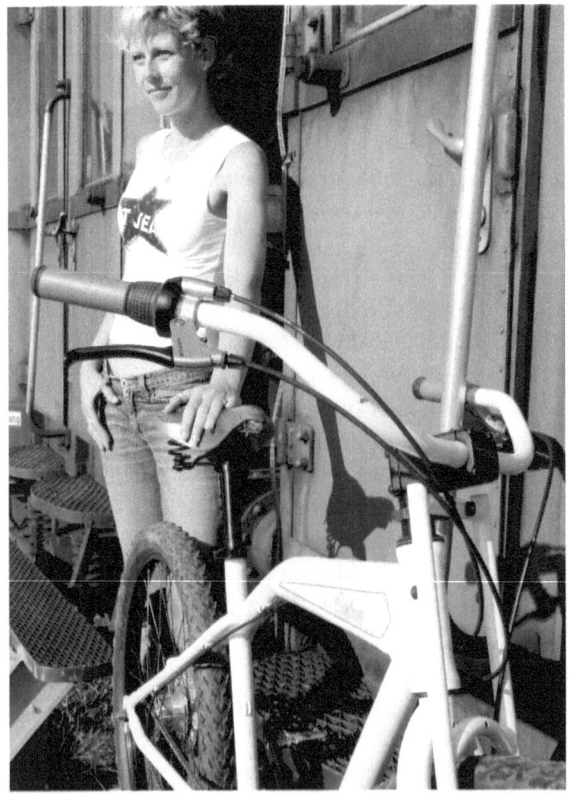

In 1999, Susanne Brüsch, a language graduate at Heidelberg University, coined the word *pedelec* (PEDal ELECtric) to describe vehicles in which the pedal activates the motor. This word has become universally accepted in the 21st century (ExtraEnergy.org/Hannes Neupert).

promotional events, where there was a need to clarify international communications on the different types of light electric vehicles. Taking an idea suggested by Frank Jamerson, PhD, and with the help of *ExtraEnergy*, Bike Europe, the Japan Cycle Press and other media, she officially created the word *pedelec* as a designation of electric bicycles in which pedaling actuates the motor; it comes from *PEDal ELectric* and was first used in Brüsch's thesis "Pedelecs: Fahrzeuge der Zukunft" [Pedelecs: Vehicles of the Future], published in April 1999. It is now a word regularly used in the 21st century, as common as the word *drone*.

6

Urban E-Bikes Worldwide

Thanks to investment in innovative electrochemical couples such as the nickel-metal-hydride and lithium-ion polymer battery, urban-oriented pedelecs and scooters, like their aerial equivalent drones, have proliferated into hundreds of millions, often as additions to conventional bicycle manufacturers' range. Each and every inventor has been adding their own touch to this product.

In 1989 Mark Aubrey Searles of Winchester, England, set up a bicycle company called Modern Times Ltd. and began work on a water-bottle-shaped battery pedelec he called Cytronex C1. Launched in 2008, several front-hub motor models followed: the Cytronex Cannondale Capo, Cytronex Cannondale Super Six and Cytronex Trek FX models. In 2010, Searles was awarded the Entrepreneur of the Year in the Business Awards.

In 1999, Jean-Yves Dubé, founder of Electric Propulsion Systems in Asbestos, Quebec, Canada, applied for a patent for a brushless, high-performance electric motor and control for retrofitting an existing bicycle, calling his system BionX. EPS was the only bike-wheel motor manufacturer in Canada. In his workshops, even the tools were manufactured by him for his 25-strong team. By 2005, production had risen and the units were selling in 200 sports shops across Canada, including 135 in Quebec alone. Dubé was planning to sell 10,000 units by 2006. Police officers from Saint-Jérôme had retrofitted their bicycles with the BionX system on a trial basis. EPS also spent three years working with the American giant Smith & Wesson (the famous firearms maker) to design a police pedelec, while German automaker BMW was exploring the possibility of marketing its own range of bikes with the BionX motor. In 2008, EPS was purchased by Manfred Gingl, head of the Magna Marque auto-parts giant, headquartered in Aurora, Ontario, Canada. BionX continued to provide 250–500-watt motor/555-watt-hour battery packages for pedelec makers in Europe and North America. In February 2018, BionX declared bankruptcy and sold all assets at auction.

6. Urban E-Bikes Worldwide   97

In 2001 Canadian Steve Miloshev was working on a draining project in China when he discovered electric bikes and scooters. Taking one back to Vancouver, Miloshev used it to ride around Yaletown and downtown, constantly stopped by people asking him about the scooter. In 2002, the Canadian Motor Vehicle Safety Act was changed in BC and Quebec to exclude electric bicycles, and some types of electric scooters, from the vehicle category, providing they were compliant with Transport Canada regulations. They were instead classified as power-assisted bicycles and could be used without a driver's license or registration. Five years later, those changes were enacted for all of Canada and the United States. Miloshev set up a company called Motorino and imported a container of Chinese pedelecs and e-scooters to Vancouver. Unfortunately, they were poorly made, with heavy lead-acid batteries, requiring improvements before they could be sold. Since the Canadian government limits all electric bikes and scooters to 500-watt continuous power, regular bikes and scooters were lacking the necessary torque to make them practical on inclines. So, in 2008, Miloshev and his team came up with a continuous current transmission (CCT) system to make their scooters competitive with the torque and hill-climbing ability of 50cc gasoline motor scooters, which in turned increased sales.

Just in time for Christmas 2002, Bosch introduced the first lithium-ion battery cordless screwdriver, the IXO. Sony had succeeded in optimizing lithium-ion battery technology, which at the time was just 11 years old, previously only suitable for very low currents (slow discharge), even for high currents (fast discharge). For Bosch, this meant a victory over cheap screwdrivers from China; for pedelecs, it was another breakthrough.

In 2003, Panasonic launched a folding pedelec called the WiLL, with its 20-inch rear and 18-inch front wheels and lithium-manganese battery, as did China-based eZee with the Quando.

Badly managed high-capacity lithium batteries do not like hot weather. In 2005, Said Al-Hallaj and Jan Robert Selman and a team of engineers working at the Illinois Institute of Technology, in conjunction with the U.S. Department of Defense's Future Force Warrior Program (regularly out in the Middle East), developed and patented a battery management system material that evens the heat in the battery pack to avoid hot spots. This problem is also encountered by electric scooters and motorcycles, the latter with high driverange and power requirements but limited room available for batteries. Al-Hallaj and Selman then founded AllCell Technologies to make and sell their product.

Since the late 1990s, Thomas Grübel of Munich had been developing an electric scooter with one of the first interchangeable lithium-ion battery management systems for scooters. In 2001, with backing from Farid Francis Al Zweigniederlassung Rahi and Michail Kapouniaris, Grübel co-founded E-Max with a production facility in Oberhaching, Germany The first prototypes of the E-Max range, designed by Paolo Valcic in Italy, were shown in 2006 at the EICMA Motorcycle Fair in Milan, Italy. From then on, the company built up distributors across Europe to include Germany, the United Kingdom, France, Italy, Sweden, Norway and Slovenia. It started mass production in October 2007 at its factory in Wuxi, near Shanghai, China, with the factory under a German management team. At the time, Grübel obtained a patent for framework for managing a variable lithium-ion battery. The E-Max 140L had a top speed limited to 28 miles per hour (45 kph) and a range of 62–75 miles (100–120 km) on a full charge.

In 2001, two Russian electrical engineers, Boris A. Maslov and Alex Pyntikov, working with investor Allen Anderson (and Anderson's hired president Joe Perry), started WaveCrest Laboratories to build and market TidalForce electric bicycles with a 36-volt electric-hub brushless motor built into the rear-wheel hub and a 36-volt nickel-metal hydride battery pack built into the front-wheel hub. The Russians had more than $100 million of investment money, a retired army general as CEO, and an emphasis on grabbing military contracts. Three models were available: the M-750, the S-750 Traditional hard-tail mountain bike and the iO-750 Cruiser. WaveCrest went out of business in 2006, with Maslov and Pyntikov going their separate ways.

In 2001, Dennis J. Eichenberg, John S. Kolacz, and Paul F. Tavernelli, engineers at NASA's Glenn Research Center in Cleveland, Ohio, normally involved with science and technology for use in aeronautics and space, modified an EV Global electric bike with ultracapacitor batteries. The performance was extraordinary. The range of 34.8 miles that was achieved with an initial speed of 5 mph with no grade is almost twice the advertised range of 20 miles. The vehicle operated for 5.7 hours under these conditions. The ultracapacitors would never have to be replaced in most applications. While ultracap buses are being used more and more, ultracap motorcycles have not gone beyond the prototype stage.

In 2003, Sparta in Appeldoorn, Holland, continued its progress by teaming up with electronics and embedded software firm 3T BV to produce the Ion pedelec, working on the basis of a pedal force sensor. This sensor registers how much force the driver puts on the pedals, transmitting the registered signal to the ION® computer. The computer then compares the effort made with the driving program the rider has chosen. Based on this calculation, the powerful motor is directed to giving more or less energy. Due to this innovative system, Sparta became the European market leader in bicycles with electric pedal assistance from 2004. Six years later, Sparta launched the E-Motion series, following which the Pick-up, the Granny and the Country Tour were introduced with electric support. In that year there were also other electric specials such as the E-Kargo (cargo bike), Fold-E (folding bike) and the Double-E (Tandem).

6. Urban E-Bikes Worldwide

In 2003, Sparta of Apeldoorn, Netherlands, launched the Sparta Ion series electric bicycle. Most competitors in the bicycle world did not recognize this bike, and even if they did, they did not see the power in it. After overcoming several technical issues, the Ion was sold very successfully, earning so much profit during the following five years that the mother company, Accell, was able to go shopping every year for one or two other major bicycle companies in Europe to add to its group portfolio. This success was repeated several years later when Accell launched the Haibike electric mountain bike, which has been the key money maker for Accell in recent years (ExtraEnergy.org/Hannes Neupert).

Returned to Bengal, India, e-scooter pioneer Anil Ananthakrishna had not given up. In 2004, his company Eko Vehicles Pvt. Ltd. launched the Eko-Cosmic scooter, which could run for 31 miles on a single charge. The company sold more than 15,000 units of its first product under the brand names Cosmic and Velociti. The EV-60, Eko-Strike and ET-100 hybrid have followed since.

Richard Brian Thorpe of Chessington, United Kingdom, a former McLaren Cars design engineer with a 25-year career working in the motorsports and light electric vehicle industry, set up Karbon Kinetics Ltd. with the aim of creating the perfect e-bike. Following considerable research and development, KKL's Gocycle was made available to the public in April 2009. Inspired by F1 high-performance and automotive design, the Gocycle's front-hub-motor and rear-pedal-drive concept was innovative; the drive was connected to the front wheel, which is the motor assist, while the rear wheel has the standard pedal-drive mechanism. The Gocycle was also the first injection-molded magnesium alloy bicycle in history, complete with a rear shock absorber to ease riding over potholes, as well as pit-stop-style quick-release wheels front and back. It could sustain momentum for up to 20 miles without pedal assistance at a top speed of 15 miles per hour but took just under two hours to fully recharge from the mains. Having won the Best Electric Bike Award at Eurobike 2009, Thorpe developed Gocycle G2, launched at Eurobike 2012 as the first production electric bike to be digitally connected via Bluetooth. It again won the Best Electric Bike Award. In April 2016, KKL introduced the Gocycle G3 in Europe, with its automotive-inspired daytime running light (DRL), another first in the industry.

In Japan alone, sales of pedelecs amounted to 450,000 units. Pedelec sales were also expanding rapidly in Europe, particularly the Netherlands and Switzerland. In Germany, Heinzmann of Schonau continued to supply its pedelec system to the German and Danish post offices and to the official FifaVelo taxis for the World Cup Soccer Championship of 2006. A total of 700,000 pedelecs were sold in Europe in 2010, up from 200,000 in 2007 and 500,000 units in 2009.

Sanyo came back in with an improvement of its electric hybrid bicycle, which boasted a "loop charge function" that both generated electricity and charged the low self-discharge nickel-metal hydride rechargeable battery while in use. Both the battery and the bike were named the Eneloop. However, when Panasonic merged with Sanyo, bike production came to an end.

Meanwhile, Malcolm Currie started Currie Technologies with staff that were mostly from the product development side of EV Warrior. Currie's biggest commercial success was its scooter, which was sourced first from Taioku and later from Bangkok Cycle. Eventually, the company declared bankruptcy, was bought by Ace Trikes, went bankrupt again, and was bought by a turnaround investment group, which restored profitably and then sold the company to Accell. Since then, the name of the company has become Accell North America, selling mostly under the Raleigh brand. Currie did license Mongoose and Schwinn labels for its scooters for a few years, and this causes some confusion. In terms of innovation, in 2007 Currie Technologies presented the iZip Express pedelec, featuring the NuVinci Continuously Variable Planetary transmission.[1]

In 2008, brothers K.C. and J.C. Mahindra, of the Mahindra & Mahindra Ltd. steel trading company in Maharashtra, India, decided to enter the e-bike market by teaming up with Kinetic Motors, founded by H.K. Firodia, which had been making and selling its Kinetic Luna moped to Argentina, Brazil, the United States, and Sri Lanka. Mahindra discontinued the Luna, which had been very cheap (15,000 rupees, or about £160) and sold in huge numbers (millions). At the same time, Vasily Shkondin founded Hero Eco in New

Delhi to develop electric two-wheelers, which would lead to the manufacture of the A2B Metro electric bike at a factory in Ludhiana.

Patrick Dennis Davin, an entrepreneur from Perth, Western Australia, co-founded Capital Pacific Pty. Ltd. and Optima Corporation. In 1999, Davin also established a scooter production company called Vmoto using his long-term association with Chinese industry. Seeing E-Max of Germany's success, in 2009 Vmoto acquired the German company lock, stock and barrel. In 2013, Vmoto launched its own electric two-wheel scooters with an innovative handlebar-controlled forward and backward speed-adjusting system, patented by Jiqun Jing and Baoguo Weng for mass production in Nanjing, China. Soon after, Davin decided to move on. In 2016, he founded MUTE in London, a platform that enables both businesses and individuals to lease electric scooters, which, thanks to almost £1 million raised by crowdfunding, is already active in Bali, Perth and Shanghai.

Meanwhile, Thomas Grübel, E-Max's co-founder, had left when Vmoto took over. With Nicholas Holdcraft and Gerald Vollnhals, Grübel founded Govecs GmbH, headquartered in Munich, Germany. The main product line is one of electric scooters, using a lithium-ion accumulator without memory effect. Of particular note is the electrification of a former German gas-moped, the Schwalbe (of which, between 1964 and 1986, over one million came off the production line in Suhl, then in the German Democratic Republic, making it the most successful single-brand European scooter in history). Working with Bosch technology, Govecs launched the e-Schwalbe with its maximum speed of 28 miles per hour in the summer of 2017.

Also in Germany, Markus Riese and Heiko Müller of Darmstadt, south of Hesse, graduated from the Technical University of Darmstadt and began to innovate in bicycle design, particularly folding bikes. In 2009, Riese & Müller, based in Weiterstadt, presented its first pedelec, called the Delite Hybrid 500S. From then on, the company built up an eleven-model variant 27.5-inch build, making use of Fallbrook's CVP NuVinci smooth transition gearing and Gates' carbon-drive belt system, as well as a cargo e-bike. In 2016, when Bosch produced the DualBattery package, designed for quick, simple mounting, charging and riding, Riese & Müller was the first to implement the range-extending system. For 2018, the company announced its entry into the U.S. market with its Packster cargo e-bike model and the Delite GT signature including Riese & Müller's control technology, DualBattery technology from Bosch, Syntace and Fox Factory components with a Kashima coating, Shimano XTR Di2 gears and high-grade disc brakes. Every Delite GT signature is numbered and comes with a certificate signed by Markus Riese and Heiko Müller.

Since 1954, Polaris Industries, based in Roseau, Minnesota, had become known worldwide for its snowmobiles; in 2009, it also decided to invest in light electric vehicles with a company called EVantage. The backbone of the project was a patent, taken out by the innovative Michael Krieger of Vector Products Inc., for a motorized bicycle with trainer mode. EVantage's first streamlined e-bike, the Polaris 1.0, was launched in 2011. It was equipped with EVantage's DuoDrive system, which allows the motor to use both speed and high torque, switching from a SpeedDrive configuration on flat or low-intensity terrain to a TorqueDrive configuration on hilly or other high-resistance terrain. In the first twelve months, more than one hundred dealers signed up in the United States, Canada and Latin America. Before long they had developed a range of 3 different lines with total of 7 models to fill all niches. The Vector line included all around rugged e-bikes designed to go from the trail to the street and every place in between. The Strive line featured touring models, built for comfort and ease. The Meridian line targeted the urban commuter with its sleek European styling, fenders and front LED lighting. By 2015, Version 2.0 of the Polaris was launched globally, with three new proprietary technologies in bicycle gearing, battery regeneration and auto terrain-sensing controls, making it the only bicycle geared like a sports car. Two years later, Polaris announced plans to launch an electric motorcycle under its Indian brand marquee, with a range of 120–140 miles. Polaris also owns Victory, which produces the 40-kilowatt Brammo technology motorcycle (see chapter 7).

Historically, the Harley-Davidson and Indian brands first began competing 115 years ago. Today they are once in commercial competition, but now electrically.

In 2009 Thomas Binggeli of Switzerland founded a company called Stromer (Rover) to create a more muscular pedelec capable of speeds of up to 28 miles per hour (45 kph) with rider assistance, as opposed to the 15 miles per hour (25 kph) characteristic of conventional pedelecs. The 500-watt ST1 was produced in 2011 and met with a mixed reception. It had a greater speed and range and was seen as the poor man's Zero. Used irresponsibly, however, it was potentially dangerous to other users of bike lanes and cycle paths. Speed pedelecs (SP), with up to 1 kilowatt of power, are also made by such companies as Bulls (E45), FLX (750 watt), Koga, Riese & Muller, and others, and they have set urban authorities worldwide the challenge of regulation. Categorized as a light moped, the SP must have a number plate, mirrors, brake light and horn; it must also be insured, and the rider must wear a helmet. Some countries are limiting these vehicles to 22 miles per hour (35 kph) and suggest that they be confined to the roadway.

Another addition to the speed pedelec fleet will be VanguardSpark, a team composed of Erik Buell and F-X Terny of Vanguard Motorcycles in New York City and Frédéric Vasseur, founder of Spark Racing Technology, Île-de-France (the company that built the 40 chassis for the inaugural Formula E electric racing series). Their Speedbike will offer a healthy and classy alternative to mopeds and small scooters, while their Commuter will be for urban use.

In 2010, Torun Tokushige of Shibuya, Tokyo, Japan, founded Terra Motors to develop and make pure electric motorcycles for export to Asia: India, Vietnam, Bangladesh, Nepal, Cambodia, Indonesia and Myanmar. As Japan's four major motorcycle manufacturers are arguably the best in the world, Tokushige hired professional engineers from these companies (for example, Shinji Minomiya and Hiroshi Shitakani from Yamaha and Tamakasa Masuzaki from Honda). This resulted in the A4000i, with a top speed of 37.28 miles per hour (60 km) and an iPhone system. Terra Motors aimed to ship 10,000 units by the end of 2013, and 100,000 in the next two to three years.

The numbers have continued to rise. According to Citylab, somewhere between 700,000 and 1,200,000 e-bikes were sold in 2012, twice as many as in 2009 and eight times as many as in 2006 (the story has been similar every year since). Many of those sales were made in the Netherlands and Germany. In the Netherlands, some 17 percent of all new bikes sold were e-bikes. In 2012, the French Post Office launched its program of electric-vehicle mail delivery, going on to acquire some 18,000 pedelecs built by Arcade Cycles in La Roche Sur Yon and Cycleurope in Romilly-sur-Seine.

In 2012, Momentum Electric, with its credo of "Moving Everybody," was founded by Glasgow School of Art–trained product designer and ex–Hoover innovator Yin Tsao Tan and athlete Andreas Törpsch in Bromley-by-Bow, East London, England. Their Model-T e-bikes incorporate the innovative Autorq technology. In 2016, after three years of research and development, Momentum Electric launched the most powerful legal electric bike, the VIT-S, on crowdfunding campaign site Kickstarter. VIT-S is a play on the French word for speed (*vitesse*) and the letter "S" also symbolizes the S-shaped frame as well as speed. The frame was designed in collaboration with award-winning Milan-based industrial design consultancy Meneghello Paolelli Associati. The front forks are lightweight and made from carbon fiber. The innovative handlebar is shock absorbing, reducing fatigue from road vibrations. With a maximum power of 700 watts, 95 newton-meters of torque and a range of up to 99 miles (160 km) on a single charge, the VIT-S meets EU- and U.S.–rated power requirements of 250 watts and 350 watts. The motor is the result of a joint venture between Nidec and Itochu as they break into the e-bike motor OEM market. Nidec is the world market leader in precision motors, and Itochu is the largest company in Japan. Momentum Electric is the first company to launch an e-bike using the Nidec motor, the results of one of the smallest e-bike companies in Europe teaming up with one of the largest companies in Japan.

In 2014, Germany's Deutsche Post DHL purchased a small start-up called StreetScooter based in Aachen. Within 18 months, it had developed its own basic, electric postal vans to zoom around crowded cities, delivering post and parcels—and handling that all-important "last mile" of delivery. StreetScooter now makes fully electric pickups, vans, bikes, and trikes, which it also sells to third parties. It says that its roughly 5,000 e-vehicles have driven almost 8.4 million miles so far and saved more than 16,000 tons of CO_2 annually. DHL plans to ramp up production of StreetScooters to 10,000 units a year and is building a second factory in Germany in 2018, allowing it to sell more vehicles to third parties. In May 2018 Milk&More, a Chicago-headquartered dairy company, further expanded its UK EV fleet with 200 new StreetScooter electric vans.

The Eurobike Show in 2016 marked a turning point where the pedelec reached parity with the rest of the cycling industry, taking up equal floor space at the exhibition, which had taken nine years to achieve. A new record was reached in 2015 when 535,000 pedelecs were sold in Germany. In 2016, Heinzmann launched its CargoPower RN 111 Motor, with its tremendous torque of up to 100 newton-meters on the drive wheel (not on the pedal crank, as with mid-mounted motors) and available with nominal speeds of 190–380 revolutions per minute. A speed of 15.5 miles per hour (25 kph) can therefore be achieved with a wheel diameter of 20–28 inches. And, of course, 28 miles per hour (45 kph) is also possible for speed bikes with a wheel diameter of 25 inches or more. This high torque and power density is achieved with a high-performance planetary gear, combined with innovative oil lubrication and oil cooling. Also in Germany, Kalkhoff of Cloppenburg has been manufacturing bicycles since 1919, and during the 1950s it expanded to 1,200 employees with a daily production of 5,000 frames. In 2015, Kalkhoff launched its folding pedelec, the Sahel Compact.

Urban e-bikes have gained in importance, and not without cause. In November 2017, in an event known as the Great Smog of Delhi, the air pollution spiked far beyond acceptable levels. Levels of PM2.5 and PM10 particulate matter hit 999 micrograms per cubic meter, while the safe limits for those pollutants are 60 and 100, respectively. Electrotherm, a company whose main business is industrial ovens and furnaces, based in Samakhiali in Kutch District of Gujarat, had started its research and development operations for developing electric vehicles in 2004; after two years, it became the first company to introduce electric two-wheelers in India with its YObykes. Electric scooters accounted for about 1 percent of the Indian motorcycle and 2-wheeler market in 2009, at about 120,000 units. The market was expected to grow to about 320,000 units by 2012. With a capacity of manufacturing 288,000 units per year, ET stands to meet the growing demand for e-vehicles. The YO EXL is powered by a 1-kilowatt BLDC hub motor with energy from a VRLA deep-discharge battery. On September 14, 2015, as part of the Global Himalayan Expedition, two YObykes became the first electric scooters to scale the world's highest-known motorable road, the treacherous Khardong La pass at an altitude of 18,380 feet. The expedition was completed in 4 hours and 12 minutes by Jaideep Bansal and Paras Loomba, a solar energy expert.

In July 2017, the British government announced plans to ban the sale of new diesel and gas cars and vans in the United Kingdom by 2040 in a bid to tackle harmful nitrogen dioxide emissions in a move that would shake up the whole motor industry. "With this announcement, the UK government is reinforcing the direction they've already taken by introducing the £1500 grant for two wheeled electric vehicles this year," said Umberto Uccelli, managing director of Zero Motorcycles Europe.[2]

In January 2018, the City of London Corporation's Environment Committee announced that a cargo bike scheme run jointly with zero-emission delivery operator Zedify, formed from established cargo bike delivery companies Recharge Cargo and Outspoken Delivery (which currently provide services across six UK cities), would be rolled out to all local businesses in the Smithfield and Farringdon areas. Couriers would use electric cargo pedelecs and trikes with load capacities of 220 and 550 pounds (100 and 250 kg), respectively, to make deliveries to and from a hub located at West Smithfield. The cargo bikes could drop the goods off anywhere within the Congestion Charge zone. The aim is to fill a gap that diesel vans may leave, as running one through the city center is becoming increasingly costly.

With 2,600 premature pollution-related deaths every year, Iran is among the top five countries in terms of air pollution mortality. In January 2018, Tehran Municipality began to develop a scheme to replace gasoline-powered motorbikes with electric two-wheelers. Loans at low or zero interest rates are to be offered to at least 2,000 people in the initial phase.

Innovations have continued apace, including the electric foldable Brompton. In 1975, Andrew Ritchie, a Cambridge graduate engineer and landscape gardener, started designing a folding bike in his flat overlooking the Brompton Oratory in South Kensington, London. Cedric Lynch recalls:

> Andrew Ritchie also worked on developing production tools for an early version of my motor in the mid–1980s, financed by London Innovation. He was working at Nick Ouroussoff's engineering firm Ouroussoff Engineering in the London suburb of Kew. He was working on the Brompton Bicycle at the same time and I remember being amazed by how fast and how small it folded. He showed great foresight; at that time Kew Gardens station was served by trains built in the early 1950s on which you could take a normal bicycle even at peak times.[3]

By 1987 the patented Brompton won the "Best Product" award against an international field at the Cyclex exhibition, and full-time production of the Brompton began shortly afterward.

The Brompton bike exploded in popularity due to its convenience and excellent design. The main reason for the Brompton bicycle's popularity in the United Kingdom was that between the 1980s and the early 2000s most British suburban trains were scrapped and replaced by new ones that, unlike the old trains, do not have guards' vans. Passengers are no longer allowed to bring bicycles on suburban trains at peak times unless the bicycle folds or can be dismantled so small that it can be placed on the luggage rack. Uniquely at the time of its introduction, the Brompton Bicycle could be folded in a few seconds to meet this requirement, without the use of tools and without getting the user's hands dirty. This made it for some years the only bicycle one could take on a train and then ride from the station to one's workplace or home. Soon, many rail travelers in England had a folding Brompton bike. The company also earned the Queen's Award for Export Achievement in 1995. In 2017, led by Will Butler-Adams, Brompton launched its foldable pedelec with front-wheel motor and a 300-watt-hour battery bag clipped on the front luggage block. These additional parts make the bicycle heavier at 30.2 pounds for the 2-speed version.

In 2004, inspired by Dean Kamen's Segway (see chapter 11), Grant and Shaun Ryan and a team at Christchurch, New Zealand, developed a carbon-fiber composite, 23.8-pound (10.8 kg) foldable electric mini-farthing scooter they called the YikeBike. With a folding time of 15–20 seconds, it has speed of 15.5 miles per hour (25 kph) and a range of 6–18.5 miles depending on the lithium-ion battery pack. The model V comes with an optional third

Will Butler-Adams of Brompton and the foldable pedelec with its front-wheel motor and a 300-watt-hour battery bag clipped on the front luggage block (Brompton Bikes).

wheel. Riders sit upright and steer with their hands at their side, using safety features such as LED lights and electronic anti-skid regenerative brakes. Once folded, the rider can even wear it using the supplied shoulder strap to go on a bus or subway. Released in 2009, YikeBike was ranked 15th on *Time* magazine's 50 Best Inventions and went into production in 2010.

Facing great air pollution pressure, Taiwan aims to phase out fuel-powered motorbikes by 2035. With a population of some 23 million, Taiwan is home to about 14 million motorcycles, the highest density of motorcycles in the world. At the beginning of 2018, the island decided to install 3,310 charging stations over the next five years. Currently, there are 1,800 charging stations for electric motorcycles installed and the new facilities will bring the total to around 5,000. Other incentives to switch to electric motorcycles include subsidies, special license plates, dedicated parking lots and parking discounts. Among the more than one million motorcycles sold in Taiwan in 2017, only 40,000 were electric. The total on the island is only about 100,000. However, a recent survey showed that nearly 60 percent of motorcycle users in Taiwan were willing to shift to electric.

To meet this demand, early attempts were made by KYMCO (Kwang Yang Motor Co. Ltd.), with its Queen electric scooter, and Sam Ever Industry Co., with its Ever model, not forgetting the aforementioned Giant's Lafree. Gogoro Inc. of Taipei was founded in 2011 by Horace Luke and Matt Taylor, former executives at HTC Corp. Their Smartscooter is powered by a G1 aluminum, liquid-cooled permanent magnet synchronous motor and runs on swappable Panasonic lithium-ion 18650 batteries. Smartscooters have a top speed of around 60 miles per hour, a beautiful digital dashboard, and smartphone connectivity. The Smartscooter's sensors collect information such as speed, battery level, consumption rate, system failures, and scooter falls. This information is presented to riders via Gogoro mobile apps. In the month of July 2017 alone, Gogoro delivered 4,042 new and licensed scooters. Gogoro, which has sold more than 30,000 Smartscooters in two years, operates nearly 400 battery-swapping GoStations, one less than every 0.8 miles in western Taiwan, from Keelung in the north to Pingtung in the south. On average, 14,000 battery swaps occur every day. Abroad, Gogoro has also launched electric scooter-sharing service with Robert Bosch GmbH in Berlin, made up of 1,000 Smartscooters; the same service has been launched in Paris. In September 2017, Gogoro raised U.S. $300 million (S $404 million) from Singapore's Temasek Holdings and other investors to pay for expansion and research and development. Generation Investment Management (co-founded by Al Gore), Japan's Sumitomo Corp, and French utility Engie SA also invested.

Klever Mobility Inc., the Cologne-based subsidiary of the KYMCO Group, has come up with a rear-drive gearless system called Biactron. Instead of mixing existing technologies, adding motors or batteries to ordinary bicycle frames, they designed the frames around the Biactron system, which also comprises an electronic motor lock and alarm function that will buzz and lock down the rear wheel in cases of unauthorized access. Biactron also makes it possible to upgrade the battery and the software. For example, Klever's 850-watt-hour battery can also be used for the first e-bikes that the company launched 7 years ago; Klever's speed pedelecs will be manufactured in Taipei.

In March 2018, KYMCO presented its new electric scooter, iONIX, at the Tokyo Motorcycle Show. The concept includes the scooter itself as well as an entirely new concept battery. The scooter not only contains a solid mounted battery but also has space for up to three removable batteries, which can be charged externally and then in turn charge the integrated battery.

In July 2017, Honda and Yamaha announced an experimental electric scooter rental service in Saitama City, north of Tokyo. This was directed by Hiroyuki Yanagi (L), president and representative director of Yamaha Motor Co., and Hayato Shimizu (R), mayor of Saitama City. Called E-Kizuna (*Kizuna* means "bond" in Japanese), the project aims to put 30 small electric two-wheelers for rent, with high-voltage charging and battery-swap stations. The Honda Super Cub and the Yamaha twin-engine PES2 and PED1 electric street bikes are being used.

Ronald Jozef Maria Meijs of Maastricht, Holland, has designed furniture and lighting, child products such as baby buggies, and a 2-kilowatt Retro-style electric moped he calls the MEIJS Motorman, with a top speed of 28 miles per hour and a range of 43 miles. Meijs was inspired by the early board track racers that zipped around motordromes at the beginning of the last century, such as the Schwinn cruiser or the 1915 Harley-Davidson—hence his vehicle's balloon tires, oversized headlight, and spring-mounted leather seat. Built by Mylane BV in Heerlen, the Motorman is being used in cities and towns across Europe. One Motorman owner, based in London, has done more than 1,240 miles in just over a year.

From Italy comes another longstanding company: Vespa ("wasp" in Italian). Since 1946, Vespa has built millions of gas-engine scooters. From 2009, Vespa's parent company, Piaggio of Pontedera, Italy, began to look into hybrid scooters such as the Vespa LX50 and the Piaggio X8 125. In 2016, Vespa announced that it was working on the Vespa Elettrica, with a 62-mile range. The Elettrica, to be launched in 2018, comes in a chrome grey color, but buyers can choose between seven color options for the decorative trim.

Another traditional gas-automobile tradition to lend its name to the electric scooter is the Ford Motor Company of Detroit, Michigan. In 1896, Henry Ford presented his first vehicle, called a Quadricycle or horseless carriage, with its two-cylinder engine; with the Model-T, Ford became a legend. The "OjO" was conceived in early 2014 by a group of well-seasoned inventors and entrepreneurs—Don Ratner, Dale Seiden, Alan Shapiro and Bill Woodward in Oxnard, California—who came together to create a new form of sustainable transportation for the bike lane. The vehicle has 25 miles of range, which can be doubled with an add-on battery pack. It has a top speed of around 20 miles per hour and is properly quick in the highest performance setting. A patented ergonomic design, a suspension system on both wheels and a rigid aluminum unibody structure keeps the ride smooth and stable. The name OjO was chosen because the letters O, J, and O suggested two wheels and a framework. Dale Seiden was at a trade show when he struck up a conversation with Ford about licensing, as the traditional Ford blue oval on the saddle or bodywork would give confidence to potential customers. The range of Ford OjO Commuter Scooters, an officially licensed product of Ford Motor Company, was launched at CES 2018. Color options include Ford race red, lightning blue and ingot silver and racing stripes as true Ford branded colors. Custom OjO colors include black, orange, graphite, and the vintage-inspired seafoam woody, vintage orange woody and vintage surfboard woody.

Alongside Ford, General Motors, already famous for its Chevrolet Bolt, is entering the electric bike market, as announced by GM chief executive Mary Barra. With twenty new electric vehicles planned by 2023, at least one of these will be a two-wheeler. Indeed, on August 7, 2017, GM filed to register two trademarks with the U.S. Patent and Trademark Office for Merge and Maven Merge, implying an e-bike sharing business.

Innovations will surely keep on coming. Structural engineer Behyad Ben Tarassoli founded Propella Electric Bikes in Seattle, Washington, to make an improved pedelec. It has resulted in a 34.5-pound (15.6 kg) two-wheeler with distinctive blue inner rims whose 3-pound (1.4 kg) Panasonic battery pack, no bigger than a water bottle, power-assists either a single-speed or a seven-speed model.

In April 2018, Ford Global Technologies obtained a patent for a "Vehicle with an Integrated Electric Motorcycle," where the two-wheeled bike, stored between the two front passenger seats, might actually fit into the front panel of a gasoline car. Ford imagines the car would work Batman-style, with "an ejector mechanism" that would "discharge the motorcycle from the carrier vehicle under the action of force," according to the patent. The bicycle or motorcycle—Ford uses both words in the patent—would notably be able to tap into the car's system and display, including an on-board computer, radio and navigation system, even after being separated from the main vehicle. The motorcycle would have a rechargeable battery, and both the car and the bike could keep moving even after being disconnected.

Based on the selectivity available on e-commerce, Benjamin Cochard and Antonin Guidicci at the Jambon-Buerre customized motorcycle concern in Angers, France, have developed the Gloria electric bicycle for the smartphone generation. Via an online design platform, customers' motorcycle selfies can finally reflect the taste and fashion sense of each unique rider, with a range of vintage shapes, futuristic equipment, and street fashion trends. J-B has teamed up with Pymco, a French start-up that specializes in battery management systems.

As this book goes to press, nations and towns around the world are making increasingly positive efforts to encourage the use of pedelecs. The Finnish Ministry of Transport and Communications proposed a 400€ incentive to Finns buying an electric bicycle: a total of 16.3 million euros—a budget sufficient for a total of 40,615 electric bicycles—will be earmarked for the incentive program between July 1, 2018, and December 31, 2021. Not only is the Finnish energy concern Fortum establishing a network of recharging points across the country, but it has also pioneered a sustainable system for converting horse manure into electricity using anaerobic digestion. Mexico City, whose EcoBici sharing program has more than one quarter of a million registered users, has placed an initial 340 pedelecs at bike stations through the capital. These are just two examples. In April 2018 *Statista* announced forecasts stating that global e-bike sales will reach approximately 40 million units sometime in 2023.

The rise in pedelec usage does have a downside. Official figures from the Netherlands' Central Bureau of Statistics show a near doubling of deaths on electric bikes in the last 12 months, three-quarters of which involved men of 65 years or over, with cycling fatalities in the country surpassing the number of people killed in cars. As of 2017, approximately 294,000 e-bikes had been sold in the Netherlands.

Since 2010, bicycle-sharing enterprises that have added e-bikes to their already vast fleets have proliferated. These include Jump in San Francisco and Washington, D.C.; Lime in Seattle and parts of the Bay Area San Diego; SoBi in Californian cities; and Spin in Miami and on two university campuses. Nere, a company currently operating under the name Smide in Switzerland, planned to enter the American market at the end of 2018. Then there are Mobike of Beijing, present in more than 200 cities around the world; oBike EVS in Singapore; Nextbike in Leipzig; Call-A-Bike, run by Deutsche Bahn (DB) in several German cities; and Bicincittà in Genoa and Monaco. In April 2018, the ride-share provider Uber added a new tool to its case: Jump Bikes became available via the Uber app.

This situation led to glut crisis in San Francisco, an incident otherwise known as "Scootergeddon," "Scooterpocalypse" or "Scooter Wars." This began when, without any warning to local residents or lawmakers, in an Uber-inspired strategy of "launch first, ask for forgiveness later," three start-ups—Bird, Lime, and Spin—dumped thousands of dockless, rentable e-scooters across city in the same week at the end of March 2018. Local residents soon complained that the unregulated schemes were a nuisance, as irresponsible users dumped the e-scooters on the sidewalks and even tossed them into trash cans and lakes. Other people tripped over the vehicles on the sidewalk, complaining of broken toes and dangerous collisions. It was the techies versus the tech-nots. City officials then sent cease-and-desist letters, warning that authorities would "impound" the motorized devices to stop the "dangerous" and "unlawful operation." On April 17, San Francisco Municipal Transportation Authority voted to regulate electric scooters, requiring companies to apply for a permit before operating on city streets. The legislation was passed unanimously. Immediately, at least seven companies, including Bird, Lime, Uber, and Lyft, vied for a maximum of five scooter permits in San Francisco. Bird snagged $150 million in a Series C funding round, giving the start-up a $1 billion valuation, while Lime raised $250 million in new funding at a $750 million valuation. Scootergeddon has repeated itself in a number of smaller cities across the United States, including Nashville, Tennessee; Scottsdale, Arizona; Charlotte, North Carolina; and Oahu, Hawaii.

The United Kingdom Stage Carriage Act 1832 first introduced the offense of endangering the safety of a passenger or other person through "furious driving." On December 9, 1868, the first non-electric gas-lit traffic lights were installed outside the Houses of Parliament in London to control the traffic in Bridge Street, Great George Street, and Parliament Street. They were proposed by the railway engineer J. P. Knight of Nottingham, who had adapted this idea from his design of railway signaling systems, and constructed by the railway signal engineers of Saxby & Farmer. The main reason for the traffic light was that there was an overflow of horse-drawn traffic over Westminster Bridge, which forced thousands of pedestrians to walk next to the Houses of Parliament. The design combined three semaphore arms with red and green gas lamps for night-time use on a pillar operated by a police constable. The light was called the semaphore and had arms that would extend horizontally, commanding drivers to "Stop," and then the arms would lower to a 45-degree angle to tell drivers to proceed with "Caution." At night a red light would command "Stop," and a green light would mean "Caution."

In subsequent decades of this 21st century, efficient regulation for silent electric transport congestion, scooters and or drones will remain of paramount importance.

7

EM Hotshots

Although, compared to the ubiquitous pedelec, electric motorcycles capable of going more than 50 miles an hour are few and far between, they have been making an ever greater impact both on the open road and around the track. But it has been a hard road, in which a number of products have fallen by the wayside despite determined efforts.

One dynamic project was started in 1996 by Andrew J. MacGowan of Newport, Rhode Island. A former vice president of Quadrax Advanced Materials, MacGowan was responsible for the relationship between Quadrax, the U.S. Air Force and its principal contractors for the F-22 Advanced Tactical Fighter program. Quadrax is a multidirectional, lightweight, high-strength interlaced material. The corporation had been awarded the contract for primary and secondary structure skin and door systems by Lockheed Martin Corporation. During a meeting at Lockheed Martin's Marietta, Georgia, facility in 1997, MacGowan struck up a deal with Lockheed: he would provide business assistance to Lockheed if the aerospace company would lend technical and engineering expertise to MacGowan's as-yet-undefined entrepreneurial effort.

The chosen name, Vectrix (similar to the word Quadrax), was based on the words "velocipede" and "electric," and the prototype was designated VX-1. Three engineers were recruited for the project. Peter Hughes (with a BS in electrical engineering from the University of Massachusetts) became the chief technical officer who would lead research and development, including component and systems design, prototyping, tooling, testing and commercialization initiatives, based in New Bedford, Massachusetts. He was joined by David Dugas, an electrical engineer from Mansfield, Massachusetts, and soon after by Craig Bliss, an innovative engineer from the field of washer/dryer machines. In the process, the Vectrix team would create 13 "test-bed" prototypes and 18 pre-production fully styled demonstration scooters. They focused on incorporating a 27-horsepower brushless air-gap DC motor supplied by SBA Parker Hannifin (Milan, Italy) into the electronically controlled scooter's rear wheel. For the battery, electrochemist Jun Furukawa of Furukawa Battery Co., Ltd.'s R&D center in Iwaki city, Fukushima Prefecture, had developed the nickel-metal hydride (NiMH) couple, increasing capacity 30 percent from 1,100 to 1,400 milliamp-hours. For the VX-1, the battery (weighing in at approximately 185 pounds) was mounted low in the chassis to keep the rider on top of the center of gravity, giving the bike a nimble and controllable feel. The VX-1 was also rechargeable in 2.5 hours from a domestic socket. This powerback was encased in a streamlined aluminum packaging provided by Alcoa. Regenerative braking would add 14 percent to the range before recharge time. Thus equipped, the scooter had an autonomy of 68 miles on a flat road, while, in the real world of hills and traffic and brief full-speed blasts on the freeway, it could manage about 40 miles tops.

Having lined up an assembly plant in Wrocław, Poland, in early 2004, Vectrix took its prototype to a Peugeot test track in France for a drag race against a top-of-the-line gas-powered competitor; the electric vehicle won. Two years later, Vectrix publicly launched its scooter. The company had also been working on the VX-2 and the three-wheeled VX-3. There were high levels of VX-1 customer satisfaction. Magazine editors and test riders everywhere praised it, while stars like Jay Leno and Leonardo DiCaprio became owner riders; both the Providence, Rhode Island, and the New York police departments launched trials, as did the government of Canada. Vectrix showed a 125-miles-per-hour (201 kph) superbike concept vehicle at the 2007 Milan motorcycle show, to be produced if 500 deposits were received. But a flawed distribution strategy coupled with a high retail price and the consumer credit crunch hindered Vectrix's success.

Vectrix had also been working with Parker Hannifin on a VX-FCe fuel cell hybrid that would contain a 500-watt Protonex NGenTM fuel cell in the helmet compartment. It would accelerate from zero to 31 miles in 3.6 seconds, with a top speed of 62 miles per hour and a range of 155 miles. In May 2008, Michael J. Boyle replaced Andrew MacGowan as CEO and chairman, dropping the VX-1's $11,000 price by $2,250, laying off half the company's workforce and increasing distribution outlets by a staggering 321 percent. Pre-production models of both MAXI bikes were shown at the New York International Motorcycle Show in January 2009, as well as at the Birmingham Motor Show. On September 28, 2009, the company announced a Chapter 11 bankruptcy filing in Delaware and declared that a New Vectrix might buy the assets of Vectrix to recapitalize a new company. In late 2009, the assets were sold to Gold Peak battery group, which manufactured lithium-ion batteries. For much of 2010, the company rehired old and new staff and began supporting old owners with issues. As 2011 rolled around, Vectrix introduced the 5.2-kilowatt-hour VX-1 Li/Li+ into the product line, displaying it at some shows. In 2012, New Vectrix (re)-unveiled the super bike prototype at the

SWISS-MOTO 2012 show in Zürich, announcing that it was taking orders and might produce the bike with as few as 200 preorders. But such orders were not forthcoming, obliging the company to cease all U.S. operations as of December 31, 2013, filing for Chapter 7 bankruptcy liquidation, with its remaining assets auctioned off the following June. Finally, Peter Hughes and David Dugas, who had been with the project for fifteen years, went their separate ways. Recently Daimler-Benz and Smart have been looking at the Vectrix concept.

Another venture to create an electric motorcycle started in 2006 in El Rancho Drive, Santa Cruz, California. Neal T. Saiki had been passionate about bicycles since he was a schoolboy, when he worked on a state-funded program examining how electric propulsion systems would be the only viable transport system for the future. When older, he built and flew model airplanes. Studying for his master's degree in aeronautical engineering at the California Polytechnic State University, San Luis Obispo, Saiki and a fellow student, Kyle Naydo, designed the world's first human-powered helicopter. On December 10, 1989, their craft, Da Vinci 3, ascended eight inches and stayed aloft for eight seconds, though this was not enough to fulfill the requirements to earn the $250,000 Sikorsky Prize awarded to the first controlled human-powered flight. But the achievement eventually helped Saiki become a designer for NASA, and then it helped another employer develop a high-altitude airplane for spying and investigating global warming.

When Saiki's wife Lisa gave birth to their first child in 1996, the ever-innovative Saiki designed and patented a self-unfolding portable hanging cot. He also started working for Santa Cruz Bicycles, designing the early iconic mountain bikes such as the Hekler, Bullit and Superlight. For his test track, Saiki made good use of the several miles of multiple bends and steep gradient of Felton Empire Road. In 2003, he designed a revolutionary mountain bike with suspension where the crankset was mounted on the swing arm, receiving a patent for this design as well. As someone who preferred riding bikes downhill and not uphill, in 2006 Saiki, helped by his wife Lisa, founded a company called Electricross to build an electric-assisted bike in their garage in Scotts Valley. In the early days, the couple worked around the clock, taking turns caring for their newborn, sweeping floors, and creating a marketing plan around the new technologies, including a viable longer-lasting battery system. Saiki handled engineering and manufacturing, answered phones and technical questions, and dealt with sales. Lisa handled accounting and marketing, in addition to making fliers and window displays, and, with a handful of employees, they both did everything else they could to carve out a nascent niche in the electric vehicle market.

At this time, a number of accidents in which lithium-ion batteries caught fire had given this battery a diminished reputation. Apart from designing every piece of the motorcycle himself, Saiki innovated a heat-dissipating, flexible and rugged revolutionary battery-interconnect system that allowed 168 high-power lithium-ion battery cells to be yoked together in a confined space (a motorcycle) and could operate at maximum efficiency under extreme loads without bursting into flames. The patent for this system was eventually awarded in 2010.

Electricross's aircraft-grade aluminum "Drift" electric motorcycle was hand-built. Saiki used shops in Soquel, San Jose and Santa Cruz to make the parts; then he did the final assembly in his 1,140-square-foot workshop at the back of the store's display area. With a made-in-China Briggs & Stratton rare-earth neodymium motor, performance was impressive: 17,000 watts of instant torque-producing power, 60 miles per hour in about four seconds, and 25-foot jumps off a dirt ramp. There were two models: a $5,500 all-terrain bike and a $6,300 motocross-ready version complete with shocks from Fox Racing. Sales were made from the Saiki garage, through Electric Cyclery in Laguna Beach and online at electricross.com.

In 2006, the Drift competed in the American Motorcyclist Association (AMA) Formula 100 race on September 16, but a problem with the drive sprocket prevented it from finishing, according to the company's website. Dal Smilie, chairman of the 250,000-member AMA, characterized the demonstration of an electric off-road motorcycle as a "pretty radical departure" for the AMA.

In 2007, Electricross' name was changed to Zero Motorcycles (a reference to zero carbon emissions), and by 2008 the staff at Santa Cruz had increased to 25 enabling manufacture of a street-legal version. On the day it was launched, there was so much interest that the company's website crashed! Comedian and vehicle collector Jay Leno took a Zero for a ride and called it the "future of motorcycling," adding that "you could go through the bird reserve and not ever bother anybody."[1]

Zero's progress using lithium-ion batteries was being followed both afloat and in the air. In 2007, Torqeedo of Starnberg, Germany, was building up its range of electric outboard motors with an integrated lithium-manganese battery pack. That same year, pioneers in the United States, France, Germany and Slovenia built and flew their first electric prototypes using lithium-ion batteries. Smith Electric Vehicles' Ford-based Newton electric truck, an all-electric commercial vehicle, was also the first HEV to use lithium-ion batteries was out on the roads. It was a key year for e-transport.

To thoroughly test its off-road vehicles, Zero went to the Anza Borrego desert in California, beginning a long tradition of testing in far-flung locations. Soon, the stalwart R&D staff would travel to Death Valley for hot weather testing, to Oregon for extended wet weather riding, and to Pismo Beach to subject motorcycles to sand and salt. From there, the Zero "wrecking

This 2008 photo shows Neil Saiki and the team at Zero Motorcycles (Zero).

crew" went on to torture its motorcycles in Baja California (Mexico), complete the Rubicon Trail in the Sierras, and establish a tradition of weekly trips to the local OHV Park at Hollister Hills. The company also opened its first foreign office in Holland, as well as public trials riding at the Sydney Motorcycle Show in Australia.

On April 4-5, 2009, Neal Saiki and Zero Motorcycles organized the "24 Hours of Electricross" event at the 408MX Motocross Track in San Jose, California. Teams came from across the United States, Mexico, Canada and even the United Kingdom to participate. 50 riders were invited to ride ten Zero X electric motocross bikes for 24 hours of nonstop racing. With a maximum of 3 batteries, the teams had to consider their speed, use of braking systems, and how often to switch out and charge their batteries. Teams would ride for an hour and swap batteries to the fresh pack, so there were always two packs charging. Zero's system allowed the pack to switch manually within a minute or so, not even requiring tools. The primary issue was the motors heating, and the teams took to squirting water on the motors during the pit stops. The Zero X had two switches: one was for torque, and the other was for top speed. In "low/low" it was pretty tame, but in "high/high" it stunned riders with its instant torque and power. More than a few were "looped" (went over backward in a wheelie). The HotChalk came out on top with a dizzying 1,015 completed laps—502.1 miles, at an average speed of 21.1 miles per hour—setting a world record in the process. This could be described as the first serious e-motorcycle contest.

Over in the United Kingdom, on the Isle of Man, whose Tourist Trophy

(TT) motorcycle race had been dominated by gasoline engines since 1907, an electric motorcycle event appeared. Azhar Hussain, a telecom engineer, was promoting his SlingSim system to Manx Telecom when it occurred to him that sponsoring an electric motorcycle event in the TT would be a great promotion. Other islanders with the same idea supported Hussain. On June 14, 2009, the first Time Trial Xtreme Grand Prix (TTXGP) all-electric-street-motorcycle race took place, with 13 machines taking part. The rules stated, "The technical concept is for motorcycles (two wheeled) to be powered without the use of carbon based fuels and have zero toxic/noxious emissions."[2] The Isle of Man government offered a prize of £10,000 for the first entrant to exceed the prestigious 100-miles-per-hour (22 minutes and 38.388 seconds) average speed around the Mountain Course.

Agni Motors' Cedric Lynch and Arvind Rabadia decided to enter. As Cedric recalls:

> We initially considered a feet forwards bike, but we couldn't find a rider willing to ride it. And so, Plan B we got our rider first. We were very lucky to secure Robert Barber and we asked him what bike he thought we should convert. Barber was familiar with the Suzuki GSXR 600 or 750 that he was riding in the Supersport 600 petrol bike class so he arranged for us to buy one without the engine in and we converted that starting in early April. Our twin Agni motors together developed up to 35kW power with a maximum 60kW with energy from forty-two 70 Ah Kokam lithium polymer pouch cells connected in pairs to make 140 Ah.[3]

Riding the Agni X01, Barber completed the 37.73-mile (60.72 km) course in a winning 25 minutes, 53.5 seconds, with an average speed of 87.434 miles per hour (140.711 kph). The highest speed the Agni-Suzuki recorded was 102 miles per hour on the Sulby straight. In the pits, the barefooted, long-haired inventor was ready to make any modifications necessary.

By this time the staff of Zero Motorcycles had grown to more than 60, able to ship the most robust lineup of four electric motorcycles in the United States, including the new Zero XU in volume. But when news of Cedric's motor arrived at Zero Motorcycles, he and Arvind were invited over to California to help adapt this motor to the Zero bikes. Cedric recalls:

> We arrived at their works in Scotts Valley which is a very nice place with a very decent climate. They modified an off-the-shelf controller by putting a front end on its control circuits, also a Canadian-made lithium-ion battery called the Molicel which gave 3 to 4 kWh and they had developed a good management system so the charger would not overrun when it was full charged, wouldn't over-discharge, etc. A lot of other battery management systems at that time had awful things wrong with them, like slowly discharging the cells at one end of the battery more than the ones at the other end and this could ruin the expensive battery if the vehicle stood unused for more than a few weeks. They would test their motorcycles on the Felton Empire Road off Highway 9, which goes up the mountainside between the California redwood trees for several miles with hairpin bends.[4]

Zero changed over to the Agni motor on the Model Year 2010 S and DS. In February 2010, Agni Motors announced that it would take part in all three regional championships of the 2010 TTXGP. Sean Higbee won the first TTXGP competition held in the United States on a Zero Agni machine, a joint entry by Zero Motorcycles and Agni Motors. This bike was Agni's 2009 TTXGP vehicle, repainted and with new stickers on it. Higbee completed the 25-mile (40 km), 11-lap race (held on the Infineon Raceway) in 25 minutes, 33.6 seconds. Agni Motors finished second in the 2010 TTXGP North American series. The company had already gained a huge racing resource when it hired Kenyon Kluge (now director of electrical engineering). Besides his skills as an electrical engineer from nearby Silicon Valley, Kenyon was a nationally ranked road racer and former AFM 750 champion on gas bikes. It didn't take long for him to put his skills to work representing Zero, and he won the first-ever TTX75 class, riding a production-based Zero. In the Road America event, Zoe Rem finished the 4.05-mile (6.52 km), 5-lap race in 2 minutes, 55.874 seconds. Team Agni's Jenny Tinmouth won the first ever UK Electric Bike Racing Championship (TTXGP), in addition to finishing third in the World Electric Bike Racing Championship in the same year aboard her Agni Z2 and finishing fourth in the TT Zero race during the Isle of Man Tourist Trophy. Robert Barber finished second in the 2010 TT Zero on another Agni bike; the race was won by the Moto Czysz machine.

In 2010, Arnold Schwarzenegger, then governor of California and an avid motorcyclist, cited the environmental benefits of electric motorcycles such as the Zero and the state's new incentive program to encourage their use publicly.

In 2010 the Isle of Man gave further recognition to electric motorcycles when it organized the TT Zero, a time trial in which riders must complete one lap on the endlessly difficult and extremely deadly 37.75-mile Mountain Course. The winner of the 2010 race, American Mark Miller on his MotoCzysz E1 built in Portland, Oregon, was timed at 96.82 miles per hour, and in the next two years MotoCzysz would dominate, raising the lap speed to 110 miles per hour. Since 2012, one of the main teams has been the Japanese Mugen, founded by Hiotoshi Honda, the son of Honda Motor Company founder Soichiro Honda. Initially started as a university project, before long Team Mugen was seriously investing millions in development, with top riders helping with testing and securing the podiums.

One of these top riders was Honda jockey John McGuinness (a.k.a. "The Morecombe Missile"), winner of 18 of the 23 TTs in which he had competed. His decision to compete in the 2012 TT Zero attracted the attention of the international press. In the first two years McGuinness placed second behind Michael Rutter on the MotoCzysz. Then, in 2014, despite injuries received in other races, McGuinness won the race with an enormous lap record of 117.366 miles per hour, while in 2015 he increased this speed to 119.279 miles per

In this 2010 photo, Arnold Schwarzenegger, then governor of California, inspects the Zero range (Zero).

hour (192 kph), riding the 120-kilowatt Honda Mugen Shinden San (Japanese numeral Three) electric superbike. In 2016, the TT Zero was won by teammate New Zealander Bruce Anstey; McGuinness had paused mid-lap due to accidentally engaging the "kill switch."

For 2017, McGuinness would be joined by Guy Martin, not merely a motorcycle racer but also a television personality, thanks to Britain's highly popular Channel 4 series *Speed with Guy Martin*, where he set speed records in a variety of human and engine powered vehicles. Since 2004 Martin had achieved 15 gas-engine podium finishes in the TT. Their mount was the slightly lighter Mugen Roku (Japanese numeral Six) with which Honda hoped to get its fourth consecutive TT Zero win. In the spring, McGuinness and Martin went out to Japan to test ride their mounts at Sodegaura Forest Raceway in Japan; Martin became the first person to crash a Honda Mugen when he slid off the first corner on the tight circuit during the second test session in Japan. Then, in May, McGuinness suffered serious injuries while practicing for the Superbike race at the North West 200 event in Northern Ireland, including broken vertebrae and ribs and compound fractures to his right lower leg bones; surgeons had to remove 2 inches (50 mm), and he needed an external fixator cage to "grow" new bone. This incident ended McGuinness' race participation for the remainder of the season.

The TT Zero was won by New Zealander Bruce Anstey with a race time of 117.710 miles per hour, faster than his Mugen Shinden teammate Guy Martin at 113.632 miles per hour. Although the 120-miles-per-hour (193 kph) average lap speed barrier had eluded them, speeds on the straights exceeded this number. Guy Martin commented:

> It's been an interesting week with the missed laps I've been behind and it's Bruce's fourth year. I've had to adapt and it's like riding a 250. You can compare it to the Wall of Death and ride it with a glass throttle. I feel honoured to be asked to be involved in the Mugen project. Those boys are different league. This is the future and I'm over the moon to be involved as I'd been really looking forward to it.[5]

The Shinden Roku, scheduled to compete in the 2018 electric TT Zero at the Isle of Man with riders McGuinness and Martin, is little changed from the previous year. It weighs in 4.5 pounds lighter, at 546.7 pounds, while the motor has the same power rating, 160.9-horsepower (120 kW) with 210 newton-meters (154.89 pound-feet) of torque. The bike reportedly has a new battery that will extend its range.

In 2011, Neal Saiki pulled away from Zero Motorcycles so he could re-enter the Sikorsky Human-Powered Helicopter Competition. The result was the 95-pound Upturn II, built with a new team at CalPoly. The aircraft had two blades 85 feet in diameter and two 48-foot-diameter blades with 6-foot-diameter propellers at the tips to drive the rotor. Although it did not win, the Upturn II made a 10-second first flight in June 2012. Saiki's company, NTS Works, subsequently donated the aircraft to CalPoly, which has focused on reducing weight and improving stability.

Ever innovative, Saiki next came up with the Lifetime Rebuildable Battery Technology, whereby a new battery can be rebuilt if the lithium-ion cells go bad. With this product, he developed the LockerCycle, a 2 × 4 electric cargo bike with a carrying capacity of 100 pounds (aside from the driver), a top range of 40 miles and an innovative front-axle steering system. The company logo featured a simple six-petal design from the Saiki family crest. The bike had a USB charger for GPS or cellphones. The following year, Saiki produced the NTS SunCycle, in which the solar panel (with a rated power of 60 watts) was on top of the cargo carrier.

Others had also been busy. In 2001, Electric Motorsport of Alameda, California, had begun to import Vespa-style electric scooters but quickly found that many of its customers wanted more performance out of their vehicles. In 2007, the company gutted a Yamaha R1 and filled it with batteries and an Agni electric motor. It looked a bit rough but worked pretty well. From this, Electric Motorsport produced the GPR-S, a lithium battery–powered model with a top speed of 60–70 miles per hour and a 35–60-mile range. Although the bike was the open-class winner at the 2009 IOM race, Electric Motorsport subsequently produced a less expensive commercial model.

7. EM Hotshots

2011: Derek Dorresteyn (center), Jeff Waldo Sand (holding handlebar) and the BRD team with the RedShift MX off-road motorcycle, soon after renamed Alta (Alta).

In 2008, Mark Fenigstein, a design strategist at Frog Design, working with inventor-designers Derek Dorresteyn and Jeff Waldo Sand, founded BRD Motorcycles in South San Francisco, California, to design and make their competition electric 250 Redshift MX off-road motorcycle. The prototype was unveiled in August 2011 at the Dainese D-Store in San Francisco. On the test track, the RedShift proved four seconds faster on a 1:10 lap than the KTM 250, a comparable gas-powered bike.

The company subsequently changed its name to Alta Motors (Alta in California, where American motocross originated). The Redshift uses energy-dense and compact 18650 lithium-ion cells (the same that Tesla uses for its sportscars). Alta produced two models: the Motocross (MX) and the Supermoto (SM) urban commuter, each using 5.8 kilowatt-hours of batteries to power, with a maximum of 350 volts said to provide 40 horsepower and 120 pound-feet of torque and 3 hours' autonomy. Recharging took four hours at 120 volts, and just two and a half at 240 volts. From there, the weight, suspension, wheels and geometry differed from model to model to tailor the bikes to perform best for their respective purposes. There is but one gear on the Alta, and once the e-motor is on, it's always there for you. No clutch, no shift, no stall, no worry—hence Redshift.

In 2016 Alta Motors opened a new factory in Brisbane, 17 miles northwest of Tesla's factory, saw its sales increase 18 times in 2017, and added 36 new distributors to its dealership network. Alta Motors added to the network again in 2018, bringing it to a total of 41 dealers in 18 states. That year, having secured backing from some of the most innovative minds in battery tech (Martin Eberhard and Marc Tarpenning, two of the original cofounders of Tesla before Elon Musk became CEO), Mark Fenigstein announced plans to eventually sell the proprietary battery pack and drivetrain to other companies working on lightweight vehicles and delivery drones.

Despite having produced electric automobiles and a semi-truck, Elon Musk himself has declared that he has no plans to make a Tesla motorcycle. In South Africa, for about eight years, he and his brother used to ride dirt-track gasoline motorcycles all the time; then, at the age of 17, he was almost killed by a truck.

In 2005 Claudio Dick of Lugano of the canton of Ticino, Switzerland, a former gas automobile and motorcycle dealer, decided to develop an electric motorcycle brand that he called Quantya (after quantum theory). Quantya combined the traditional ingenuity with attention to detail of Swiss watch makers such as Longines and Rolex in order to deliver its first production model: the FMX. The FMX was a high-performance electric motorcycle for the sports enthusiast who did not want to compromise performance and quality. Quantya reached a new milestone in 2007, when it obtained the international TUV certification for a street-legal version in Europe, which was called the Strada. In 2008, Quantya teamed up with former world champion snowboarder Chris Karo and Shredelectric, an action sports retailer, to promote the brand. The Strada went into service with California State Park's Off-Highway Motor Vehicle Recreation Division and the U.S. Army.

The electric motorcycle finally arrived in India in 2016, when Tork Motorcycles in Pune, India (founded by Kapil Shelke), received funding from a host of investors, including Bhavish Aggarwal and Ankit Bhati (co-founders of Ola) and Harpreet Grover (co-founder and CEO of CoCubes), to get its prototype, the T6X, on the market. Tork had already competed in the Isle of Man TT, and it also won the world's premier electric motorsport race series, TTXGP. The motorcycle has features like cloud connectivity, integrated GPS, and in-built navigation capabilities, thereby making it the first smart motorcycle. Connected with a mobile app, the platform will map driving cycles and provide real-time information about the bike. TIROS (Tork Intuitive Response Operating System) is the intelligence that drives the T6X. Apart from analysis and compilation of data for every ride, power management, real-time power consumption and range forecasts, TIROS also learns how you ride.

Gas motorcycles bearing the name Royal Enfield "Bullet" have been on the roads since the early 1900s. In 2015, considering the firm resolve of the Indian government to go entirely electric by 2030, Siddhartha Lal, managing director and CEO at Eicher Motors owners of the Royal Enfield now in India, announced that he would be developing an electric version of the Royal Enfield Bullet 500 using 11 Nissan Leaf automobile batteries to obtain a speed of more than 62 miles per hour. The batteries were stacked in six over five, sitting on a customized aluminum frame.

Science-fiction has continued its long-standing love affair with powerful electric motorcycles. Daniel Simon, originally from Germany, is a concept designer and automotive futurist. He designed the "light cycles" for *Tron: Legacy*, a 2010 American science-fiction action film, and the vehicles for Captain America, a fictional superhero appearing in American Marvel comic books and movies. Simon's latest creation is the Cosmic Motors Detonator, as featured in the fantasy book *Cosmic Motors: Spaceships, Cars and Pilots of Another Galaxy* (2012). The Detonator is a 11.5-foot electric motorcycle powered by a 1.5-gallon V2 Cratomium engine with elliptical pistons, using li-po power to cruise 80–100 miles on a one-hour charge with a maximum speed of 120 miles per hour. Within the book, this ridiculously magnum-sized street cruiser is for wealthy droids on planet Tarra I. The bike's extremely modular design never pleased Cosmic Motors founder Osni Redua, but its high demand after a leaked prototype led to a limited production run of ten numbered machines in a variety of color combinations. The slightly different prototypes No. 1 and No. 2 remained with the company's research labs, while bikes 3–9 were sold within days, and the final production number ("0") is owned by Redua's daughter LaGata.

Italy came to the electric motorcycle in 2010 from a well-established Formula One precision part concern, CRP Racing in Modena. Livia Cevolini was 36 years old when, with her family, she decided to lead the design and construction of the eCRP, an electric racing motorcycle. The team, led by Giampiero Testoni, included Giovanni Gherardi, Simone Martinelle and Eleonora Montanari. The eCRP 1.0 was unveiled during the Cleaner Racing Conference in Birmingham, United Kingdom, on January 13, 2010. That October, the eCRP 1.2 competed at Brands Hatch and won the title of European Champion TTXGP 2010. The use of additive manufacturing and the innovative materials of the Windform product line represented a crucial stage in the construction of the electric racing motorcycle, carried out in collaboration with CRP technology. The chassis of the eCRP 1.4, the runner-up world champion and European champion electric racing motorcycle, featured a cast aluminum frame, welded aluminum swing arm and racing suspension. After two years of racing, the eCRP team started working on the road version: Energica.

In just six months, a high-performance e-motorbike was created. The

2012: Livia Cevolini with the two Energica motorcycles (photograph by Massimo Sestini).

first prototypes were manufactured using 3D printing and F1 technologies. The result was the Ego, unveiled in 2012—a 568.8-pound (258 kg) superbike powered by a 136-horsepower, oil-cooled three-phase AC permanent magnet motor with energy from a battery-managed 11.7-kilowatt-hour lithium (Li-NMC) pack, giving it 145 pound-feet of torque. Components included Pirelli Diablo Rosso Corsa tires, which are made mainly for racing but have type-approval for road use. Two years later, the limited edition luxurious Ego45 superbike, with carbon-fiber fairings specially covered with a ceramic finish by English company Zircotec, was unveiled at Top Marques, Monte-Carlo. Soon after, the Energica Eva made a one-day, 450-mile ride up Highway 1 from Los Angeles to San Francisco by using DC fast-charging stations, which allowed rider Bill Levasseur to recharge in an average time of 23 minutes.

For 2018, Energica is launching the "EsseEsse9" named after the Via Emilia, the major road that crosses the Italian Motor Valley; with more of a classic look, including a round headlight and more upright sitting position, it has a top speed limited to 125 miles per hour but produces a supposed 132.7 pound-feet (180 Nm) of torque. Energica's vehicle control unit (VCU) is a multi-map system that manages the power and battery (even when the bike is turned off), and it is said to deliver a maximum range in "Eco" mode of 25 miles. The rider gets a 4.3-inch TFT color screen with an integrated GPS receiver, Bluetooth, and an ambient light sensor, and it can even show you the closest charging stations when connected to the MYEnergica app. Demonstrating the potential of the technology, a 50-kilowatt fast-charge station has been installed in the Dolomites—in partnership with renewable energy company Alperia—and is free to use for Energica customers. The EsseEsse9 will also be available as a "Special" from 23,690 euros, with spoked Marchesini wheels and Öhlins suspension. In addition, Energica used 3D printing provided by CRP Technology to create a new dashboard for the Ego that allows the rider to access and utilize the motorcycle's extensive configuration options. The process took only two days, using Windform LX 3.0 (a GRP-reinforced polyamide composite) as the construction material.

Ego logged a seventh-place finish at the 2017 Isle of Man TT Zero, a challenging 37.73-mile race for electric motorbikes that saw the Energica average 78.8 miles per hour. In December 2017, Dorna, the promoter for MotoGP, announced that the Energica Ego motorcycle will form the basis of its upcoming pure-electric racing class, FIM MotoE World Cup. Enel X, the title sponsor, will provide smart and CCS Combo fast charging, advanced energy services, green energy supply, and storage. The Italian bike will join the global motorcycle racing championship as a support series at select venues beginning in 2019. The inaugural MotoE season in 2019 will consist of five races with 18 motorcycles. Seven private teams will get two bikes each, and four more bikes will be reserved for Moto2 or Moto3 teams. The MotoE races will be short, with only 10 laps, primarily due to range constraints on the EgoGP. On March 27, 2018, former 500cc British Grand Prix winner Simon Crafar took the EgoGP electric superbike for a demo lap at Qatar's Losail International Circuit after the premier class race.

For more than a century, the legendary V-Twin Harley-Davidson, with its gleaming tubular welded-steel metalwork and melodious "potato-potato-potato" sound, has been a household word for motorcycles, with such iconic memories as Peter Fonda riding his chopper-style motorbike in the 1969 film *Easy Rider*. Now, led by Jeff Richlen, with the approval of Bill Davidson (vice president of the Harley-Davidson Museum in Milwaukee and great-grandson of company founder William A. Davidson), an electric two-wheeler was created in Milwaukee with a 74-horsepower (55 kW) unit that linked to a 7-kilowatt-hour battery, which gave it 0–60 miles per hour in less than 4 seconds, or 52 pound-feet of torque. The demonstration bikes were charged using 240-volt Level 2 chargers, taking about 3.5 hours to fully replenish the battery pack. Although the traditional steel was replaced by aluminum, the final drive to the wheel was by a belt, typical of gasoline Harleys. Harley-Davidson added a housing that creates a resonance when in operation, a whirring sound somewhere between a jet turbine and an oversized vacuum. When the Project LiveWire Experience launched June 24, 2014, in New York

City, it was compared to the status-symbol Tesla electric sportscar. For promotion, the vehicle was ridden to 30 Harley-Davidson dealerships in 30 U.S. cities before wrapping up in Jacksonville, Florida, on December 20. Three years later, Harley-Davidson had yet to deliver a consumer edition of LiveWire but announced that it would release 100 new motorcycles in the next 10 years, including the "H-D Revelation," an entire range of electric bikes. In March 2018, Harley-Davidson made an equity investment in Alta Motors whereby the two companies would collaborate on electric motorcycle technology and new product development, with the first products to appear in 2019. "The EV motorcycle market is in its infancy today, but we believe premium Harley-Davidson electric motorcycles will help drive excitement and participation in the sport globally," Matt Levatich, Harley-Davidson's president and CEO, told the *Milwaukee Business Journal*. "As we expand our EV capabilities and commitment, we get even more excited about the role electric motorcycles will play in growing our business."[6]

In 2011, Chris Bell of Boulder City, Nevada, founder of Bell Custom Cycles (BCC), presented the first in the Brutus line of family-built electric motorcycles, with names such as the Brutus Café, the V2 Rocket and the Brutus V9, a retro machine that harkens back to the old highway patrol police motorcycles and is clearly aimed at the Harley-Davidson cruiser market. The Brutus V9 is powered by a 125-brake-horsepower (93 kW), 9-inch DC motor and up to 33 kilowatt-hours of energy storage with a city range of 280 miles and 165 miles on the highway and a top speed of 115 miles per hour. A law enforcement option is available exclusively to registered law enforcement agencies.

After amassing a small fortune from selling e-commerce solutions, Craig Bramscher of Ashland, Oregon, decided to build the ultimate American electric supercar: the Brammo Rogue GT. To do this, he recruited Aaron T. Bland (BSc from the University of Wisconsin–Madison). Available electric technology was judged inadequate for that application, but it seemed perfect for a two-wheeled commuter vehicle—and thus the Brammo Enertia motorcycle was born. Then, in 2008, Brammo's director of product development, Brian Wismann, heard about the zero-emission TTXGP at the Isle of Man. Together with Aaron Bland, Bramscher and Wismann worked after hours and on weekends to convert the pedestrian Enertia into a proper racing machine, featuring a 40-kilowatt Parker GMV IPM water-cooled AC motor, IET™ high-performance 6 speed transmission and Brammo's unique BPM 15/90 lithium-ion (NCM Chemistry) battery modules. Brammo's Empulse R participated in the first all-electric motorcycle race and was podiumed. Brammo was also the first racing team to win an electric vehicle race at Daytona International Speedway and the Indianapolis Motor Speedway, where the bike reached speeds in excess of 170 miles per hour—a new electric motorcycle world record for a race circuit. In October 2009, Wismann and Bland went on a 10-day trip, coined "Shocking Obama: Brammo's journey to present our president with the most energy efficient electric vehicle in America." While on this journey through America's heartland, Wismann and Bland educated people about the benefits of electric bikes and advocated for the Advance Vehicle Technology Act. In total, they stopped in 21 cities, meeting with leaders, charging their bikes at local hot spots and crashing on the couches of fellow electric vehicle advocates. Soon afterward, Polaris, the conglomerate that owned cruiser-focused Victory Motorcycles, acquired Brammo. By tweaking the formula with a slightly bigger 10.4-kilowatt motor, improving battery capacity, and sharpening handling, the Empulse TT offered an incrementally better EV than its predecessor. Then Brammo was purchased by Cummins, which required the manufacture of battery packs and electric drivetrains for electric trucks and electric helicopters, and the Empulse motorcycle was shelved.

Canada's entry into the field came with the initiative taken in 2009 by Jean-Pierre Legris to found LITO Green Motion Inc. in Longueuil, Quebec, and produce a hand-built luxury electric motorcycle. Having formerly worked for Honda in Japan, Legris combined the name Lito (which means "light") with Sora (a unisex Japanese name meaning "sky"). The LitoSora is a distinctly styled piece of industrial design that took 60,000 man hours to develop. Power is provided by a liquid-cooled 3-phase AC induction motor TorqueCrank: 90 newton-meters (66.37 pound-feet, 0–6,000 revolutions per minute) with energy from a 12-kilowatt-hour lithium-polymer battery pack to give a range of approximately 124 miles (200 km). Among its features are a carbon fiber bodywork, Öhlins suspension, a Safe Range system that gauges speed and acceleration patterns and projects estimated riding distances onto the bike's 5.7-inch GPS touchscreen, adjustable seat support, Motogadget gauges and keycard ignition custom-made and programmed for the owner. The price tag for this product is $77,000. The higher-end Signature Series, which owners can customize to their liking for a $27,000 premium, also comes with lightweight carbon-fiber wheels and components sourced from around the world, like Beringer brakes from France and Rizoma mirrors from Italy. In 2010, the LitoSora achieved unprecedented fame when it appeared in season 6 of *Hawaii Five-0*, a popular police procedural based in the Hawaiian Islands. Watched by 10 million viewers, Chin Ho Kelly, head of the SFPD Five-0 Task Force, often rides his LitoSora to work. Fiction ultimately became fact when LITO Green Motion supplied two specially adapted Soras for use by the Longueuil and Montreal Police Departments. The vehicle went into production in 2014. Featured in the Concours D'élégance Beverly Hills, California, in 2015, two years later Jean-Pierre Legris received Patent 20170050535 for his power management system.

At Zero Motorcycles, the technical innovator who replaced Neal Saiki as CTO was Abe Askenazi. A native of Mexico City, Askenazi had done his MA thesis at UC Berkeley on "The Dynamics of Motorcycles"; then he worked at the Buell Motorcycle Company for fifteen years, where he rose to the position of senior director of analysis, test and engineering process, reporting to Erik Buell and Harley-Davidson Inc.'s Senior Leadership Group. At Buell, Askenazi was responsible for the development of 26 high-performance motorcycle models (including those of two customers) on the basis of four different platforms; the result was more than 130,000 motorcycles produced and more than $ 1 billion in revenue. Askenazi has numerous patents on motorcycle components and has published a book and several articles on analytical engineering.

In 2010, Askenazi was recruited by Zero as vice president of engineering and product development, and on-and-off electric motorcycles, leading his team in the development phase of the 2011 lineup. This was a major development, as more than 80 percent of each existing model had to be redesigned or improved and three new models added to the lineup: Zero XU, the ultimate urban commuter (featuring a removable power pack so city dwellers could charge their batteries away from the motorcycle), along with the road-homologated versions of the Zero X and Zero MX bikes, delivered from design to production in exactly 10 months. The rapid development of this comprehensive range available worldwide was a first for the electric motorcycle industry. It seemed natural that when Neal Saiki pulled out, Abe Askenazi should take over. In 2011, with its factory capacity doubled, Zero was able to ship more than 100,000 miles of power with the most robust lineup of five electric motorcycles in the United States, including the new Zero XU, in volume (X, MX, S, DS and XU models, plus two dual-purpose derivatives, the XD and MXD). The year 2011 also saw the introduction of a carbon-reinforced belt-drive to replace the noisiest, most annoying component in an electric motorcycle: the chain.

In 2012, Zero developed and patented a new system and method of using high-energy packs, using the "ZF9 Power Pack" with the Zero S and DS models, increasing autonomy to an unprecedented 100 miles, with the potential for more than 300,000 miles of battery life via powertrains that were completely maintenance-free. This development was due to new battery technology that utilized "pouch" instead of cylindrical cells. In 2012, Brandon Nozaki Miller rode the first production electric motorcycle to break 100 miles per hour (161 kph), a Zero S ZF6, at Bonneville Salt Flats. Fabio Lanzoni, an Italian American actor/fashion model and spokesman who appeared on the covers of dozens of romance novels throughout the 1980s and 1990s, added a Zero DS to his already large motorcycle collection and became a spokesperson for the U.S. EV advocacy organization Plug In America.

In 2013, the powertrain architecture of all Zero models was completely redesigned. Three different batteries were developed using both a manufacturing and a user-modular design, the latter of which was patented, increasing capacity up to 11.4 kilowatt-hours. The company's first proprietary motor design, a brushless permanent magnet AC motor, was also introduced. In addition, the 2013 Zero FX dual-sport model (with the aforementioned patented modular removable power pack) was introduced. CHAdeMO fast charging was also available on 2013 models. In 2014, the optional 2.8-kilowatt-hour "Power Tank" became available to further extend the range of S and DS models. That year also saw the addition of the Zero SR to the range, a higher-performance version of the Zero S, incorporating a more powerful controller and a motor with higher temperature magnets. The 2015 models increased battery pack size to 12.5 kilowatt-hours, for a maximum capacity of 15.3 kilowatt-hours (including the optional Power Tank and a range of 185 miles). Also introduced in 2015 were standard ABS brakes (first ever production electric motorcycle offered with ABS) and Showa suspension. Due to the uncertainty of competing public DC fast-charging standards, CHAdeMO fast charging was eliminated as an option, leaving instead an optional quick charger accessory at added cost (which was first offered in 2011).

In 2015 Kota Nezu and a team at Snug Design of Tokyo, Japan, took a 50-kilowatt, 144-newton-meter, Zero Motorcycles–sourced electric motor and built the futuristically styled *Zec00* around it, claiming a top speed of 99 miles per hour, 144 newton-meters of torque, and a range of 99 miles. There was a limited production run of 49 machines, handmade and customizable to each customer's individual requirements.

In 2016, Zero announced the DSR and FXS models. The DSR is based on the DS, but with the SR model's more powerful motor and controller. The FXS is a supermoto version of the FX. Additional changes for the model year included the availability of a "Charge Tank" accessory, which is an on-board Level 2 charging system compatible with the J1772 plug that nearly tripled onboard charging power. Battery pack size improved again to 13 kilowatt-hours (3.3 kilowatt-hours per FX power pack), for a maximum capacity of 15.9 kilowatt-hours (including the optional Power Tank). The air-cooled motors on the SR, DSR, and FXS were revised to an interior permanent magnet (IPM) design to improve manufacturing robustness and reduce heat produced during high output.

For 2017, all models had the IPM motor. Battery architecture was further simplified, and the integrated ZF6.5 power pack was introduced. Most models also received a larger-capacity controller, which provided an increase in maximum torque and horsepower output, up to 116 pound-feet on the SR and DSR models. All models but the newly introduced 2017 S/DS ZF 6.5 received a wider, high-torque carbon-fiber-reinforced belt.

Other changes for 2017 included a locking tank box and more durable paint on the S, DS, SR, and DSR models, as well as the ability for owners to update their bike's firmware through the mobile app. The company has also worked hard to improve its battery tech, and some bikes in Zero's 2017 lineup promised 200 miles per charge. That compares to electric motorcycles with a 40-mile range made by Zero just a few years ago. With modern batteries, the 2016 SR ZF13.0 with a Power Tank (i.e., the largest battery configuration available) delivered close to 200 miles in the city and almost 100 miles at 70 miles per hour. This is already a very capable product for a variety of usage cases. And when energy density doubles, one could build a similar bike with twice the range, or one with similar range and half the battery weight and cost. The latter option means being able to eliminate close to 100 pounds and thousands of dollars.

For 2018, Zero unveiled its 6-kilowatt Charge Tank accessory, which can be used by the company's Zero S, Zero SR, Zero DS, and Zero DSR bikes. The new accessory enables the Zero S and DS ZF7.2 to be charged in roughly an hour when plugged into a Level 1, 110-volt outlet, while larger batteries found in the SR and DSR models can be charged in around two hours using a Level 2 charger. As for the vehicles' range, the models equipped with the ZF7.2 and ZF14.4 power packs can now travel 10 percent farther thanks to improved battery chemistry. How far they can go largely depends on the area where they are ridden, but Zero notes that the range will top out at around 223 miles. With European riders heading further afield on their electric motorcycles, Zero has launched its new Zero DSR ZF14.4 Black Forest Edition, which boasts a touring kit and off-road-going tires. The SR is the most powerful of Zero's models, delivering 69 horsepower (52 kW) with 146 newton-meters (107.7 pound-feet) of torque. Faster charging would allow batteries to be charged as quickly as gas motorcycles are filled up. For example, if a 15-kilowatt-hour battery on a 2015 Zero S could use a Tesla Supercharger at 135 kilowatts to charge, it would take only about 7 minutes.

During the scorching summer heatwave that hit the United Kingdom in 2018, Zero Motorcycles took its range of electric motorcycles on a tour to eight venues, going from Wales north to Scotland and back to Surrey, giving riders the opportunity to try out a Zero for themselves; they simply needed to bring their own protective gear (helmet, jacket, gloves, etc.) and a valid license.

One advantage for electric vehicles is their ability to sneak up on criminals. As long ago as 1889, Customs officers of the Chinese Empire recognized the silent superiority of an electric motor over a 30-horsepower clattering steam engine during the tricky process of catching an opium smuggler unawares at night on his junk. The mission was to find a boat that could be used to fight opium smuggling in the China Sea. The boat commissioned for this purpose was a 30-horsepower Trouvé electric launch. It was steel hulled, weighed 8 tons, and measured 50 feet (15 meters) long, with a bronze propeller of about 20 inches (50 cm). Capable of going 11 miles per hour (18 kph), it also had an electric spotlight capable of projecting a beam of light with a range of 3 sea miles (6 km). The Emperor Guangxu of the ruling Qing Dynasty, who since his childhood had been fascinated by clocks and gadgetry, was so impressed that he commanded a scale model for exhibition at his Palace Museum in the Forbidden City in Peking.[7]

Starting in 2012, officers in Bogota and Hong Kong began patrolling their streets and trails using fleets of Zero S and DS police motorcycles. In 2014, Zero Motorcycles provided a DSRP for the Los Angeles Police Department for evaluation. The motorcycle was praised over the traditional bulky Harley-Davidson and BMW bikes for its stealth, low operational costs, immediate tactical advantage, and green environmental impact. By 2015 more than fifty departments had adopted the Zero DSRP, outfitted with equipment such as police lights, sirens, crash bars, and storage accessories. For example, police in Cobb County, Georgia, were using this vehicle to patrol the 77 parks within the county parks system, along with patrolling the 13-mile Cobb section of the Silver Comet Trail (a heavily traveled, 61-mile paved trail stretching from the Atlanta area to the Georgia-Alabama border).[8] In July 2017, the Vancouver Police Department in British Columbia, Canada, became the 100th fleet in North America to leverage Zero's stealthy electric motorcycle lineup. In North America, 15 university and college police departments also chose Zero as their vehicle of choice, and 12 departments went on to purchase additional motorcycles after their positive experiences with their initial purchase. A military version has also been released that has infrared lights and an "override" switch to escape from enemy gunfire.

The military is also interested in the stealth advantages of electric motorcycles. In 2013, U.S. Special Operations Command acquired a Zero MMX but found that a pure electric vehicle presented a problem: Each battery holds a two-hour charge and needs to be recharged or replaced to keep the bike moving. To go longer than that distance in one trip, a soldier must carry extra batteries; however, this is a space a soldier would rather reserve for ammunition and food. The solution was to go hybrid. The Pentagon's DARPA (Defense Advanced Research Projects Agency) developed SilentHawk as a collaboration between Logos Technologies, a Fairfax, Virginia–based contractor (whose multi-fuel genset had already been used for a UAV program), and Alta Motors. SilentHawk can run on gas most of the time and on electricity when it needs to be quiet. And it is not limited to gas but can run on diesel, as well as JP5 and JP8 jet fuels, so that the special forces using the vehicle in the field can power it with whatever fuel is available. When running on fuel, the SilentHawk recharges its own batteries and any electronic devices

By 2013, Zero Motorcycles had supplied more than 100 police forces in North America (Zero).

the troops might have, like radios, GPS receivers, or tablets. The idea is to go 50 miles, and when the rider gets within 10 miles of the objective, they can shut off the multi-fuel engine and go all-electric. When running on fuel with the generator activated, the bike's noise level is about 75 decibels, or the sound of a garbage disposal. Switched to all-electric mode, it produces less than 55 decibels, or about the sound of normal conversation. SilentHawk has an on-demand front-wheel-drive hub motor for improved handling on loose terrain and steep inclines. In addition to SilentHawk, DARPA is sponsoring work on another hybrid-electric bike: Nightmare is being developed by LSA Autonomy in Westminster, Maryland. At 400 pounds, Nightmare weighs more than SilentHawk, but it also generates greater horsepower.[9]

Another legendary name to convert to electric is Curtiss. Glenn "Hell Rider" Curtiss (1878–1930) was an American aviator, industrial designer, and motorcycle pioneer known for mounting aircraft engines onto his own Hercules bicycles. In 1903, Glenn Curtiss set the very first motorcycle speed record riding one of his original Hercules bicycles, which used a 1,000cc V-twin, taking him up to 64 miles per hour (103 kph). Later on, he wowed the world by stitching four engines together to create an incredible 4,000cc V8, which he mounted on another Hercules bike to set a 136.27-miles-per-hour

(219.31 kph) speed record in 1907. (This record would not be beaten for another 23 years.) More than a century later, in 2017, Confederate Motors of Alabama (well known for its custom-built, big V-twin gas two-wheelers), having decided that still being associated with the Confederate States of America was a bad look, announced that it was changing its name and working with Zero Motorcycles to create the Curtiss Hercules. Curtiss will deploy a modular architectural system, the design upon which numerous patents have been filed, such as the optimal foundation for an all-new twin-engine powertrain supplied by Zero. In May 2018, Curtiss unveiled its twin-engine Zeus at the 10th Quail Motorcycle Gathering in Carmel, California. The Zeus's chassis is machined billet aluminum, opting for bolted members over welding. The rear suspension uses a center-line cantilever mono-shock, and the front suspension uses a four-link girder mono-shock. The two Zero motors working in tandem are good for 393 newton-meters (290 pound-feet) of torque and 170 horsepower (127 kW), taking their energy from a 14.4-kilowatt battery pack. Awarded the coveted "Most Innovative Motorcycle," the Zeus will go into production in 2019.

In 2009 Pierpaolo Rigo of Santena, near Turin, created a company called Tacita (named after the Roman goddess of silence) to make the T-Race Enduro range of three electric off-road motorcycles in line with the company motto, "Chi sceglie Tacita sceglie uno stile di vita" ("Whoever chooses Tacita chooses a lifestyle"); this lifestyle also includes a "bio" clothing line of organic cotton shirts and a solar-paneled recharge trolley for the bike. In 2012, Tacita became the first electric motorcycle to race in the grueling African sand dunes as part of the Merzouga Rally. In September 2017, at the AIMExpo show in Columbus, Ohio, Rigo and his American associates launched the Tacita T-Cruise, with adjustable ergonomics and a five-speed gearbox with hydraulic clutch. Three different 120-volt lithium-polymer battery packs are offered, starting with the 7.5-kilowatt-hour base kit for a maximum range of up to 50 miles (81 km) before the motor enters reserve mode. The second pack includes a 15-kilowatt-hour battery, good for 93 miles (149 km); yet the most interesting development is the long-range 27-kilowatt-hour battery that can propel the T-Cruise for as long as 168 miles (270 km).

Then there is Ducati of Bologna, Italy. To put the destructive memories of the Dieselgate emissions scandal behind it, in 2017 the Volkswagen Group pushed toward electrifying its entire range of automobiles and trucks by 2030. As VW owns Ducati motorcycles, it seemed logical that Ducati, which had been making gas motorcycles since the 1950s, should follow suit with a range of electric scooters and motorcycles that would comply with the Euro 5 emission norms that would come into effect in 2020 for two-wheelers across Europe. In 2016, Pininfarina Design of Cambiano, Italy—a legendary name behind the elegant design of such gas automobiles as Ferrari, Alfa Romeo,

Peugeot, FIAT, GM, Lancia, and Maserati—teamed up with Diavelo, a member of the Accell Group (focusing on state-of-the-art technology in the bicycle sector), to produce the Fuoriserie Evoluzione Alloy, with a 250-watt, high-end mid-motor from German Brose and full carbon frame. The flush-set computer sits just above the bend in the top tube, creating a smooth, integrated cockpit. The Evoluzione was unveiled at the 2017 Taipei International Cycle Show.

Nathan Siy is a fourth-generation Canadian Chinese who has been in China for the past 10 years. In 2010, Siy set up Beijing Electric Bike tours for those who wanted to explore the city with a guide. He is also a voiceover artist at Ming Sheng Studios in Beijing. In 2014, Siy and Chris Lee Riether set up Evoke Motorcycles, and the following year they presented the Urban S and the Urban Classic, Italian-inspired street bikes with a 100 percent electric drivetrain. With a 19-kilowatt, 117-newton-meter hub motor, its patented lithium-cobalt battery system offers a top speed of 81 miles per hour (130 kph) and a 125-mile (200 km) range at city speeds with one single charge of around 4 hours. Highway range is approximately 75 miles (120 km). In 2018, Evoke announced that it was developing a reverse gear for its Urban range. With first-time and inexperienced riders in mind, the reverse gear is meant to aid motorcycle parking in compact spaces and will have a top speed of around 3 miles per hour (5 kph). Riders will be able to activate the reverse gear through the LCD touch-control panel.

In terms of one-offs, Chris Jones and Mike O'Hanlon of Perth, Australia, took a Suzuki RG and retrofitted it with a pair of Agni motors fused at the shaft and wired in parallel from a 1,200-amp Kelly controller and 6 kilowatt-hours of Turnigy A123 lithium battery. With speeds of up to 111 miles per hour (180 kph), they entered it in Round 1 of the 2014 Australian electric Formula Xtreme Challenge held at Queensland Raceway. Five electric superbikes made the record grid, with the O'Hanlons' Voltron, ridden by Danny Pottage, winning all four heats.

Shanon Parker and Marc Parker (a.k.a. the Parker Brothers) of Port Canaveral, Florida, made the dream of many fans of the 1982 sci-fi film *Tron* come true with their 100-miles-per-hour, 100-mile-range Electric Tron Light Cycle. Inspired by this one-off, in 2011, Evolve Motorcycles presented its Xenon at the Milan International Motorcycle Show. Designed by Darren Gilford, this model has a 40-kilowatt motor, with custom lithium-ion batteries giving it a speed of 100 miles per hour. The neon blue glow was made possible thanks to OLED light tape.

Another e-motorcycle thoroughbred that fell by the roadside was the Voxan Wattman. In 2009, Voxan, based in France's Sarthe region (which had aspired but failed to become France's first serious motorcycle manufacturer), was purchased by Gildo Pallanca Pastor of Venturi Automobiles in Fontvieille,

Monaco. Pastor wished to create a luxury and the world's most powerful electric motorcycle, which would be built at the Voxan works on an order-by-order basis. It was designed by Sacha Lakic around a one-piece aluminum frame to contain the batteries, motor, gearbox, and electronic components. Its 200-horsepower, 200-newton-meter belt-drive permanent magnet motor was liquid cooled and derived its energy from the 12.8-kilowatt-hour battery pack. Weighing in at a little more than 770 pounds (350 kg), the Voxan Wattman could accelerate from zero to 60 miles per hour in a mere 3.4 seconds, and it could travel 110 miles (about 180 km) on a single charge. It was launched as a concept bike at the 2013 Paris Motorcycle Show, primed to take on the motorcycle market. But, following a host of complications, the project was dropped in 2015, as Venturi decided to recenter on car racing and record-breaking. In car racing, Pastor teamed up with Leonardo DeCaprio and various pilots racing the Spark-Venturi VM200, although with no first-place podium. However, in September 2016, the Venturi Buckeye Bullet-3, piloted by Roger Schroer, established a new world speed record for an electric vehicle of 341 miles per hour, making it the world's fastest electric car. Power was 3,000 horsepower made up of four motors and eight battery packs comprising 2,000 lithium-ion cells.

In 2017, Rajeev Mishra, CEO of the UM Lohia Two Wheeler based in Miami, Florida, revealed UM Motorcycles' intention to venture beyond its 125cc gas motorbikes into the electric field. At Auto Expo 2018, Miami-based UM Motorcycles unveiled the Renegade Thor, which is also the world's first electric cruiser, along with the Renegade Duty S and the Renegade Duty Ace. The Renegade Thor produces an impressive 30 kilowatts of power along with 70 newton-meters of torque, and it is equipped with a 5-speed transmission gearbox, along with a hydraulic clutch and a liquid-cooled motor with a controller. The Renegade Thor also comes equipped with reverse gear, allowing for easy maneuvering. The Renegade Duty S and the Duty Ace are fitted with a 223cc single-cylinder motor connected to a 5-speed gearbox. The four-stroke, oil-cooled engine churns out 17 hp at 8,000 revolutions per minute and 17 newton-meters of torque. Weighing at 313 and 308 pounds (142 and 140 kg), respectively, the Renegade Duty S and the Duty Ace have the potential of being ridden on-road as well as off-road, allowing the light weight to aid in their nimble handling and maneuverability. UM has a distribution network in 25 nations with 1,200 outlets.

From Herstal, Belgium, comes Saroléa, founded in 1850 by Matthias Joseph Saroléa, who first specialized in armory and bicycles. The first motorcycle was produced in 1900, and manufacturing continued until the 1960s. Brothers Bjorn and Torsten Robbens decided to revive the legendary Belgian bike brand as a high-performance, 100 percent electric racing machine. Following their purchase of the company in 2008, all components were designed and built by Torsten Robbens, already a composite expert with an impressive motorsport background—including McLaren F1, Porsche and Audi World Endurance, Aerospace (ExoMars, Proba-V, Solar Sat)—as well as experience in military engineering. With the first prototype running in 2010, during the next three years, a succession of prototypes underwent continuous improvement. In 2014, Saroléa competed in the Isle of Man TT Zero. Skilled road racer Robert Wilson took the all-carbon SP7 to fourth place, at an average speed of 93.50 miles per hour, just 0.4 seconds off the podium. There were significant technical improvements for the 2015 IOM TT Zero, which resulted in an increase in the average speed to 106.51 miles per hour and a solid fifth place overall. At the 2016 IOM Zero, Saroléa riders Dean Harrison and Lee Johnston raced a completely new machine that was built on the steady progress of the past two seasons. In 2017, the company launched a limited series of its street-legal superbike, the MANX7, which is able to move its 436.5 pounds (198 kg) at the maximum speed of 200 miles per hour (320 kph) and go from zero to 62 miles per hour in 2.8 seconds, with an autonomy of 185 miles (300 km). In keeping with the brand's heritage, all Saroléa bikes are built by hand in-house. The first ten bikes were sold in 2017 without even having photos to show to customers. Some went to Walloons and Flemish while others were shipped to Australia, the United States or Thailand. The plan was to sell 100 more vehicles in 2018 to reach a production of 250 motorcycles maximum per year for this first model from 2019. In April 2018, invited by the ACO (Automobile Club de l'Ouest), the Saroléa SP7 did two demonstration laps in front of more than 75,000 spectators before the start of the Le Mans 24-hour motorcycle race.

In March 2018, Giovanni Castiglioni of Cagiva, formerly one of the largest names in Italian motorcycles and once owner of Ducati, Moto Morini, Husqvarna, and MV Agusta, announced its plans to enter off-road electric motorcycles, with production starting toward the end of 2019.

In mid–April 2018, the lithium battery technology company Alternet Systems of Dallas, Texas, announced its plan set up a subsidiary company called ReVolt Electric Motorcycles to make an electric version of the classic 1938 BMW R71 sidecar motorcycle, as used by German troops during World War II (and by Steve McQueen to outrun them in the 1963 film *The Great Escape*). The motorcycle will be based on the CJ750, a Chinese-made replica of the Soviet-era M-72 sidecar motorcycle, which itself was a replica of the original BMW R71. Alternet Systems holds 10 U.S. patents for lithium battery technology.

In 2019, electric motorcycles designed by Kalashnikov, known for its AK-47 assault rifle and other military and civilian weaponry and manufactured by the state corporation Rostec, will not only go into service with the Moscow Police, but will also will join President Vladimir Putin's "Kortezh," or official motorcade. Weighing 510 kg (1,124 pounds), the motorcycles will have a top speed of 250 kph (155 mph). Also in the Moscow force will be an electric three-wheeler named the IZH Ovum built by the Izhevsk Machine-Building Plant, a fleet of which were trialled at the World Cup.

After seven years of research and development involving more than 18,600 miles (30,000 km) of testing, India-based eMotion Motors (better known for its electric bicycles and scooters) expanded its focus and debuted its new Surge electric motorcycle. Its top speed of 75 miles per hour (120 kph), and 0–37 miles per hour (60 kph) acceleration in under 4 seconds, is helped by a high torque setup, with 20 newton-meters produced at the motor and geared down to a massive 517 newton-meters at the rear wheel. However, eMotion Motors wanted to push the torque even higher on the Surge, and thus opted for a 4-speed gearbox.

England, with its tradition of gas motorcycles such as Brough Superior, Triumph Bonneville, Norton Commander, Matchless Silver Hawk, and Royal Enfield Bullet, to name but a few, entered the electric field in good faith, led by Lawrence Marazzi. At the age of 11, Marazzi had made his first operational three-stage rocket; he also engineered a 12-cylinder, two-stroke engine for a hill-climb racer when he was 14 and then, just five years later, secured a job that saw him designing components for Formula One cars. In 2001, Marazzi passed the famously grueling acceptance course required to become a member of the Royal Marines Reserve, and he later served on the front line in Afghanistan. Qualifying as an aeronautical engineer at St. Mary's, London, he worked as a design engineer for firms such as Formula One teams Fonmet 1 and Venturi Larousse. In 2008, he founded Agility Motors in the basement of the Celtic Hotel in Bloomsbury, London, where he drafted the specs for an electric motorcycle with a short wheelbase, excellent handling and brakes, exciting performance and, crucially, a practical range between charges.

A key element to realizing this project would be linking up with Arvind Rabadia and Cedric Lynch of Agni Motors for their revolutionary axial-flux pancake motor. In 2015, Agility Global and Agni Motors merged; given his Italian background, Marazzi called the new company Saietta, which means "thunderbolt" in the Italian Apennine dialect. For more working space, Saietta moved from London to Heyford Park near Bicester, Oxfordshire, an ex–RAF/USAF base (it was actually a USAF base but officially called RAF Upper Heyford; the associated housing estate has American fire hydrants, and the houses have American mains sockets—which are no longer connected to anything—in addition to UK sockets) with access to 20 miles of private test tracks for testing. The actual manufacture of the motors continued in the solar-powered factory in Gandhidham. The machines in the factory have Agni/Saietta motors and are powered by solar panels on the factory roof;

there is also a battery that allows several hours of running at night when required and is recharged by the solar panels the next day.

The design of the Saietta motorcycle was revolutionary, featuring a wheelbase similar to that of a 250cc GP race bike; a Hossack front suspension; a lean angle of 55 degrees with low front-end lift fairing, which partially enclosed the front suspension; an eye-popping fairing design; and a crazy degree of mass centralization that could only be achieved with battery cells. The vehicle had a top speed of 80 miles per hour (130 kph) and a range of 60 miles (100 km); called the Saietta R, it was unveiled in 2013. This was to be replaced by the Saietta S, intended to have a 0–60 miles-per-hour dash in 2.7 seconds and a top speed of 150 miles per hour.

In 2016, Saietta launched Next Generation Saietta (NGS), boasting a number of technological firsts, including a revolutionary electric motor; an innovative lightweight, immensely strong structural monocoque; industry-leading battery capacity and range; 3D printing of the body; and even a new, highly distinctive roar! By June 2017, Saietta had raised more than 70 percent of the £5.85 million it needed to expand its activities. However, NGS never met the projected budget.

Among those using the Saietta-Agni motor was a team led by industrial engineer Marc Barceló, whose Volta BCN City, Sport and My Volta are made in Figueres, Girona, Catalonia, Spain. In 2010, with frame and technology in hand, Barceló enlisted the aid of both the IED (Istituto Europeo di Design) and design firm ÀNIMA Barcelona to help create a stunning, sporty shape for his new motorcycle. In the process, he joined forces (and development funds) with co-founder Joan Sabata of ÀNIMA, and Volta's first prototype (EV.1) was launched in Barcelona in April 2011. It would have a 25-kilowatt output, a top speed of 74.5 miles per hour (120 kph) and a range of between 45 and 60 miles. The lithium-ion batteries must last over 2,000 recharge cycles. The Volta BCN, with 85 percent of its components coming from the Catalan region, was launched in November 2011 at the EICMA Motorshow in Milan. In December 2015, the Catalonian General Council and the City Council of Barcelona signed a convention for the creation of the Catalan Electric Motor Industry Consortium, for which Volta Motorbikes, Scutum, Torrot Electric and Rieju manufacturers would jointly manufacture a 100 percent Catalonian scooter with the intention of producing 10,000 units per year. For 2018 Volta launched the BCN Forest.

Saietta is still planning a racing version of its motorcycle; meanwhile, Cedric Lynch and Arvind Rabadia are currently negotiating with companies in Asia to retrofit their well-proven Agni motor into auto rickshaws. EMBARQ India's analysis regarding the size of the auto-rickshaw market in select Indian cities, based on government records, indicates that Tier I cities in India (with population greater than 4 million) typically have more than 50,000 auto-rickshaws, while Tier II cities (with population between 1 and 4 million) have between 15,000 and 30,000 auto-rickshaws.

Meanwhile, Cedric, the irrepressible 62-year-old, long-haired inventor, continues his innovations. The latest is an improved efficiency AC/DC motor with multiple applications. Cedric continues commuting the 50 miles to work in his streamlined two-wheeler, having logged more than 60,000 miles through commuting to various venues. He recharges it with solar panels, some at his home and others at the workplace.

8

China
Almost 300 Million E-Bike Riders

China is the world's leading producer of e-bicycles. It is estimated that there were roughly 120 million e-bikes in China in early 2010; as of 2018, that number was fast approaching 300 million.[1] Of course, the majority of new e-bike sales today are to replace worn-out bikes, so the increase in fleet size is only about 25 percent of the new unit sales. It's hard to imagine now that there was once a time when the Chinese had not even heard of a bicycle.

In the aftermath of the Second Opium War (Second Anglo-Chinese War), which ended in 1860, Robert Hart, the head of China's Imperial Maritime Customs, suggested to the ruling Qing authorities that they send an exploratory diplomatic mission to some of the principal countries in Europe. After Thomas Wade, by then British minister at Beijing, seconded this opinion, the Qing government decided to send a mission, albeit a strictly informal one.

The Chinese took advantage of Robert Hart's 1866 furlough to include his language secretary—with temporary third-degree official rank—and several students among those who made the trip to Europe. After landing in Marseilles in March, they moved on to London, Paris, Copenhagen and Berlin before returning to China. The members of the mission have left interesting diaries, primarily describing the strange social customs and cities, but very little commentary on the politics of the countries they were visiting, instead evaluating the latest technological innovations and considering whether they could be used for imperial military purposes.

One of the officials, Binchun, discovered a fantastical sight on the streets of Paris. "On the avenues," Binchun writes in his book *Chengcha Biji* (Travels Abroad), edited by Zhong Shuhe,

A conveyor belt at Taioku in Zhangjiegang, Jiangsu province, one of China's 470 e-bicycle factories (courtesy Ed Benjamin).

> People ride on a vehicle with only two wheels, which is held together by a pipe. They sit above this pipe and push forward with movements of their feet, thus keeping the vehicle moving. There's yet another kind of construction which is propelled by foot pedaling. They dash along like galloping horses.[2]

The Chinese were also "surprised beyond measure at the numerous applications of which the electric fluid is capable," even though the storage of electricity (battery) was discovered in 1800 and the first electric motor invented in 1834 in Europe.

The bicycle industry in China began in the 1930s, when assembly plants for foreign-made bicycles were first established. In 1936, a Japanese businessman built the Changho Works factory in Tianjin, northeastern China, and started to make "Anchor" bicycles. The brand name was subsequently changed to "Victory," and then renamed Flying Pigeon. In January 1958, Chairman Mao Zedong launched the second Five-Year Plan, known as the Great Leap Forward, of the People's Republic of China (PRC); it aimed to rapidly transform the country from an agrarian economy into a socialist society through rapid industrialization and collectivization. The Flying Pigeon was at the forefront of the bicycle phenomenon in the People's Republic of

China. This vehicle was the government-approved form of transportation, and the nation became known as *zixingche wang guo* (the Kingdom of Bicycles). A bicycle was regarded as one of the three "must-haves" of every citizen, alongside a sewing machine and a watch—essential items in life that also offered a hint of wealth. The Flying Pigeon bicycle became a symbol of an egalitarian social system that promised little comfort but a reliable ride through life. Mao Zedong had one himself.

By 1958, China was producing more than a million bicycles annually. As part of this development, during the late 1960s, the Communist Party commissioned an investigation of electric bikes. However, under the so-called Gang of Four (led by the late Mao Zedong's fourth wife, Jiang Qing), early efforts to develop and commercialize these electric vehicles failed.

During the 1980s, a group of entrepreneurs from Shanghai, as well as Jinhua Grankee Vehicle Co., Ltd. in Zhejiang and Flying Pigeon in Tianjin, gathered to revive the fledgling industry. In 1987, the Electric Vehicle Institute of China Electrotechnical Society was founded. Total annual e-bike production reached 10–20,000 per year. This peak, however, lasted only 3–4 years. This introduction of e-bikes was short lived for several reasons. First, e-bike technology was not advanced enough to fulfill the demand of consumers. In particular, battery quality was low in terms of performance and lifetime. Second, the e-bike price was relatively high due to the high battery costs. E-bikes failed during this phase because they could not compete with inexpensive gasoline motor scooters.

Chinese e-bikes experienced a second surge during the early 1990s due to the government's push for energy efficiency. In 1991, the National Science Board named the e-bike as one of 10 main technology projects during the ninth Five Year Plan period. Carefully observing the appearance of the Yamaha PAS e-bike in Japan during 1993, Shanghai founded an electric vehicle industrialization development center. Tianjin also banned the sale of gasoline-powered scooters. In 1995, Prime Minister Li Pong declared his support for electric vehicles, leading to the "Seminar for E-bike Development in Light Industry General Society."

Taking part in this development was a first batch of e-bikes produced by Cranes Electric Vehicle Co., based in the Pudong section of Shanghai, and backed by the government. But that batch was far from perfect; after barely three months of use, the motors burned out and the lead-acid batteries—designed to be removed from the bikes and taken inside for plug-in charges—could no longer take a charge. During the next two years, Cranes developed 150- or 180-watt brushless hub motors that delivered higher torque, a more reliable electronic controller on the handlebars, and 24-volt, 7-amp-hour lead-acid batteries that delivered a range of up to 37 miles (60 km) and lasted up to two years. In 1996, the first national forum on e-bikes was held. Sales mounted, and Cranes' success attracted competition, bringing both start-ups and conventional bike manufacturers, such as T and Di Continental Dove of Nanjing. Yongjiu (Forever) in the Shanghai suburbs, one of China's most popular bicycle makers, teamed up with the U.S. company Zap for motors and batteries and designed an electric bicycle that ran for up to seven hours without being recharged and could reach a top speed of about 15 miles per hour (30 kph).

In 1996 Shanghai stopped granting licenses to gasoline-powered vehicles downtown, in order to, as its mayor declared, "gradually eliminate gasoline-powered assist vehicle and actively develop and promote electro-assist technology." Meanwhile, Cranes rolled out its first commercial batch of e-bikes powered by a 150–180-watt motor, with a 7-amp-hour battery capacity. Guangzhou, Shijiazhuang, and Suzhou followed suit by banning the sale of gasoline-powered scooters. Many other medium/large cities would do the same in the following years. In addition, Shanghai began holding annual inspections of gasoline-powered scooters, eliminating those in which exhaust gas emission was unacceptable: 53,000 in total. The mayor then stated his desire to replace *all* gas scooters with electric bikes during the next five years.

Another company was the Suzhou Small Antelope, founded in December 1997 and manufacturing electric bicycles from July 1998. Eventually its annual output would reach 350,000 electric bicycle units per year. The motor makers at Small Antelope, Qinghua Wang and Mr. He, moved on to found Bafang Motor Company (still at Suzhou)—the largest supplier of e-bike motors to Western markets.

Although bicycle companies Daluge, Chizuru, Red Flag and other manufacturers were experimenting with electric vehicles, it was in 1998 that Ma Guilong, a professor at Tsinghua Research University in Beijing, developed and patented a speed switch, pedal sensor and pulse width modulation for electrically assisted tricycles. Manufactured at the Wuyang factory in Guangzhou, having passed Japanese testing standards, these devices were exported to Tokyo. In 1999, an industry panel suggested that e-bikes should be limited to a maximum load capacity of 88 pounds (40 kg) and a speed of roughly 12.5 miles per hour. These seemingly arbitrary specifications have met with fierce resistance from consumers ever since. Ma, who became chief scientist of the China Electric Bicycle Association, was later featured in an episode of a China Central Television documentary series commemorating top industrial innovators in 2009, largely because he gave up his claim to nearly 100 patents so manufacturers could share the technology freely.

Founded by Winston Chung, Shenzen Battery Ltd., based in Shenzhen, Guangdong Province, China, produced its first batch of white Thunder Sky lithium batteries in August 1998. In 1999, Shanghai Economy and Trade Committee listed e-bikes as one of 12 main construction projects in the "Highland."

E-bike licenses were granted in Shanghai, Tianjin, Jiangsu, Zhejiang, Guangdong, Cichang, Yunnan, Anhui, and Hebei. Administrative coordinators nationwide recommended promotion of e-bikes to the Department of State. Such a strategy would enable e-bikes to emerge into the market during the end of the 20th century to witness an exponential growth.

But then came a turnabout in fortunes. In 2002, the city of Beijing issued a statement declaring that it would cease offering e-bike licenses beginning in 2006 in order to promote safer four-wheel automobile development. China, following the path of Western countries, was rapidly redesigning its cities around automobiles. Houses are springing up in the suburbs, just as they did in the West decades ago. The automobile is king in this model, because, in the absence of extensive public transit, cars are the only way to get from distant suburbs to offices and industry parks. Therefore, e-bike penetration is noticeably different from city to city. Some cities have low adoption rates, like Beijing (less than 10 percent), while others have high adoption rates, like Chengdu (more than 50 percent).

In 1996, Mrs. Jihong Hu, starting in a 15-square-meter garage, completed the design and refit of the first e-bike. Although the company originally ran at a loss, nine years later Luyuan Electric Vehicle Co., located in Jinhua on the outskirts of Shanghai, was building and manufacturing a good product. The company's rise was exponential. The Japan Cycle Press yearbook for 2005 stated that Luyuan manufactured 47,500 e-bikes in 2002 and increased production to 85,600 units in 2003. But that year officials in Fuzhou, capital of the neighboring Fujian province, decided to ban electric bicycles in favor of automobiles—shutting off what until then had been one of Luyuan's best markets. Fuzhou not only ceased issuing licenses for electric bicycles but also seized 20 electric bikes from a bicycle shop. So Jie Ni, Luyuan's CEO, gathered a coalition of 126 electric-bike manufacturers and citizens and filed suit against the city in its own municipal court. The coalition scored a partial win against the city government, forcing it to return the seized bikes. Far more valuable, they received from national media and the warning that attention sent to other municipalities.[3]

In 2003 e-bike sales surged again after the outbreak of the SARS coronavirus, when many riders shifted away from public transit. Annual domestic e-bike sales in China soared from 40,000 in 1998 to 10 million in 2005—about 3 times the number of automobiles sold. The following year, Shanghai's e-bike population reached 1.35 million, the highest ownership level of any city in China, while overall e-bike production in China in 2006 was projected to reach a staggering 18 million, and this out of a total population of 1.311 billion Chinese.

In terms of manufacturing, from the ten original equipment manufacturers in 1998, there were officially 481 by 2005, although unofficial estimates range from 1,000 to 5,000; output varies accordingly, from thousands of bikes per year to 300,000 per year. However, such growth has come at a cost, particularly emissions from primarily smog-producing coal power plants and increased lead waste from battery use.

One example of the power of Chinese production is the Jiangsu Xinri E-Vehicle Co. Ltd., a civilian-run, joint-stock listed company based in Anzhen, Xishan District, Wuxi, with its SUNRA range. It has six major production bases in Wuxi, Tianjin, Dongguan, Xiangyang, Henan and Xuzhou, with a total of 5,000 employees (including 500 engineers), resulting in an annual production capacity of 4 million electric vehicles of various models: bicycles, scooters, motorcycles, tricycles and cars.

Yadea Technology Group Co. Ltd., another major producer of electric bikes, scooters, tricycles and other special vehicles, has four production bases: Jiangsu (headquarters), Zhejiang, Tianjin, and Guangdong. In August 2008, the company, with 5,300 employees and annual sales of 3.2 million units, launched its Z3 e-scooter model in Beijing, targeting high-end e-scooter consumers across the world. The company said it would export the model to 66 countries, including the United States and Germany. Since then, Yadea has been the only electric vehicle manufacturer in China to export to more than 50 countries.

Starting in 2013, China set and implemented regulations for the specs and size of e-bike lithium batteries while a battery management system was also launched. In October 2014, China reached a strategic collaboration agreement with Germany. With that, the Chinese electric car brands will adopt the same charging standards as BMW and Audi. During the first half of 2014, the production of lithium-battery-equipped e-bikes reached 1.7 million units, an increase of 36 percent and accounting for more than 50 percent of the total e-bike export.

By 2016, despite an estimated 200 million e-bikes manufactured by 700 companies in regular use, Beijing, Shanghai, Guangzhou and Shenzen had forbidden the use of e-bikes across large swathes of the cities. Dr. David Hon of the China Bicycle Association published a letter to the government, speaking out against these regulations.

The Luyuan Company now has an annual turnover of 176 types of LEVs, more than 4,000,000 e-scooters and 7,000,000 batteries, which means that Luyuan can provide everyone in a mid-size city with one e-scooter in a single year. It holds 253 completely independent patents and has 7 manufacturing bases (Shangdong, Jiangsu, Zhejiang, Fujian and Vietnam) with a total area of 1,300,000 square meters. The Luyuan frame automatic production line is equipped with 50 welding robots, which makes Luyuan the first company to import such devices. Electric vehicles sales in China are nearly 30,000,000 per year, and there are almost 2,000,000 customers choosing Luyuan. Since

E-bike traffic in China (courtesy Ed Benjamin).

November 2016, Luyuan has had around 12,700,000 users.[4] This is just for one company.

In October 2017, China was accused of flooding Europe with hundreds of thousands of cheap electric bicycles. Imports of Chinese e-bikes to Europe had increased from almost zero in 2010 to an estimated 800,000 in 2017, according to the European Bicycle Manufacturers Association (EBMA). As stated by EBMA, there were more than 430,000 Chinese e-bikes sold in the European Union in 2016, representing a roughly 40 percent increase compared to 2015 levels. Preliminary forecasts for 2017 were in the 800,000 range. The industry group had had enough: it filed a complaint with the European Commission that accused Chinese manufacturers of dumping e-bikes into the European market at rock-bottom prices. The complaint argued that subsidies offered by the Chinese government allow its manufacturers to sell e-bikes in Europe for less than what they cost to produce. The association cited an economic planning document produced by the Chinese government that "sets a clear 2020 goal that the 'export of electric bicycles will be dramatically increased.'" Global e-bike sales are expected to increase from $15.7 billion in 2016 to $24.3 billion by 2025, according to Navigant Research.[5]

In recent months, China has expressed its intent to be the world's first all-electric vehicle nation. Alongside many thousands of cars, buses and trucks, the manufacture and sale of electric motorcycles and bicycles will contribute to this.

Although it does not fall within the brief of this transport history, one would be accused of looking through rose-tinted spectacles if one did not play devil's advocate with three questions. What to do so that the carbon footprint of an electric vehicle battery does not become an ecological disaster? What to do so that its recycling does not become an ecological disaster? How to find sufficient raw materials to make the cells and the chemicals for batteries in the long-term? If the history and the future of the electric two- and three-wheeler, etc., is to have a beneficial impact, such questions must be addressed by those responsible.

At the time of this writing, major motorcycle manufacturers are entering the e-bike industry at full speed as demand from the motorcycle market shrinks. China's motorcycle manufacturers, like Haojue, Zongshen, and Dayun, are all investing in e-bikes. This stronger competition forces the current e-bike makers to upgrade their operations in order to survive.

In the summer of 2018, U.S. President Donald Trump in his "Make America Great Again" trade war against China imposed a 25 percent tariff (product code 284) on the imports of electric bicycles and parts including motors, electric speed controllers, e-bike batteries and other common components. While there are a few companies in the United States building their own e-bikes, they still generally use a large portion of Chinese-made components. In an ironic twist, some of the biggest losers were U.S. companies that designed, marketed and sold their e-bikes locally but manufactured them in China. To dodge this, a growing number of Chinese companies shifted e-bike production to countries such as Vietnam, Serbia and Mexico.

9

Marathons

There is no better proof of the reliability of electric vehicles than marathon journeys. *Turanor Planet Solar*, the solar catamaran, voyaged twice around the world, while *Solar Impulse*, the solar monoplane, flew around once.

Kanichi Fujiwara is a Japanese long-distance motorcycle rider and writer. Between March 2004 and May 2008, he made a 31,412-mile (50,552 km) journey circumnavigating the world on a Yamaha Passol electric scooter, following a route that covered 44 countries, including Australia (going from Sydney to Perth), Thailand, India, South Africa, Kenya, and America (from New York to San Francisco). This journey may have been the first global circumnavigation by an electric two-wheeler. Fujiwara visited and documented the sites of sacred trees in various countries to spread awareness of green transportation. The scooter he used in the 2004–2008 circumnavigation, sponsored by Yamaha, weighed 99 pounds (45 kg) and had a top speed of 18.6 miles per hour (30 kph) and an endurance of 12 miles on a battery charge. However, even with six batteries giving a 60-mile range, Fujiwara's partner Hiroko had to shuttle charged batteries to him in order for Fujiwara to cross Australia's Nullarbor Plain.[1]

The Sun Trip

From his childhood growing up in the Auvergne-Rhône-Alpes region of the French Alps, Florian Bailly had loved cycling, competing in several races around the local mountains, where he particularly loved climbing the peaks and seeing the other side of the frontier. One day, with friends, he cycled almost 225 miles (360 km) to Marseilles. He also cycled around the peaks of Mont Blanc, a distance of 205 miles (330 km). In short, he loved long-distance cycling.

In 2006, Bailly, 24, studying at the University of Chambéry Savoie, took three months to ride his pedal bicycle more than 6,200 (10,000 km) from his home to China. The adventure was an eye opener, and he knew that he would soon make another marathon trip. By 2009, Bailly, now press attaché for Savoie Council, obtained a leave of absence to make a 100-day journey to Tokyo, Japan. For this trip, he would use a VTT (Velo Tout-Terrain, or mountain bike) pedelec towing a single-wheel trailer covered with 15.4-pound (7 kg) solar panels providing energy to 17.6-pound (8 kg) lithium-iron phosphate batteries. The e-trike rig had been worked out by Olivier Wiss, an engineer at the National Solar Energy Institute, recently set up in Savoie, which was largely devoted to the installation of solar panels on buildings. During this journey (called "On the Road of the Rising Sun!"), Bailly took four months, covering almost 75 miles (120 km) per day, to cross empty deserts, mountains and countrysides, traveling through ten countries to arrive on time in a city with a population of millions. The following year (2010), Bailly rode his Sunrise No. 1 to China and the Pavilion in the Puxi Urban Best Practices Area of the Shanghai World Expo with its theme "Better City, Better Life."

No longer wanting to make such trips alone, in 2013, Bailly organized the Sun Trip, modeled on the Vendée Globe yacht race: 35 sunbikers, including

Florian Bailly in Shanghai after his ride in 2010 from France to Japan. He was received at the Shanghai Universal Exhibition (courtesy Florian Bailly).

Day 15 of the 2018 Sun Trip: Thirty-five adventurers prepare to enter Kazakhstan. One, Raf Van Hulle, who rode about 2,400 miles in 15 days, would have gone even farther with better sunshine (courtesy Florian Bailly).

entries from Belgium, Kazakhstan, Austria, Switzerland, France and Italy, rode almost 5,000 miles from Savoie, France, to Astana in Kazakhstan. Bailly made a documentary of the event. In 2015, the second edition of the Sun Trip was a loop of 4,660 miles (7,500 km) from Milan (Italy) to Anatolia (Turkey). The conflict in Ukraine and instability in countries bordering Iraq forced Bailly, as president of the Sun Trip Company, to change the route of the race. The winner, Bernard Cauquil, had an average performance of almost 175 miles per day, although on some days he reached more than 215 miles.

In 2017, after two bigger events on the roads of the world, the Sun Trip Company launched the 745-mile Sun Trip Tour around the Auvergne-Rhône-Alpes region. The Sun Trip 2018 covered a distance of more than 8,000 miles from Lyon, France, to Guangzhou, China, making it the largest terrestrial adventure in the world. A batch of eZee Solar Delta Longabikes, with 360-watt PV roof panels, capable of an average speed of 21.75 miles per hour, were shipped over to Lyon so that competitors could ride them back to Guangzhou. The route crossed 10 countries along the New Silk Roads to commemorate the 30th anniversary of the Lyon-Canton (Guangzhou) twinning, the cities being, respectively, the second- and third-biggest cities of France and China. The Sun Trip 2018 official start took place in Lyon on Friday, June 15, at mid-day. The start proper took place in Chamonix on the morning of June 19. As opposed to earlier Sun Trips, the solar panels weighed only 700 grams per square meter and were paired with far more reliable batteries. In all, 36 competitors took part. The Sun Trip 2018 took 57 days. By September 11, there were 13 finishers and 12 still en route. Raf Van Hulle rode about 3,900 km (2,400 miles) in 15 days. Behind him, a group of 10 teams maintaining their average around 200 km/day clearly stood out.[2]

Another long-distance adventurer is Susanne Brüsch, who officially coined the word "pedelec" in 1999. In 2011, Brüsch started organizing multi-week adventure tours on electric bikes together with a specialist team. She began with 620-mile (1,000 km) tours through Morocco using a 500-watt GoSwiss Drive hub motor, and then, in Mongolia in 2012, she used speed-pedelecs equipped with the center-motor from Bosch. In 2013, Brüsch and her adventurers went on a 2,485-mile challenge through Iceland's northern territory. Next, Brüsch, along with trial world champion Marco Hösel and vehicle designer Norbert Haller, took brand new Trefecta e-bikes on a discovery journey through Berlin and its surrounding woods. Following the COP21 UN climate change conference in Paris in early December 2015, with the start of E-Bike Africa, Brüsch and Bruce MacLeod set out on a journey of more than 12,400 miles from Glasgow to Cape Town; her work gained another dimension when she joined forces with a Scottish charity, the Purple Heart Network, to raise awareness of climate change. The epic traverse of the western United States, with its stunning landscapes and extreme contrasts, was her biggest adventure to date: 3,100 miles long and more than 187,000 feet climbed—a new record. A film documentary about the "Sand to Snow" tour has just appeared on DVD in English. This year, Brüsch is touring through Germany giving presentations on her pedelec adventures and sharing her best tips and tricks on e-bike travel at various events while making plans for new adventures.

Hot-Shots have also covered long distances. Zero Motorcycle marathoners have proved themselves several times, beginning on October 31, 2011, with "Electric Terry" Hershner of Santa Cruz. Hershner, who studied electrical and mechanical engineering at North Carolina State University, decided to break the rules to embark on a social and technical experiment of powering lives using alternative energy instead of fossil fuels. In 2012, using the public charging electric vehicle network, Hershner made a 500-mile (800 km) trip to Miami, Florida, and then a 1,200-mile (1,900 km) trip to the Bonnaroo Music Festival in Manchester, Tennessee, which he said was the longest distance ridden on an electric motorcycle at that time. Having further modified his bike, in June 2013 Hershner, on a 2012 Zero S ZF9 outfitted with a Craig Vetter streamlined fairing, became the first person to ride cross-country on a Zero electric motorcycle, going from San Diego, California, to Jacksonville,

Florida, in five days, or 135 hours, with no support and using existing charging infrastructure. In July, shortly after his arrival back on the West Coast, Hershner placed second to a Tesla Model S in the BC2BC All Electric Vehicle Rally, riding from Canada to Mexico. Subsequently, on November 24, 2013, Hershner and his passenger, Chelsea Liggatt, became the first to travel "two up" across the United States by electric motorcycle. In 2014, Craig Vetter and students from Virginia Tech helped Hershner rebuild the tail section of his motorcycle out of aluminum to hold 21 kilowatt-hours of batteries, as well as up to 24 kilowatt-hours of chargers that would run off four J1772 Level 2 plugs, at 6 kilowatts each. Later, on August 29, 2014, Hershner became the first electric motorcycle rider to win the historic Craig Vetter Fuel Economy Challenge, traveling 172 miles (205 km) on a single charge, at speeds up to 80 miles per hour (130 kph), for 1.3 cents per mile cost in electricity. On September 15, 2014, the first day of National Drive Electric Week, "Electric Terry" became the first electric motorcycle rider to earn an Iron Butt Award (Saddlesore 1000) from the Iron Butt Association. He rode more than 1,047 miles (1,685 km) from the ChargePoint headquarters in Northern California to the Mexico border and back, in 22 hours and 57 minutes, using only ChargePoint charging stations. On May 7, 2015, Hershner became the first electric motorcyclist to ride 300 miles on a single charge. He carried 27 kilowatt-hours of battery on board. When Hershner wasn't setting records, he was often spotted on his Zero electric motorcycle with his partner: a mini Husky bitch by the name of Charger, who perhaps loves riding even more than Hershner does!

Alongside Hershner, there is Ben Rich, a former swing dance instructor. In 2007, Ben took the Basic Rider course to get his motorcycle license; then, in 2007, he got his first electric motorcycle, a blue Vectrix electric motorcycle, so he could travel without using gasoline. Changing over to a Zero S, in 2012 Ben traveled across the United States from Mexico to Canada. In 2013, he rode on his Zero from east to west, traveling 4,500 miles (7,240 km) from Charleston, South Carolina, to Google Headquarters in Mountain View, California. He charged up primarily at 120-volt outlets and occasionally used Level 2 charging at 3 or 4.5 kilowatts. Terry Hershner had completed a similar trip a couple of months earlier, going from Los Angeles to Jacksonville, Florida. Hershner and Rich met in person on this trip and assumed that others would soon follow.

In 2014, Ben Rich rode his Zero S on his own trip, visiting friends and riding parts of Skyline Drive, the Blue Ridge Parkway, the Natchez Trace Parkway and the entire Tail of the Dragon. On that journey he traveled 6,000 miles from New Jersey to North Carolina, St. Louis, Chicago, and New Hampshire before returning home. He could ride up to 80 miles at a time and charge at 4.5 kilowatts. In 2015, while on break from his job as a sustainability coordinator and physics teacher at Montclair Kimberley Academy (New

Electric Terry Hershner and his Husky, Ranger, on their marathon Zero motorcycle (courtesy Terry Hershner).

Jersey), he took a 2014 Zero SR on a 7,000-mile (11,200 km) New Jersey loop road trip from New York City to Florida, Mexico, and Montreal, before returning to New York. With a larger 14.2-kilowatt-hour battery pack and the ability to charge at 6.3 kilowatts, using a system made by Hollywood Electrics, Rich's range and charging both increased. He was able to ride the entire Skyline Drive on one charge (130 miles), as well as the entire Blue Ridge Parkway (500 miles [800 km]) and the entire Natchez Trace Parkway (441 miles [710 km]). Rich was featured on the cover of the February issue of *American Motorcyclist* magazine, where he wrote, "Riding the open road is a treasure and a mystery waiting to be experienced."

On June 10, 2013, IT-sector businessman Nicola Colombo, together with bike industry brand manager Valerio Fumagalli, started an electric bike trip, the "Meneghina Express," from the Shanghai Universal Exposition to Milan, Italy. Forty-four days, 7,691 miles and 12 countries later, via Ulaanbaatar (Mongolia), Astana (Kazakistan), Volgograd (Russia), Odessa (Ukraine), and Belgrade (Serbia), they reached their destination. Based on the lessons learned from this experience, and assisted by Adriano Stellino (a graduate from IAAD in Turin and a designer for first-class automotive firms including Lamborghini and Bertone), Colombo and Fumagalli set up the Volt motorcycle company to produce the Lacama, rated for an electronically limited top speed of 112 miles per hour (180 kph) with a maximum power of 94 horsepower (70 kW).

In September 2014, 23 students at Eindhoven University of Technology (TU/e) in the Netherlands began to plan an 80-day, 14,300-mile (23,000 km) around-the-world journey on two self-built electric motorbikes. They called their mounts "STORM Wave." They designed and built special lithium-ion battery packs giving a promising range of 236 miles (380 km) between charges. Each honeycomb-shaped modular pack comprised 24 separate cartridges shaped into the body of the motorcycle and provided 28.5 kilowatt-hours of energy. It would be possible to change a full battery pack within seven minutes. If a rider were going to take a long trip, all the batteries would be used, but for short trips they could use the minimum quantity of 12 cartridges, thus traveling lighter.

The Storm World Tour began at Eindhoven on Sunday, August 14, 2016, and the loop was due to be completed on November 2. Despite some minor setbacks, the team took it in turns to ride through 16 countries, visiting 65 cities and covering a total of almost 14,300 miles (23,000 km). In late September 2016, the Wave motorcycles were air-freighted from Shanghai, China, to Seattle, Washington. Then, after the first European e-motorcycles had crossed the United States, they were again air-freighted from New York to Paris. On November 2, day 80 of the journey, STORM Eindhoven drove the last 250 miles (400 km) from Paris to Eindhoven, where the team arrived around 17:30 p.m. on the TU/e campus. Along the way, they had gathered 17,001 megabytes of data with the help of their revolutionary IoT integration, which resulted in some stunning and fun facts about the journey (for example, during the trip they changed the batteries 74 times). Back in Eindhoven, they are now preparing a commercial version of their electric motorcycle. Sapa Extrusion of Benelux will supply the aluminum cartridge cases.

On March 10, 2018, Remo Klawitter created an electric motorcycle record for kilometers ridden in a 24-hour period. Using his 2018 Zero DSR ZF14.4, with its optional Charge Tank (which increases charge speed by up to six times), the 38-year-old bicycle salesman made a looped ride from his shop

Top: The 2016 Storm Tour team: Each member took turns to ride their motorcycles around the world. *Bottom*: The 2016 the Storm Wave motorcycle without its fairings, showing the cartridge battery replacement system (both TuDelft).

in Falkensee near Berlin, along Federal Highway 96, to the Neustrelitz Land Center for Renewable Energies in the state of Mecklenburg-Vorpommern. Klawitter rode in 93-mile (150 km) stints at an average of 55–60 miles per hour (90–100 kph). After each stage he stopped and fully recharged the bike—requiring just one hour at Level 2 public charging points. He rested during the charging breaks in Neustrelitz, where a solar-powered charging station had been reserved for him. At the end of the 24 hours, he had totted up almost 692 miles (1,113 km).

In the fall of 2018, three riders plan to cover 25,000 miles (40,200 km) on custom electric motorcycles, their route tracking mostly the Pacific coastline of North and South America from Prudhoe Bay in Alaska to Tierra del Fuego in Argentina, involving fourteen international border crossings. Confirmed adventurer J.C. Davis will ride alongside Grey Smith, an engineer, and Danell Lynn, a humanitarian campaigner who is already in the *Guinness World Records* for having covered 53,000 miles (85,000 km) on a Triumph Bonneville gas motorcycle for more than one year through 50 U.S. states and Canada. Lynn is the first solo woman motorcyclist to hold this record. For the joint trip, the riders' mounts are Expedition Electric 950 KTMs, modified by Brutus e-motorcycle master Chris Bell of Boulder City, Nevada. The chassis has been enlarged to take a 20-kilowatt battery pack to extend the range to about 300 miles (484 km). Each bike includes a 119.3-newton-meter (88-pound-foot) AC motor and regenerative brakes. "Expedition Electric" will be the team's second attempt at the trip after their first attempt ended because of technical difficulties in 2016. "After we'd made it down through Alaska, through the Yukon, and were on our way into British Columbia, we had a battery failure," explained Davis.[3]

Such feats have proven that electric motorcycles now have the range of gasoline traditionals. As batteries improve, these marathons may become even longer.

10

Speed Records

The moment an electric motorcycle was timed, it was a record. The first such record was set in April 1881 by Gustave Trouvé's tricycle in Paris when it was timed at a speed of 7.4 miles per hour (12 kph) along the rue Valois in downtown Paris; Trouvé was not at the helm but observing from a window of the Hotel de Hollande. Although the inventor felt that, with a more powerful motor, he could have achieved 12–18 miles per hour (20–30 kph), this never took place. Sixteen years later, electric cycle-pacing tandems and triplets were clocking speeds of 38 miles per hour (60 kph) around velodromes. But it was to be another 60 years before an electric motorcycle achieved serious speed.

In the early 1970s, Mike Corbin, a 27-year-old ex–US Navy electrician in Somerville, Connecticut, built a street-legal commuter electric bicycle called the Corbin Electric; its three Exide 36-volt lead-acid batteries gave it a speed of around 30 miles per hour (48 kph) for 40 miles (64 km). 100 Corbin bikes were manufactured between 1972 and 1973. Corbin was the first company to be a licensed vehicle manufacturer for street-legal electric motorcycles. Provoked by frequent comments that electric vehicles were too slow, in 1973 Corbin built a motorcycle he called "Lightning," with Die Hard lead-acid batteries, and took it to Bonneville, Utah—the first e-motorcycle to run on the salt flats. It clocked an average speed of 101 miles per hour (163 kph), thus becoming the first known electric motorcycle to go more than 100 miles per hour.

The following year, Corbin persuaded Yardney Electric in Pawcatuck, Connecticut, to provide him with energy-dense silver-zinc batteries, then in use on nuclear-powered submarines. These were intended for use on a 9-foot bike called "Quicksilver." Dr. Americo W. Petrocelli, chief operating officer of Yardney, told Corbin that although the batteries would cost $100,000, the company would let him take the silver from a naval vault at the Yardney factory in Rhode Island and build a 100-cell battery that delivered 1,000 amps at 120 volts—not easy to recharge. This was the first time an electric motorcycle ran on chemistry other than lead-acid. For the motor, Corbin used two 120-volt DC starter motors from Douglas A4B fighter planes, because they had lightweight cases and silver windings, which have lower resistance than copper.

> We bought a full pallet of them from the Navy surplus, because they used to burn up. You'd get going like hell, and they'd overheat and solder would come out of the commutators. And these copper bars would fly out into the motor, and you'd have to throw the whole thing away. So I had a bunch of those....
> The controller was the hard part. We didn't have any way to rheostat that much amperage. So what we did was make a stepped voltage controller with magnetic contactors. So it'd start at 12 volts, then you'd switch to 24 volts, then you'd go to 120. If you put the 120 volts on immediately, the wheel would just spin and dig a hole right in the salt.
> So we had a flying start, we'd tow the bike up to anywhere between 40 and 60 mph (64 and 97 km/h) with a rented Nash, then I had an ejection rope, you'd spring load this thing and it'd fall in the salt, and I'd go around the car and start accelerating.
> There was very high amperage involved and the magnetic contactors could not open fast enough to avoid arching (welding shut) In series with power bars, I built a large knife switch with a 400 amp fuse in parallel. To shut down, I pulled a mechanical release and the rubber bungee cord open the knife and the fuse blew eating up the initial arc. I had to pull this first or the whole bike would not be able to shut down.

In the fall, Corbin and a team from Yardney took Quicksilver, AMA 24, weighing just over 700 pounds, to the Bonneville Salt Flats, and on August 19 they clocked an average of 165.387 miles per hour (266.164 kph), although they also clocked runs of 191 miles per hour (307 kph) and 201 miles per hour (323 kph); however, the timing wire was broken that day. "Then we came home, we recycled the batteries, we put about 99 percent of the silver right back in that vault, and the Navy never knew it!" Despite a number of attempts to surpass this feat, Corbin's record average stood for 38 years.

In 1975, using the publicity gained from this record, Corbin-Gentry Co. series-produced a 1-horsepower X-2 electric city bike capable of going 50 miles per hour (80 kph) with a range of 50 miles (80 km) using a nickel-zinc battery manufactured by Yardney Electric. The first unit was traded to Professor Charles McArthur for his hot air balloon. During the week of June 15–20, 1975, the first annual alternative vehicle regatta was held at Mount Washington, New Hampshire. The regatta was created and promoted by Charles McArthur, an environmentalist who sincerely believed that the rally was necessary to gather together and test all possible forms of alternative

Opposite, top: On August 19, 1974, Mike Corbin rode Quicksilver to a new average record of 165.387 mph (266.164 kph), although he also clocked runs of 191 mph (307 kph) and 201 mph (323 kph). *Bottom:* In this 1974 photo, Dr. Americo W. Petrocelli, chief operating officer of Yardney, talks to Mike Corbin and team around the Quicksilver record challenger (both collection Mike Corbin).

10. Speed Records

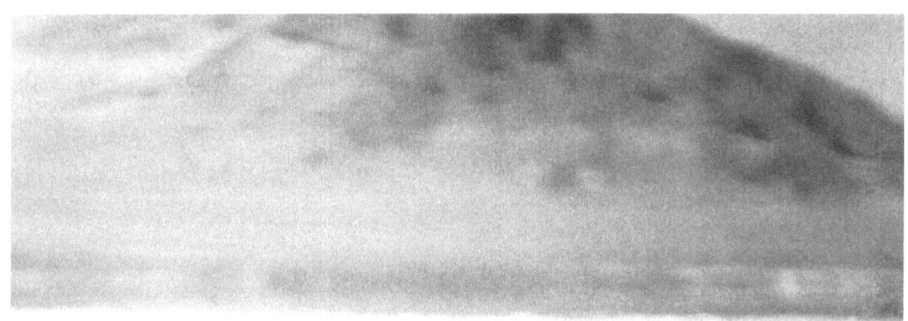

transportation. Emphasis was placed on low energy consumption and minimal pollution. As McArthur planned to use his own bike to make an ascent of Mount Washington, Corbin and Petrocelli made sure that it was equipped with the most energy-dense silver-zinc battery possible. On June 17, 1975, this super battery, with a total energy content of more than 4,680 watt-hours, successfully powered the Corbin-designed motorcycle 8 miles to the summit on an average gradient of 12 percent, through 99 hairpin turns, in 26 minutes nonstop. On June 18, this same winning combination made 2 nonstop trips to the summit, setting another record. It then coasted down the mountain and ascended again on the same charge. The Corbin XLP-1 was recharged by a windmill on the mountain made by Enertech of Norwich, Vermont, to provide free electricity for recharging any electric vehicle that made it to the top. Steve Schiffer, new products manager of Yardney Electric, and Bill Drake, president of Enertech, saw to it that the Corbin-Yardney motorcycle was recharged using this free source of power. It thus became the first electric vehicle to ascend Mount Washington twice, on one charge, and then be recharged with renewable clean energy. Based in Hollister, California, Mike Corbin later earned a fine reputation as a maker of quality seats for conventional motorcycles.

Also during the 1970s, Ed Rannberg of Fontana, California, was developing electric vehicles; he electrified his Renault Dauphine using a J&H 9-horsepower aircraft motor and a 36-volt battery system, using it to commute. He then set up Eyeball Engineering, where he converted and built a series of electric vehicles. Among his creations was a go-kart that, with an aircraft motor and 72 volts' worth of nickel-cadmium batteries, ran the quarter-mile drag strip at 94 miles per hour and in 14.02 seconds in the open air about 2 inches above the ground. Ed also designed and built an aircraft-motor/nickel-cadmium-powered drag bike called the Ampeater; its best quarter-mile performance was just a tiny bit slower than the go-kart. In 1987, a new lead-acid battery came onto the market—the Pulsar Power Pack, manufactured by Dunlop Pacific in Australia. Rannberg acquired sixteen 10P batteries and linked them to a 100-horsepower Prestolite MTC-4001 motor; then he used them to power a modified Kawasaki Ninja bike motorbike, calling his mount the Kawashocki. In 1988, Rannberg tested his Kawashocki along the Bonneville Salt Flats. Reaching a regular 124–126 miles per hour (200 kph), it could complete a quarter-mile (400 m) in 11–12 seconds.

Elsewhere, others continued the quest for speed. In 1989, Thomas Herzog and Thomas Wick of Switzerland took the electric motorcycle record to 21.75 miles per hour (163 kph), partially due to ultra-light carbon-Kevlar bodywork. In October 1994, the electric motorcycle record was increased to 104.7 miles per hour (168.498 kph) by Italian Superbike champion ace Max Biaggi on his Violet-Violent in bright purple paint 102 on the Nardo track in southern Italy. The standing-start quarter-mile speed was 47 miles per hour (75 kph).

In 1996, the French decided it was their turn. Jean-Francois Monteil (an electronics engineer and former lecturer at the Institute of Technology in Reims in central France) and a team of his former students, headed by Micha'l Cassez, took a 9.2-foot (2.8 m) Kawasaki ZZr 1100 tourer framework and reworked it to receive three nickel-cadmium aviation batteries, provided by SAFT of Bordeaux, as well as a 500-amp-hour controller from Curtis U.S. (which supplied the lunar jeep for NASA's Apollo missions) and a 47.5-horsepower (35 kW) electric motor made by Leroy Somer of Angoulême (and already used in the electric version of Peugeot's 106 car, then specially prepared and cooled by a centrifugal pump). The total weight of the projectile (without its Aéro-Style shell) was 582 pounds (264 kg). As for a name? In 1899, La Jamais Contente (The Never Satisfied) had been the first road vehicle to go more than 62 miles per hour (100 kph). This vehicle was a Belgian electric automobile with a light alloy torpedo-shaped bodywork and batteries. The electric motorcycle created by Monteil and his team was duly christened "La Jamais Contente 2" (JC2). On September 27, 1996, ridden by Bruno Bonhuil, the JC2 increased the world electric motorcycle record to 127.305 miles per hour (205 kph). The course was the Départmental 27 road, part of the Gueux circuit, near Reims. The timekeepers were the French Gendarmerie's traffic police radar. The JC2's performance was impressive: the 400 meters standing start was 87.157 kilometers per hour, then progressing to 80–180 kilometers per hour in just eight seconds without the need to change gears thanks to a 750-amp-hour booster with knife-switch contactor.

But the ultimate target remained the two-wheel record of 200 miles per hour.

Bill Dubé grew up in Cranston, Rhode Island. A member of his high school's ecology club, he graduated in 1971, fourteenth in his class—from the bottom. He subsequently enlisted in the military. After a couple of years tooling on small engines and catching jet planes for the air force, he returned home to Rhode Island and worked as a foreign-car mechanic and apprentice electrician. He started attending adult education classes in Aurora, Colorado, where his introductory algebra teacher dismissed his aspirations of becoming an engineer. Soon enough, however, Dubé enrolled at the University of Colorado at Denver—paying his own way on part-time jobs and a small check from the GI Bill—and earned a degree in mechanical engineering.

With his environmental orientation and engineering education, Dubé soon discovered electrathons in the 1980s. The events, which still take place all over the country, challenge participants to build battery-powered vehicles that can outlast the competition using only a limited amount of energy. He quickly recognized that electric vehicles should be efficient as well as powerful and that mainstream motorists would never voluntarily buy EVs (as they are known) until both characteristics were available in one package. He also believed—in part because of timid, genteel events like electrathons—that electric vehicles had a serious publicity problem. To beef up their wimpy image, Dubé and a group of other enthusiasts decided to introduce EVs to drag racing. "Racing is less sophisticated, but it's a lot more exciting," Dubé pointed out. In 1996, he helped found the National Electric Drag Racing Association (NEDRA), becoming its first technical director and drafting the organization's safety rules. Dubé and NEDRA's inaugural president, Roderick "Wildman" Wilde, successfully lobbied the National Hot Rod Association (NHRA), the primary governing body for American drag racing, to change a 56-year-old rule that required drag vehicles to have an internal-combustion engine, opening the door for EVs to compete in official NHRA-sanctioned events.

Dubé's first homemade drag EV was a cherry-red 1985 Volkswagen Rabbit convertible named the Ewetwik Wabbit. In 1998, the Wabbit vomited its transmission onto the starting line of a drag strip in Portland, Oregon. Dejected during the long drive back to Denver, Dubé daydreamed about his next project. "Conversions always have issues," he says. "Cars are heavy and expensive, so I decided on that road trip that I wanted to build a motorcycle."

He spent six months creating the KillaCycle in the basement of his Park Hill bungalow. He dismantled the finished bike to get it up the stairs; then he reassembled it and took it straight to the racetrack.

For his bread and butter, Dubé has worked for National Oceanic and Atmospheric Administration in Boulder, Colorado, with expertise in electrical engineering, electronic engineering and control systems. He coauthored such reports as "Determination of Inlet Transmission and Conversion Efficiencies for in Situ Measurements of the Nocturnal Nitrogen Oxides, NO_3, N_2O_5 and NO_2, via Pulsed Cavity Ring-Down Spectroscopy"—in other words, building advanced atmospheric sensors and instruments for NOAA airplanes, including "hurricane hunters" (the enormous surveillance planes that fly into hurricanes).

But alongside this work, for ten years, until December 2010, Dubé's 619-pound (281 kg) KillaCycle was the fastest electric motorcycle in the world. Its lithium-ion pack—made of 990 A123Systems M1 cells (small cylindrical cells also used in some battery electric drills), with a combined voltage of 374 volts, and weighing 175 pounds (79.4 kg)—was rechargeable in 10 minutes. Two Model L-91 6.7-inch DC motors, 2,000 amps each (switchable between series and parallel connection), gave 2,000 pound-feet of torque on the back wheel; power was 350 horsepower (260 kW). Acceleration was 0–60 miles per hour (100 kph) in 0.97 seconds, which was more than 2.5 times the gravity acceleration. On August 26, 2000, KillaCycle established a drag racing record of completing a quarter-mile in 9.450 seconds on the Woodburn track in Oregon. KillaCycle used lead-acid batteries at a speed of 152.07 miles per hour (244.73 kph). Later, KillaCycle, using A123 Systems nano-phosphate cells, set a new quarter-mile record of 7.824 seconds, breaking the 8-second barrier at 168 miles per hour (270 kph) in Pomona, California, at the All Harley Drag Racing Association (AHDRA) on November 10, 2007.

On May 4, 2012, Larry "Spiderman" McBride rode the Lawless Electric Rocket bike at Quaker City Raceway in Salem, Ohio, on a pass that unofficially beat the KillaCycle's fastest time in the quarter-mile drag. In September, the Rocket became the first electric motorcycle to enter the 175-miles-per-hour club, a barrier that the KillaCycle had yet to break. McBride quickly went back to his shop and built another battery pack, at a cost of unknown thousands, that increased the Rocket's output to nearly 900 horsepower. By November, the NEDRA record for the world's fastest vehicle belonged to the Rocket. And then, on April 30, at Virginia Motorsports Park, the Rocket shattered the ceiling: it went a quarter of a mile in 7.246 seconds, more than half a second faster than KillaCycle's best speed, and reached a top speed of almost 186 miles per hour (300 kph). Later, at a NEDRA meeting, the Rocket made record run of 6.940 at 201.37 miles per hour (324 kph), making it the first electric vehicle to break 200 miles per hour in the quarter-mile!

Between 2012 and 2015, Glenn E. Nielson of Denmark took his electric dragbike, Silver Bullitt, to Malmö Raceway and established several NEDRA records; perhaps the most impressive was the quickest ⅛-mile ET for an electric motorcycle, with 5.16 seconds at 138 miles per hour (222 kph). In July 2017, Nielson further improved this speed to 4.82 seconds over the ⅛-mile at the Summer Nationals at Malmö Raceway.

But where a full kilometer or mile record was concerned, a duel took place in the United States.

On one side was Richard Hatfield, who had ridden motorcycles since he was 12 years old and studied business and computing at Grinnell College in Iowa. In 1994, a group of friends were developing an electric Porsche; at the time Hatfield was racing a Formula Mazda open-wheel race car on the California circuits when they invited him to drive the Porsche. Curious, he ended up fitting out both the suspension and the handling, becoming fascinated by the whole electric aspect. They raced for a couple of years (1996–1997) in a National Auto Sport Association university series, and the Porsche proved one of the fastest vehicles. However, Optima spiral-wound, valve-regulated lead-acid batteries held them back. As lead-acid batteries go, the Optima is one of the best for racing, due to its low internal resistance; however, it is not as good as a lithium-ion battery. Then Hatfield located a source of LiFEPO4 prismatic batteries from Thunder Sky in China, and in 2006 he took a friend's Yamaha R1 race bike and, using a PMDC motor supplied by Mars, converted it to electric: its 65-horsepower and 70-pound-foot torque gave it top speed of 100 miles per hour. "It went like lightning so when we set up our company in San Carlos, San Francisco Bay, we decided to call it Lightning Motorcycles—it seemed to be an appropriate name for our motive force. Blue and silver were chosen by our designer Glenn Kerr."[1]

In 2008, Lightning developed a lithium battery induction motor ATV quad bike to be used for military, border control, law enforcement, and search and rescue. Starting in May 2010, prototypes ran at racing events. In 2010, the BUB Motorcycle Speed Trials were held on 4 miles of the Bonneville Salt Flats, Utah. Experienced motorcycle record-breaker Paul Ernst Thede of Irvine, Newport Coast, California, the owner and president of Race Tech Suspension (a successful motorcycle and ATV suspension company), rode the Lightning Bike to a new electric land speed record with an average speed of 173.388 miles per hour (279 kph). Lightning then road-raced that bike and won the AMA as well as the 2010 North American Championship; after that championship was over, they spent the next six months preparing for higher speeds. Craig Vetter gave the Lightning a streamlined fairing design based on the 470-mile (750 km) per gallon bike that won him the Fuel Economy Challenge.

The other duelist was William Morrison Yates III (a.k.a. "Chip Yates"), born on February 11, 1971, in Portsmouth, Virginia, although he spent his early years in Pittsburgh, Pennsylvania, where he displayed an early interest in mechanics. By the time he was thirteen years old, he could disassemble and reassemble complete motorcycles. At age fourteen, Yates was sent to Culver Military Academy, a co-ed boarding school in Indiana, where he received his high school education. He went on to receive a master's degree in business entrepreneurship from the University of Southern California, where he was later hired as an adjunct faculty. In 1997, Yates replaced automotive designer Chip Foose at ASHA Corporation, where he invented and patented a series of hydraulic control valves for the 1999 Jeep Grand Cherokee. He also launched a start-up company called SWIGZ to market his patented dual-chambered fitness bottle concept. From 2001 to 2004, Yates served as a technology-marketing executive of the Boeing Company and then Honeywell Aerospace from 2004 to 2015.

During this time, Yates also went in for auto racing. He competed in the SCCA Club Rally and Pro-Rally Series, driving a 1989 Toyota MR2 that he built with a half-gallon supercharged engine. In 2001, Yates won the SCCA Southern Pacific (SOPAC) Group 5 (2-wheel drive class) Rally Championship. In January 2007, at age 36, Yates switched to motorcycles and entered a beginner's motorcycle track riding course at the Auto Club Speedway near Los

Angeles, California. He became drawn to motorcycle racing, earning enough points during the 2007–2008 amateur road-racing seasons to turn professional within nineteen months of his first track experience. In 2009, Yates competed in the AMA Pro Daytona SportBike class in televised professional races at Auto Club Speedway, Infineon Raceway, Laguna Seca, and Heartland Park, before his season ended prematurely with a broken pelvis sustained in a high-speed racing crash during an AMA competition. Yates also raced gasoline-powered motorcycles at the world level through his wild-card invitation and entry in the Fédération Internationale de Motocyclisme (FIM) World Superbike Championship round in 2009 at Miller Motorsports Park near Salt Lake City, Utah, where he was the only American to qualify and finish the 2009 World Supersport Race. The following January, Yates placed second in a race against ICE superbikes using his homemade electric superbike. On April 10, 2011, at the Mojave Mile Shootout at the Desert Raceway, from a standing start, he was clocked at 190.6 miles per hour (306.7 kph), claiming "the fastest motorcycle in the world."[2]

Now it was Lightning's turn. During the Bonneville Speed Week, August 13–19, 2011, Paul Thede mounted the latest 200-horsepower black and yellow Lightning APS-Ω 8881, powered by a 345-volt, 11-kilowatt-hour LiFEPo4 nano phosphate battery pack:

> Richard and I knew there were a number of teams around the globe with their eye on being the first to break the 200 mph barrier so we were in a race more than just on the track. We were on a time crunch from the beginning. The number of mechanical failures and battery meltdowns that other teams had experienced weighed on us. Normally a bike that is capable of breaking 200 needs to be on the 5 mile long course to be able to get up to terminal velocity but since the bike had never been run on the salt we took our place in line on the 3 mile short course. To comply with the rules I had to take one run and keep it under 175. Many people don't understand that for a motorcycle to get up to those speeds it is really a drag race, on salt, wet salt so traction can be sketchy. When it was finally my turn Richard gave me the thumbs up and I rolled off the line. We had a controller issue so I had to "baby" it up to 150 or it would shut down. The Lightning pulled so smoothly and strongly that when I finished the run of 174 mph we immediately calculated what gearing we needed to go over 200 and got back in line. In order to qualify for the long course we needed to go over 175 but I didn't want to waste the time as the wait between runs can be in excess of 3 hours and we didn't know what our competition was up to. I "gently" rolled on the throttle and the Lightning once again pulled strongly barely noticing the added strain created by the higher gearing. Once up to 150 I let it rip and the bike pulled like a jet plane with afterburners. I was stunned at how hard it pulled at those speeds. I literally had to use most of my strength just to hold on as it accelerated. My view from the cockpit was very limited as my helmet was smashed down on the "gas tank" (battery cover) to be as aero as possible. I kept one eye on the GPS speedometer and one eye on the line that marked the course. The speed kept climbing and before the 2 mile marker we were over 200 and stayed there through the end ot the 3rd mile. We had done it! First to break 200! I was so overwhelmed with emotion I started yelling

and whooping it up as I eased it down from speed and pulled it to the service road. Funny, no one could hear me but I knew we had just done something important. To be able to go that fast, so easily (and quietly) on so little energy was a game changer. It was one that the world needed. We backed up the run the next day and set the official record at over 200 mph. We geared it up even higher on the next few days and broke our own record eventually setting the top speed at over 218.96 (351.8 kph). I think it is important to note that by changing bodywork, this same motorcycle has been successfully road raced and is a pretty impressive ride to work![3]

Electrical energy was equivalent to 50 miles per gallon. It had cost 16 cents. Although this did not qualify as a Guinness World Record, as it wasn't timed by the FIM timing association, Lightning decided to rename its production model the LS-218, following Jaguar, which in 1992 had named its latest two-seater supercar the XJ220 after its speed potential. Thede told journalists, "What blows my mind is that a motorcycle that can go 218 mph on the salt would also be an economical choice for commuting back and forth to work."

Meanwhile, unable to race due to his broken pelvis, Chip Yates had recruited two volunteer aerospace engineers, Ben Ingram and Robert Ussery, to develop an electric racing motorcycle capable of meeting his goal of equaling

2011: From left, Jeff Major, Paul Thede and Richard Hatfield with the Lightning e-motorcycle, which had just established a speed of 218.96 mph on the Bonneville Salt Flats (courtesy Paul Thede).

In August 2011, Paul Thede accelerated Lightning to a world speed record average of 215.907 mph and a top speed of 218.96 mph. Thereafter the LS-218 model would be sold to customers worldwide (photograph by Thomas "Pork Pie" Graf).

gasoline-powered motorcycle lap times. Yates announced plans to ride the hand-built prototype in the newly formed TTXGP and FIM e-Power electric motorcycle race series. To accomplish gasoline performance parity, Yates and his team developed and filed patents on several new electric vehicle technologies including a kinetic energy recovery system ("KERS") designed to capture braking energy from the front wheel of the motorcycle. Three weeks after Lightning's record, Yates and the SWIGZ.COM team arrived at Bonneville with their 258-horsepower electric superbike. Robert Ussery stated "When it became clear to us that we wouldn't be able to beat Lightning Motorcycle's unofficial record of 215.907 because of our batteries [being] handicapped by only having 45 minutes to try to recharge them between runs because of the tough FIM impound rules, we directed all our efforts to going after the FIM and AMA Official Records in the four key electric motorcycle classes. We clocked a Flying Mile average of 196.420 mph (316.107 kph), while Chip's peak speed was 200.7 mph. Not only was it incredibly fun, but pushing for the records allowed us to demonstrate the flexibility of our electric superbike and the dominating power of our UQM Technologies 258hp, 400 ft/lbs liquid-cooled electric motor. I wish we could have passed Lightning's amazing top speed."[4]

Another contender for the record might have been the MotoCzysz E1pc Digital Superbike, which was capable of accelerating from zero to 119 miles per hour (192 kph) in 7–8 seconds, created by Michael Czysz, an architect from Portland, Oregon. It was described as having 10 times the battery capacity of a Toyota Prius and 2.5 times the torque of a Ducati 1198. Although proving very competitive, winning the inaugural TT Zero electric motorcycle race in 2010, as well as the next three after that, its technical progress was halted abruptly by Czysz's untimely death in 2013 from anaplastic rhabdomyosarcoma, a rare form of cancer.

While Chip Yates retired from motorcycling to concentrate on electric airplane records, Richard Hatfield and the Lightning team continued. In 2012, at the TTXGP/e-Power race at Laguna Seca (held during the MotoGP weekend), the LS-218, with Michael Barnes in the saddle, had lap times within the ballpark of MotoGP lap times. The LS-218 was named the best electric motorcycle of the year by Motorcycle.com. In November, Jim Hoogerhyde set a new land speed record in California, piloting a *solar-powered* Lightning SuperBike electric production motorcycle, reaching 189.086 miles per hour (304.3 kph) in 1.3 miles (2 km) at El Mirage. Hoogerhyde stated, "Riding an electric bike at these speeds almost feels like cheating because it is so much easier to ride." Then, in June 2013, Carlin Dunne rode the LS-218 to win the motorcycle field at Pikes Peak International Hill Climb, making it the first electric bike to beat out all its gas-powered counterparts *by more than 20 seconds*. In November 2014, Lightning Motorcycles delivered an LS-218 electric superbike to its first paying customer; other sales in the United States and around the world followed. The current LS-218s that are being delivered to customers are virtually the same as the race bikes that ran at Pikes Peak and Bonneville except that the street bikes are significantly more powerful. The company also equipped a bike with a 23-kilowatt-hour pack, took it to Laguna Seca and let a former MotoGP rider, Gregorio Lavilla, do laps on it. He was able to do just under 50 miles at full race speed. This was unheard of even a couple of years earlier; Lavilla was probably very surprised.

Could Lightning increase its 218-miles-per-hour record, enabling it to rename its model with a new number? With a cutting-edge, higher-density battery pack developed in collaboration with Farasis, a test was made in August 2017 on a mile-long course at El Mirage, a dry lake bed outside Mojave. From a standing start the Lightning hit encouraging speeds of 211.7 miles per hour (340.6 kph), and the team was hoping that with the flying start and longer distance provided by the Utah Salt Flats, it might achieve up to 300 miles per hour (480 kph). On August 16, although Jim Hoogerhyde was timed at 209.8 miles per hour (337.6 kph) with less than 59 percent throttle, the salt condition would not allow more than 50 percent throttle without excessive wheel spin. In November 2017, the Lightning LS-218 had a head-to-head competition with a gas-engine 2016 Kawasaki H2 at the Infineon Raceway, San Francisco. Zack Courts of *Motorcyclist* and his team rode both bikes for several days. Kawasaki Heavy Industries, more than a century old with 34,000 employees, was the Goliath versus Hatfield's Lightning as David. The end of the resulting magazine article reads:

> What it means is that the end of this drag race is just the beginning of a new era. The Lightning *LS-218* isn't perfect, but the fact that there is even a conversation—that an electric bike creates feelings that are hard to describe—holds more potential than just horsepower.[5]

Much higher speeds for electric motorcycles have been the province of KillaJoule, created by Bill Dubé, the builder of the KillaCycle, and his courageous Swedish wife, Eva Håkansson. Håkansson is an ancient Nordic name, going back to the 11th century with Erik Håkansson, or Eric of Norway (960s–1020s), earl of Lade, ruler of Norway and earl of Northumbria.

When a couple of joint projects with other racers didn't work out, Eva and Bill decided to build something insanely fast and simply wipe out the competition. With a current top speed of a little more than 270 miles per hour (434 kph), they certainly succeeded. In the world of electric motorcycles, the second fastest electric motorcycle is the Lightning, a blasting 51.5 miles per hour behind KillaJoule.

Eva Håkansson was born in 1981 in Nynäshamn, Sweden, a port municipality in Södermanland (35 miles south of Stockholm) on the shores of the Baltic Sea. Both of her parents are mechanical engineers, and both of her brothers are electrical engineers. She was the last one in the family to obtain her engineering degree. Her father Sven built and raced motorcycles in the evenings and on weekends, while her mother Lena was his mechanic. Sven was the kind of character who would wake up one day, sniff the air and decide to build a 50cc desmodromic-valve engine entirely from scratch. Eva went to her first race track in a baby carrier. According to her parents, she built a "nuclear power plant" from cans and cardboard in the garage when she was four years old. From ages 10 through 16, Eva sidetracked from the technology a bit and spent her spare time taking care of competition horses, though she was more interested in the horse equipment than the horses themselves. She repaired everything from saddles to rugs and improved or invented new equipment where needed. When Eva turned 16—the legal age to drive a lightweight motorcycle in Sweden—she traded the horses for her first motorcycle. The 125cc Moto Guzzi Stornello from 1972 was bought as a pile of pieces. She helped Sven put it together in his fully equipped garage, and it started on the first kick after having been in pieces for 18 years!

In 1999, at the age of 18, Eva won the Swedish Junior Water Prize for a biological wastewater treatment project that explored eutrophication (the excess growth of weeds, algae, and so forth, due to an excess of nutrients in the waters of the Baltic Sea), proposing cost-effective, low-impact techniques for curbing excess nitrate and phosphate pollution. In 2000, she presented a project at the Swedish Exhibition of Young Scientists, proposing that purifying water with chlorine and boiling methods was too expensive and inefficient for practical use in emergency situations and suggesting that high-voltage currents or high-efficiency heat exchangers could do the job faster and for less. The presentation earned her a place at the Intel International Science and Engineering Fair in Detroit—the Olympics of academic science competitions. More than 1,200 students from 48 states and 40 countries gave presentations, but Håkansson's was one of just two that received the Schlumberger SEED International Prize.

Eva's first car was an abused Saab 900 Turbo that had belonged to her brothers; the first thing she had to do was replace the broken gearbox (transmission). After finishing high school with concentration in natural science and technology, winning several first places in the national science competitions with "clean technology" projects (which, of course, included building things), working for a year as a lab assistant at an oil company, working half a year at the Royal Swedish Academy of Sciences and spending another half a year at the oil service company Schlumberger in Cambridge, England, it was time for college. Eva decided to broaden her mind and picked an unexpected field of study. She earned two degrees at Mälardalen University: a bachelor's degree in business administration with an emphasis in ecological economics, and then another bachelor's degree in environmental sciences. She also took classes in energy technology, wind power, fuel cells, and nuclear power. Eva wrote her bachelor's thesis about political incentives for introduction of low-emission cars.

With a newfound passion for electric vehicles, but without a clear vision for her future, Håkansson moved back in with her parents and spent most of her time writing about electric vehicles for little or no pay. In 2007, again with her father, she converted a motorcycle to electric drive—a project that would fit both the garage space and her wallet. It resulted in Sweden's first street-legal electric motorcycle—the ElectroCat. Based on a CagivaFreccia C12R-90, a 125cc Italian two-stroke motorcycle, the electric version had equivalent performance to the original combustion engine motorcycle. The ElectroCat passed the registration inspection and became a street-legal vehicle in Sweden in January 2008. That spring, Eva Håkansson was invited as a guest speaker to the Swedish Parliament to talk about the advantages of electric cars. The ElectroCat was invited too, and it was most likely the first time a motorcycle had been inside the Riksdagshuset parliament building. That same year, Eva published her first book, a popular scientific book about hybrid and electric cars: *Hybridbilen—framtidenärredanhär!* (The Hybrid Car—The Future Is Already Here!). Wanting to use a picture of the KillaCycle drag-racing motorcycle in the book, she tracked down its owner, Bill Dubé, online and asked for permission to use his photo. He replied with a long email about the bike.

Eva and Bill met at an electric vehicle symposium in Los Angeles, the EVS 23, and fell in love. In order to be with Bill out in Colorado, in 2009 Eva applied for a student visa. She started out at the University of Colorado, Denver, the very same university where Bill had earned his engineering degree two decades earlier, but soon transferred to the University of Denver (DU). DU accepted Eva into a master's program, and it also provided a generous scholarship and later a teaching and research assistantship, allowing her to earn her way through both the master's and the PhD program. She graduated in 2013 with a master's thesis about galvanic corrosion of carbon-fiber-supported power transmission cables, later obtaining a PhD in the same field in 2016.

Meanwhile, Bill and Eva had married. The "chapel" was a gleaming-white prototype Boulder Electric Vehicle delivery truck. Eva rode down the aisle on the ElectroCat while Bill entered on an electric bicycle. The Swedish bride wore a traditional costume, parts of which had belonged to her grandmother, while other parts were handmade by her mother. She and Dubé exchanged nonconductive wedding rings made from zirconium dioxide, an advanced ceramic material normally used in all kind of things from Japanese sushi knives to certain types of batteries.

Although Mr. and Mrs. Dubé were now on the KillaCycle team, going for new records in the quarter-mile, they knew that this did not impress the general public, and they decided that something else was required to make people interested in electric vehicles. They targeted building a vehicle that could reach 300 miles per hour (484 kph). With neither the budget nor the garage space for a car, it had to be a streamlined motorcycle. After some failed partnerships, they decided to do everything themselves and finance the project out of their own pockets: "We thought it would take about 6 months and a budget of $10,000. It would end up taking 10 times longer and costing us $150,000 into it over the next five years. It proved a very expensive hobby." They gave the resulting vehicle a new name—KillaJoule. (The joule is a derived unit of energy in the International System of Units; one kilojoule is one thousand joules.)

To start, Eva rolled up her sleeves and began to strip wheels, axles and brakes off an old Suzuki motorcycle she found on Craigslist. With the help of two Bay Area frame-builders, Clay and Gary Gardiner, she and Bill built the 18-foot chassis and roll cage in four days in March 2010. Eva's father Sven helped design the suspension system. Early designs were optimized with computational fluid dynamics software, creating the most aerodynamic shape possible. When Eva and Bill realized that the ideal model's design of com-

Eva Håkansson working on A123 Systems's 19-kilowatt-hour lithium nano-phosphate batteries, invented by Yet-Ming Chiang at MIT (courtesy KillaJoule Racing Team).

posite fibers (the standard used for most contemporary streamliner land speed vehicles) would cost thousands of dollars, they had no choice but to switch to less expensive materials. So instead they riveted together curved sheets of aluminum to build the body, just like an airplane. For the nose cone, they molded fiberglass around one of those oversized exercise balls as are used in keep-fit gyms.

In spring 2010, Eva took a break from her studies at the University of Denver when she and Bill took the KillaJoule to the Bonneville Salt Flats for the World of Speed, an annual gathering. But during the trials their KillaJoule struggled to stay balanced, wobbling and curving, preventing Eva from making a clean, straight pass. After each run, she returned to the pits, where Bill and their pickup crew attempted to diagnose the problem. In the end, they decided that they would have to convert it into a *sidecar* motorcycle. They went home and added a sidecar wheel (among other improvements). In 2013, back at Bonneville, Eva clocked a world speed record by hitting an astounding *average* run of 212.040 miles per hour; in addition, she won the "Fastest Sidecar Motorcycle" Prize, as well as the very prestigious "Female Rider" Award. Now that the pair had the electric sidecar record, they wanted to go after the overall record, which was only 224 miles per hour. Bill and Eva predicted that this goal would be easily achievable, as their record-breaking 212-miles-per-hour run was made using only half of the available battery power.

Eva, the academic, had just moved from the University of Colorado to the University of Denver, and the challenge was at a level she had never experienced before. By 2014, her research group at University of Denver, led by Dr. Maciej Kumosa, had just received a grant from the National Science Foundation to form a research center for high-voltage and high-temperature materials, the HVT Center. As one of the more senior graduate students, and with experience in public relations, Eva was elected to be the marketing director in addition to her role as PhD student and research assistant.

The KillaJoule streamliner had been 5 years in the making, and the Dubés had not achieved the desired results. They made a few more upgrades over the winter, including changing to the latest in battery technology from their sponsor A123 Systems, maker of the 19-kilowatt-hour lithium nanophosphate batteries, invented by Yet-Ming Chiang at MIT. These gave energy to the EVO Electric AFM-250 motor, capable of producing 500 horsepower, although two Rinehart Motion System PM100 controllers had to keep all that power in check, limiting everything to 400 horsepower. At Bonneville, KillaJoule was charged by a bio-diesel-powered generator from the Dubés' Cummins Onan truck; back at home, it was done with solar power, which also powered their Nissan Leaf electric car.

In 2014, Eva and Bill returned to their hobby on the Bonneville Salt Flats. Once out on the flats, they slowly ramped up the speed with every run. On August 29, Eva clocked a speed of 240.72 miles per hour (387.32 kph), the fastest official two-way speed record ever for a female motorcycle rider:

> We thought there would be a chance to take the unofficial record for a female rider at 264 mph. This was a single run made by Becci Ellis on a regular sit-on motorcycle at an airport in the UK, quite a brave feat in itself. With a theoretical chance at 265 mph, I turned out on the track deciding to give it everything it had. The speedometer in the bike "only" showed 259 mph, but I knew that it was a bit pessimistic (the front tire grows at speed and offsets the speedometer reading a little bit), but I wasn't sure how much. When the timing folks reported on the radio that we had run 270.224 mph (434.883 kph) I knew this wouldn't be my last year of racing. I was the world's fastest female motorcycle rider, and 300 mph was simply too close to quit now.
>
> How does it feel to set a new record? I wish I could say that it is a big rush, but it isn't really. The closest I can describe it as a 2 minute long mix of horror, boredom, and magic. Setting a new record means that I am going faster than I ever have gone before, and that the bike is going faster than it ever has. Accelerating up to a speed

where I have been before is typically so uneventful that it is almost boring, but as soon as you surpass that speed you are entering uncharted territory. It is known that stability problems can occur very suddenly, so it is quite nerve-wracking. The vehicle is also extremely tight and claustrophobic. To be honest, that alone took a while to get used to. The relentless desert sun beating down doesn't make it any more pleasant. But, at the same time, the feeling when everything works flawlessly is like magic. Years of work finally pay off, and it is like time stops. When I have finished a run, all my nervousness and discomfort quickly vanishes and is replaced by a huge grin. I say, "Well, that was easy, let's do it again"[6]

Although no record attempts were made in 2015 due to the rain falling on the salt flats, the following year Eva was back with the flame red streamliner. But she was unable to beat the speed she had achieved that September day in 2014 when the planets lined up and the angels were singing.

In 2017, Bill and Eva left the United States for New Zealand. Starting in 2018, Eva was hired as a faculty member in mechanical engineering at the University of Auckland. She will be teaching "Principles of Engineering Design" to 1,000 freshman engineering students. She has a two-year contract to begin with, but it is possible that she and Bill will stay for much longer. The plan is to retire the KillaJoule and start constructing its successor. With

Bill Dubé and Eva Håkansson beside the *KillaJoule* on the Bonneville Salt Flats. In August 2014 Håkansson piloted it to 240.72 mph (387.32 kmh) (Bonneville Stories.com).

10. Speed Records

the working name "Green Envy," this bike will look very much like the KillaJoule, but the power required is now 1 megawatt (~1340 horsepower), 3–4 times that of the KillaJoule, from twin AC motors. The maximum practical diameter is around 19.6 inches, and the maximum practical length around 12.5 inches. The range of maximum revolutions per minute allowing for single reduction final drive is 3,000–12,000 rpm. (At 400 miles per hour, the wheel rpm is around 5000.) Green Envy will be 23 feet (7 m), about 3 feet (1 m) longer than the KillaJoule. Green Envy is currently looking for a motor partner. Initial trials will take place in March 2019 on the 99-mile (160 km) Lake Gairdner salt flats, South Australia, under the sanctioning of the Dry Lake Racers of Australia. The goal is to achieve a safe speed of more than 200 miles per hour! Then, in March 2020, they will return to Lake Gairdner, to target a speed of more than 300 miles per hour—perhaps even 400 miles per hour (640 kph).

Meanwhile, Eva is leading a University of Auckland Formula SAE team made up of 45 undergraduate engineering students in Melbourne, Australia. Within a year, this group of dedicated and focused students will design, build, and compete an open-wheel race car as part of an international design competition run by the Society of Automotive Engineers (SAE). "It will be an honor to be their faculty advisor for next year and help them climb to the top of the podium in December 2018!"

True to style, by January 20, 2018, Eva also obtained her New Zealand private pilot license (PPL)! It is based on her U.S. license, but she had to do a bit of flying to catch up with the New Zealand requirements. As she wrote to this author in January 2018:

> An electric speed record airplane is certainly on my vision board, and becoming a pilot myself was the first step towards it. A supersonic battery-powered car is also on my vision board. Going supersonic with battery power is right on the edge of possible with current technology, but in 10 years or so the technology should be here to do it. But for now, that is also just a vision.

11

Variations on a Theme

So far this history has recounted the electrification of saddle-based, in-line two-wheeled and three-wheeled cycles—both pedelecs and pukka motorcycles. This chapter is devoted to those lateral-thinking inventors who have stepped outside the conventional approach, more recently using electricity to realize their monocyclic dreams.

In 1869, Monsieur Rousseau, a craftsman working in Marseilles, France, built what was arguably the world's first monocycle, which perched the cyclist on the inside of a 7-foot wheel. As there was no steering mechanism, the Rousseau monocycle required a rider with a great sense of balance. In the same year, over in Connecticut, Richard C. Hemming, a British-born circus entertainer, built and patented his hand-powered unicycle or, as he called it to attract the spectators, his "Flying Yankee Velocipede." Twenty years later, Louis Schutte of Philadelphia patented an improved monocycle "transmitting and converting the reciprocating motion of the pedal-levers to a rotary movement of the single wheel of the monocycle."

Nobody during this period seems to have tried out an electric monocycle. Without power electronics, it would have been difficult (or even impossible) to have sufficiently responsive control of the motor to achieve longitudinal balance if the center of gravity was above the axle; however, the device described below probably had the center of gravity below the axle. With the arrival of the gasoline engine, in 1903 at the Turin Motor Show, the Milan-based House of Garavaglia exhibited a monocycle belt-driven by a 4-stroke engine. It consisted of a drive wheel of 78.74 inches in external diameter, with internal gear teeth of the rack type and a frame to hold the seat, the steering wheel and the 4-stroke engine that transmitted the motion, with belt and pulley, and a pinion inserted into the rack. Regarding Signor Garavaglia's monocycle, *La Vie de l'Automobile* commented:

> This arrangement is certainly amusing and jolly, but it is strange to note that this fantastic apparatus is however more perfect (in theory) than the ordinary motorcycle, since it implements direct command, without intermediaries uselessly absorbing power! It is however, much less perfect in practice. Note the suspicious-looking wheel out on the left. A stabiliser? Shouldn't there be one on each side?[1]

In 2007, Christopher J. Hoffmann of Portland, Oregon, was working for a firm making high technology and pheromone-based products for insect monitoring and disease control when Lauren, his 13-year-old daughter, asked whether it was possible to build a one-wheeled motorcycle she saw on the television show *Dragon Ball*. There is also a *Ratchet and Clank* computer game where the toughest weapon is the R.Y.N.O. (Rip Ya a New One). Hoffmann had no formal engineering degree, but he had worked in design, engineering and invention in Detroit, Michigan, before moving himself and his inventing career to Portland in 1996. He now set about working on a prototype in his garage.

Hoffmann's first attempt at building a one-wheeled electric vehicle failed when the link to the circuit boards and the motor caught fire. Eventually, working with Tony Ozrelic, an engineer and inventor with a keen interest in self-balancing machines, they came up with a twin-motor single 25-inch motorcycle tire, which, using SLA or lithium-ion batteries, reached 10 miles of travel on a full charge and speeds up to 10 miles per hour, using a combination of gyroscope sensors and accelerometers to balance itself. That, combined with a strategic weight distribution and an intuitive acceleration and braking method, makes this motorized unicycle feel safe. Once Hoffmann's daughter Lauren had been satisfied, he and Ozrelic founded RYNO Motors (using the video game's acronym), though they updated the acronym with new name: Ride Your New Opportunity. RYNO would inspire a lookalike family of self-balancing electric unicycles (commonly abbreviated EUCs), made in China: Airwheel X3, Ninebot OneE+, Gotway MSuper 18, Kiwano KO1, and so on.

In 1986, Emeritus Professor Kazuo Yamafuji and Zaiquan Sheng at Tokyo's University of Electro-Communications invented a small, self-balancing, riderless "parallel bicycle," including a two-wheeled, single-axle design and the stabilizing mechanism device that kept it from tipping over.

> In this paper, the dynamic characteristics of a human riding a unicycle are analyzed following observation. From the observation and analysis, we found that the rider's trunk, thighs and shanks form two closed-link loops, and this special mechanism plays an important role in the stability of the unicycle. Based on this idea, we developed a new model with two closed-link mechanisms and one turntable to enable a robot to emulate a human riding a unicycle.[2]

The Japanese team did not, however, go as far as developing their inventions into a transportation device, although they were eventually granted a patent in Japan in 1996.

Although the Segway is basically a two-wheeler, its rider stands up. In the 1990s, Dean L. Kamen, a maverick American engineer, inventor, and businessman from Bedford, New Hampshire, developed a balancing technology for the iBOT wheelchair at the University of Plymouth, in conjunction with BAE Systems and Sumitomo Precision Products. iBot was nicknamed "Fred Upstairs" (after the singer/tap dancer Fred Astaire) because it could climb stairs. In 1999, Kamen transferred his technology to a personal transporter (PT) that he patented soon afterward (US20030226698). Although it was originally code-named "Ginger," after Astaire's regular film partner, Ginger Rogers, Kamen came up with the marketing name "Segway," derived from the word *segue* (/ˈsɛgweɪ/), meaning smooth transition. The Segway is an electric, self-balancing human transporter with a computer-controlled gyroscopic stabilization and control system. The device is balanced on two parallel wheels, each with its own 2-horsepower electric motor, and is controlled by moving body weight. The machine's development was the object of much speculation and hype after segments of a book quoting Steve Jobs, Jeff Bezos, and legendary venture capitalist John Doerr on its society-revolutionizing potential were leaked. The Segway PT (U.S. Patent PTO #6302230) was unveiled on December 3, 2001, in New York City's Bryant Park on the ABC News morning program *Good Morning America*. It was first sold to the public in 2002. Very soon afterward, the U.S. Senate passed a federal bill approving the use of Segways, with only Hillary Clinton and one other senator voting against the scooters. The majority of U.S. states soon rubber stamped the use of "Electric Personal Assistive Mobility Devices" (legalese for Segways) on public sidewalks.

In 2002, the U.S. Postal Service began testing the two-wheeled Segway for mail delivery but ended its evaluation after a few years. The Segway could not go the distance on one charge, nor did it have adequate storage capacity, and its lack of suspension made for rough rides. And yet, as part of an event to promote Stonyfield yogurt, in 2003 Gary Hirshberg and colleague "segged" from the Londonderry plant in Manchester, New Hampshire, to Providence, Rhode Island, just over 100 miles (160 km). There was a chase vehicle stocked with a pile of spare batteries and a mechanic. They seemed to have done the math as far as scheduling and logistics. The following autumn, filmed by Hunter Weeks, Josh Caldwell rode his Segway HT on a 100-day, coast-to-coast journey from Seattle, Washington, to Boston, Massachusetts. Weeks' documentary film, titled *10 mph*, takes its name from the Segway's average speed, although it can reach a top speed of 12 miles per hour. With modifications such as larger wheels, a Segway could go even faster. On August 30, 2003, the official World EPAMD Speed Title was set by Christo at the first annual Segway Time Trials held in Black Rock Desert. His fastest run was 20.54 miles per hour (33 kph), and the fastest average of the upwind and downwind runs was 19.1 miles per hour (30.7 kph).

Once they realized its advantages, police, fire, airport operations and emergency management in cities all over the world adopted the Segway. In January 2004, the Chicago Police Department became one of the first police agencies in the world to use Segway PTs when it placed a fleet of patrol units in service at O'Hare International Airport. Two years later, Chicago decided to add 100 Segways to its 50-strong fleet. By August 2007, more than 500 police and security agencies worldwide were using Segway PTs, an increase of 140 percent since the beginning of the year. O'Hare and Midway airports still use Segway PTs for security and operations, as do 38 other airports around the world, including the major international airports in Paris, Munich, Amsterdam, Philadelphia, Washington, D.C., and Orlando, as well as the world's two largest airports in Chicago and Atlanta. By October 2008, more than a thousand police and security agencies were using Segway PTs as part of their patrol operations, according to the company. Working with helicopters, police on Segways have chased down car thieves and even nabbed gun-wielding Chicagoans. In 2008, the French National Police tested what has been translated as *le gyropode* in the town center of Montpellier before it was adopted across the French Republic.

It soon became evident that Segways could be equipped with a curved billboard for advertising product while circulating around town. Mobilboard has become the international rental agency for Segway, with 50 approved agents based in France, Belgium, Luxemburg, Morocco, Tunisia and Spain.

Much gentler on the turf than a golf cart, Segway X2 Golfs were soon being used on the links. They offer a golf-bag carrier on one side, along with a handlebar-mounted scorecard holder, and, when fully charged, have enough range to last 36 holes (or 14 miles). More than 900 rounds of golf have been played at Indian Tree Golf Club on the specially equipped golfing Segways. Tiburon Golf Club now has eight Segway X2 Golfs in use at the Greg Norman–designed championship golf course.

In 2010, British entrepreneur Jimi Heselden bought Segway Inc., but soon afterward the 62-year-old sportsman died after falling from a limestone cliff while riding a Segway PT near his home in West Yorkshire. A few days before his death, Heselden had donated £10 million to the Leeds Community Foundation, which he had founded in 2008. In 2015, Segway was acquired by Ninebot Inc., a Beijing-based transportation robotics start-up. The Ninebot One E+Ninebotis are well known in Asia and Europe. Its investors include Sequoia Capital, Xiaomi Corporation and ShunWei TMT Capital. Segway boasts an international distribution network of more than 250 retail points in 80 countries. The combined company has strategic hubs in the United States, Netherlands and Beijing as well as manufacturing centers in the United States and China.

During this time a new sport was born: Segway polo. Instead of playing on horseback, each player rides a Segway PT on the field. The rules have been adapted from bicycle polo and horse polo. Two teams of five players each hit a ball with their mallets, trying to get the ball into the other team's goal. A regulation match consists of 4 chukkas lasting 8 minutes each. With a shorter 1–3-minute break between the first/second chukka and third/fourth chukka, and a longer 5-minute half-time break, matches are usually completed in 40–45 minutes. Battery autonomy will depend on the weight of the player, the surface, ambient temperature and the playing style, but on average one full charge will be good for two matches.

In 2003, a polo team sponsored by Mobile Entertainment played in the Hubert H. Humphrey Metrodome at a Minnesota Vikings halftime show. Months later, unaware of the Minnesota meet, Bay Area Segway Enthusiasts Group (Bay Area SEG) held its first meeting at the California FIRST Robotics Competition.

Although not a major sport, Segway polo is gaining popularity, and teams have begun forming in the United States, Germany, Sweden, Austria, Barbados, Lebanon, the United Kingdom, Holland and Spain, among others. Among those who have enjoyed playing is Steve Wozniak, who cofounded Apple Inc. with Steve Jobs. The International Segway Polo Association (ISPA) has been established as the official governing body for Segway polo. The Segway polo world championship for the Woz Challenge Cup was established in 2006 when the Silicon Valley Aftershocks played the New Zealand Pole Blacks in Auckland, New Zealand. The result was a 2–2 tie. In 2007, it was played in San Francisco, California, with the Aftershocks defeating the Pole Blacks 5–0. The 2008 Woz Cup was played in Indianapolis, coincident with Segwayfest 2008. The California Gold Rush defeated the Silicon Valley Aftershocks for the championship by a score of 3–2. The Funky-Move Turtles (Germany) placed third and the Polo Bears (California) were fourth.

The sport was introduced in Barbados in 2009 by Jason Gilkes, who started the business Segway of Barbados Adventure Fun Rides but wanted to find other ways to use Segways as a means of bringing his friends together for some fun. With Barbados' rich horse polo history, Segway polo was a natural fit. The 2010 Woz Cup was played at the Lion Castle Polo Estate in Barbados. Barbados Flyin' Fish won the 2009 and 2010 world championships and only narrowly lost the final in 2011. Members of the Barbados National Women's Field Hockey team also had a go at Segway polo.

In 2015, twenty teams from nine countries arrived in Cologne, Germany, to compete in the world championship of Segway polo, the Woz Cup, presented by Wozniak. By 2017, the Woz Cup, played at the Overhoff Arena in Hemer, Germany, saw 18 teams from 7 countries (including two from Barbados) participating. Once again, the team from Barbados took first place, beating the Balver Mammuts (Germany) 3–1. The current world champion

Segway polo requires great skill: The Austria Vineyard Devils' pass to Sinisa (left) goes wide and he has to slow and turn. The two Team Cornwall players, Paul Macintosh (center) and Steve Farnell (right), change direction and attack (photo by Andrew Bickell).

team comes from Barbados. There is some argument as to who is the best Segway polo player. At the last world championship, Daniel Hatch from Barbados was voted Most Valuable Player and scored the most goals, but there are players of similar caliber in Sweden and Germany.

According to Ralf Luther of the International Segway Polo Association:

> It is important to note that Segways are virtually impossible to tune (higher top speed or better acceleration). Provided that only approved tires are used (that's a rule) and the tire pressure is within regulation, then no player can gain advantage from having a "better" Segway. Hence, our slogan "The Segways are great equalizers." It only takes minutes to learn to ride a Segway, and the ability to accurately hit the ball to shoot at goal or pass to a fellow player combined with a good tactical understanding of the game are far more important. This means that unlike in most other ball and team sports, people of all ability (young, old, male, female, fit, unfit) can play on the same team or against each other. Another point worth mentioning is that the Segways appear to be extremely durable. Other than the odd broken rim we have not had to write-off any Segways from accidental collisions or Segways hitting fence posts, walls or concrete curbs after a player may have lost control. Of course, safety is the top priority, during game play all contact between the Segways is forbidden and during practice and competitive matches all players must wear helmets (other safety gear is optional).[3]

In 2008, students performed a choreographed dance using four Segways to the classic "Born to Be Wild" at the Saint Louis Science Center.

The first Segway PT tours opened in early 2002, shortly after the vehicle hit the market. Since that time, the Segway PT tour business has grown to include hundreds of tours in the United States as well as thousands of tours worldwide. In 2011, the Segway Experience Program was launched. It encouraged tours to become authorized and affiliated with Segway Inc. to create a strong, worldwide, cross-promotional network. City Segway Tours offers rides in capitals across the world, including Berlin and Vienna. The vehicle is also qualified for tours through the mountains, such as the Tyrol region in Austria. However, some municipal councils, such as those in Prague and Barcelona, have felt that too many Segways are a risk to ordinary pedestrians. In the view of the UK Department for Transport, Segways are motor vehicles and therefore not allowed on pavement under the 1835 Highways Act, which says people cannot use the footway to "lead or drive any horse, ass, sheep, mule, swine, or cattle or carriage of any description." In Canada, Segways are limited to use by people older than 14 years with a disability, door-to-door delivery personnel of Canada Post and police officers.

In 2014 Segway filed a complaint over infringement of its Patent No. 8,830,048, and in March 2016 the ITC issued a general exclusion order banning several types of self-balancing devices, often called "hoverboards." Segway Inc. filed a lawsuit against Inventist, Inc. for allegedly infringing on five patents to build the Solowheel and Hovertrax. According to the defendant, the lawsuit marks retaliation for a lawsuit against Segway filed in China as well as a cease-and-desist order sent in America. In 2016, Segway-Ninebot showed off its Segway Advanced Personal Robot, which it has developed into the Loomo bot. The rider rides the device like a hoverboard to the store. When they get off, the head swivels around and becomes a face. The bot can then follow them around autonomously, take pictures on demand, and work as a surveillance robot. Loading up with cargo, the owner can also voice-command it to follow them home. There's also an enterprise version in the works, called Loomo Go, which can pull a storage wagon behind it for deliveries.

But where was the monocycle in all this?

Janick Simeray of Argenteuil, near Paris, France, is a physicist who holds more than 120 patents and founded the company simerLab to commercialize his creations. He holds graduate degrees in electronic and mechanical engineering from École Nationale Supérieure de Techniques Avancées and Université de Valenciennes (ENSTA). His dissertation concerned the Laser Range Finder, using the Larsen Effect, for which he was awarded the prestigious Prix Yves Rocard by Société Française de Physique in 1994. Starting in 2000, Simeray applied his knowledge of physics to production and business. Among his inventions are a portable and self-contained system for maintaining prepared meals in a cool state and then reheating them, board games, an electromagnetic doll's eye and electromagnetic levitation technology. In November 2006, Janick and Marc Simeray filed a U.S. patent for a compact seatless device (U.S. 20090266629 A1, obtained in 2009). This was an autonomous and lightweight vehicle intended to transport a city dweller combined with the use of public transportation. Formed by one motorized wheel on which the user maintains (through speed) his or her lateral balance, longitudinal balance is ensured by automatic functioning driven by an accelerometer. The footrests and the guide supports that tightly hold the leg are retractable. Driving does not require the use of one's hands. The entire device goes into a bag (e.g., a backpack) and weighs less than 9 pounds.

Also in 2009, Aleksander Polutnik from Malecnik, Slovenia, applied for a patent for a two-axis balancing, human-ridable, sit-down unicycle, the eniCycle. Its Chinese brushless hub motor was powered by standard D size NiMH batteries, while it used MEMS gyroscopes and accelometers. Polutnik obtained an MsC at the Faculty of Electrical Engineering and Computer Science, Maribor.

Shane Chen grew up in Beijing, China, and attended Beijing Agricultural University for a degree in agricultural meteorology. Since China was a difficult environment for starting and growing businesses in the mid–1980s, Chen emigrated to America in search of better opportunities. In 2009, Chen, based in Camas, Washington State, invented the seatless self-balancing electric unicycle he called Solowheel using a gyroscopic sensors to balance the unit in the direction of travel. In September 2010, the Solowheel prototype was presented to the public at the Bike Expo in Las Vegas, Nevada. Chen launched the compact Solowheel in February 2011, and in the following month he concluded a licensing agreement with the Simeray brothers. By March 2012, the first of three patents was granted.

What happens when one uses a detachable single wheel to electrify a bicycle?

In 1907, Dmitry Balachowsky and Philippe Caire of Neilly sur Seine, France, had obtained Patent US1,055,598 for "an improved motor-driven wheel for electrically propelled vehicles in which the-motor is embodied in the-wheel structure, the improvements" being intended to render the wheel and its motor *readily separable* as a unit "from the axle."

Toward the end of World War II, many German scientists were taken prisoner and their inventions used by the victorious Allied forces. Werner von Braun went to the United States and worked on a program that would eventually send a man to the moon. More modest was the case of Bernard Neumann, a German engineer who had a set of blueprints in his briefcase for a two-stroke bicycle motor whereby the tank, gas engine and carburetor could be fitted to the wheel of a pedal bicycle. This device had been designed for the DKW concern but never went into production because of the war. Neumann's blueprints were placed in the hands of the Interpro Buro: an international organization (English, American and French) that had been formed to help to build up industry in the Netherlands after the war.

A company called HNG built a prototype of what it called the RadMeister, which translates as Cyclemaster; its 25.7cc gas engine was given the type number M13. While the Cyclemaster power wheel made its first public appearance at the Utrecht Industries Fair in April 1950, Interpro had also sent the DKW blueprints to England. By June 1950, Cyclemaster Ltd. had launched its product to be manufactured by EMI Factories in Hayes, Middlesex. In early 1950s Britain, few new vehicles were available for the home market, as most were exported to help the country's need for foreign exchange. Most folks had to rely on their trusty bicycles for transport, and a cheap cycle-attachment engine was a viable option to add a few more miles per hour to the daily commute. Cyclemaster, utilizing a mechanism not much more difficult than fitting a normal back wheel, proved an immediate success. In its first year on the British market, the Cyclemaster was in competition with nine other cyclemotor units, including Mercury, Vincent Norman and Phillips, and during the early 1950s UK production passed the 100,000 mark. There was even a journal called *Magic Wheel: A Quarterly Magazine for Cyclemaster Owners*. Hundreds of people gathered for somewhat noisy rallies and runs with their 32cc Cyclemasters, many of them used daily by tradesmen. Ironically, there was even a German version made by Rabeneick, the German frame builder from Brackwede. As sales of the gas-motor scooter and moped got going, the bolt-on Cyclemaster fell out of fashion. Its electric bolt-on power wheel equivalent would have to wait half a century before being revived.

In 2007, an enterprise in Alicante, Spain, introduced a 36-volt, 250-watt electric motor conversion kit called the eBici.

Watching the movie *Tron*, Michael Burtov, a software engineer in Cambridge, Massachusetts, thought there was a lot of wasted space inside the motorcycles because of their hollow wheels. So he began to think about a wheel that could be attached to any bike in less than a minute, taking the place of the front wheel. He called the concept "GeoOrbital." After making a prototype and filing patents in 2015, Burtov ended up meeting SpaceX engineer Dakota Decker at a local event; Decker subsequently left SpaceX and became GeoOrbital's CTO. Due to its shape and design, GeoOrbital does not rotate around an axis, but rather around a fixed central module. This part consists of a 500-watt brushless DC electric motor and a 36-volt Panasonic rechargeable lithium-ion battery to power the vehicle. Three metal arms run

11. Variations on a Theme

Michael Burtov and Dakota Decker brought out the GeoOrbital in 2015. The GeoOrbital does not rotate about an axis, but rather around a fixed central module; the wheel is recharged while descending, but also when pedaling (GeoOrbital).

from the center and join the wheel, allowing it to rotate around the module. With this equipment, it is possible to reach the maximum speed of 20 miles per hour (32 kph) and to expect a pedal-assisted range of approximately 30 miles (80 km). Another advantage is that the wheel is recharged while descending, as well as when pedaling. Moreover, it does not contain an inner tube since the tire is made of foam. There are two versions, depending on the wheel size of the existing bicycle. GeoOrbital is built locally in New England in partnership with local contract manufacturers and part vendors. All the structural components are made in Massachusetts and New Hampshire.

In 2011, in Boston, Massachusetts, two brothers, Yevgeniy and Boris Mordkovich, originally from south-central Asia, started Evelo and marketed the OmniWheel, developed by a Taiwanese company called DK City as a front-wheel electric assist, its 350-watt motor giving a speed of up to 20 miles per hour (32 kph) and a range of 25 miles (40 km). In 2017, the Mordkovich brothers decided to relocate to Seattle, Washington, and to concentrate on more conventional pedelecs such as their 750-watt Delta, Foldable Quest and Galaxy Cruiser.

Carlo Ratti is an Italian architect, engineer, inventor, educator and activist. He is associate professor at MIT's Department of Urban Studies and Planning and director of the Senseable City Lab. In 2008, the city of Copenhagen, which was preparing to host the UN Conference on Climate Change (the COP 15), agreed to co-finance Ratti's efforts to come up with a pedelec rear bicycle wheel. Ratti, with Assaf Biderman and student Christine Louise Outram, applied for a patent for a "hybrid sensor-enabled electric wheel and associated systems, multi-hub wheel spoking systems, and methods of manufacturing and installing wheel spokes" (granted in 2011, U.S. 20110133542 A1). With further assistance from the Polytechnic University of Milan, the Italian motorcycle company Ducati, and the Italian environment ministry, "The Copenhagen Wheel" was born, colored red and white, like the Danish flag. When it was unveiled at the 2009 United Nations climate change conference, Ritt Bjerregaard, the lord mayor of Copenhagen, stated that the wheel might well help achieve the goal of lowering CO^2 emissions in the Danish capital by getting half of its citizens to bike to work or school every day. Bjerregaard placed an initial order to be used by city workers. Between 2009 and 2012, Biderman and the team continued to develop the Copenhagen Wheel technology at MIT by testing and combining different types of motors, batteries, sensors, and control systems to assess the advantages and disadvantages of different hardware combinations. During this time, there was much speculation about whether the wheel would ever get to market, as well as criticisms about its design (and appearance), its price, and its weight-to-benefits ratio (was it worth the 17 extra pounds?), not to mention the question of its performance in real-world riding situations.

But in late 2012, nearly four years after the concept was introduced, Biderman, co-inventor of the Copenhagen Wheel, obtained a license from MIT to commercialize the unit and founded Superpedestrian Inc., located in Cambridge, Massachusetts, to manufacture the device. As a product, the Copenhagen Wheel includes a built-in 350-watt electric motor with a 48-volt/279-watt-hour lithium-ion battery, which takes four hours to charge. That motor kicks in whenever the rider pedals, adding a proportional amount of electrical assistance; top motor-assisted speed of 20 miles per hour (32 kph) is possible, and there is no throttle-only mode. One charge of the battery is good for a range of up to 30 miles (48 km), although that distance will depend on factors such as the hilliness of the ride. The wheel is controlled by a smartphone app, and it is charged externally via a battery charger, with additional charging while riding the bicycle from regenerative braking (i.e., when the rider back-pedals as in a coaster brake). A built-in computer uses

A project by the MIT Senseable City Lab, the 350-watt bolt-on Copenhagen Wheel, colored red and white like the Danish flag and unveiled in 2009, has a range of up to 30 miles (48 km) (photo by Max Tomasinelli, Superpedestrian Inc.).

sensors in the Copenhagen Wheel to analyze the topography and the rider's pedaling to determine whether to deliver power to assist the rider. The range per battery charge is stated as up to 31 miles (50 km). The device is already available in 44 U.S. states, but in 2017 Superpedestrian announced that it would be selling in the United Kingdom and Europe, including Denmark, for the first time. The comments have been favorable: Nick Bilton, writing in the *New York Times*, commented, "It's rare that a company comes along and reinvents the wheel, but it looks like that is about to happen,"[4] while the Smithsonian.com opined that "the Copenhagen Wheel does for electric bicycles what Apple did for mobile computing with the smartphone and tablets." *Time* named the Copenhagen Wheel one of the 25 best inventions of 2014.

Unfortunately, the Copenhagen Wheel has had a troubled evolution. In 2016, Superpedestrian and MIT filed patent infringement complaints against Niko Klansek of FlyKly's Smart Wheel (based in New York) and Giovanni Alli of Zehus's Bike+ (based in Milan) for manufacturing similar products without licenses; other imitators include DK City Wheel, the Electron Wheel, and so forth.

Innovations are continuing. In 2013, Stéphane Rachmuhl and Antoine d'Acremon of Montrouge, France, launched the Rool'in, an electric bicycle wheel that allows the rider to transform a pedal bicycle in a few minutes into electric bicycle by replacing the front wheel. The electric bike kit consists of an electric motor, a lithium-ion battery, a sensor and a console on the handlebars. Three levels of assistance are offered: eco, medium and sport. The "eco" mode optimizes the given force at 50 percent, compared with 100 percent and 200 percent for the "medium" and "sport" modes, respectively. Rool'in gives a range of 25–40 miles depending on the model and its use. In 2017, Rool'in launched the its solar wheel, increasing autonomy by roughly 12.5 miles. Connected to the rider's smartphone iOS or Android, the rider can select up to 3 levels of assistance, check the charge and consult the number of miles/kilometers covered. Equipped with a GPS, the rider can easily geolocate their two wheels and find the best orientation to optimize the recharge of the batteries.

Michelin of Clermont-Ferrand, France, was established in 1891 and is the second largest tire manufacturer in the world. In 2013, David Olsommer and Olivier Essinger at Michelin's research and development center in Givisiez, Fribourg, applied for a patent for a quick retrofit electric assist device that would enable the rider to switch from bike to pedelec in less than 3 seconds and to extend the vehicle's range by 30 miles. The 250-watt motor/252-watt-hour battery-pack unit, weighing 6.6 pounds (3 kg), was conceived in partnership with the French cycle giant Mobivia, under the Wayscral pedelec brand. In 2017, the Michelin E-System was unveiled at the Movin' On Summit in Montreal for sale in 2018 at 2,000 points at Norauto centers in France (as well as Spain and Italy, among other countries) and Auto 5 in Belgium. Mobivia expects to win 10 percent of the electric bicycle market, selling within four years 150,000–200,000 pieces.

What if the unicycle were part of an electric automobile? Working at the Ford Motor Company in Melbourne, Australia, the team of Johannes Huennekens, Samuel Ellis, Greg Foletta and Finn Lauri Mikael Ohra-aho came up with some innovative patents. Among these are a vehicle system that includes a detection signal indicating the presence of an unauthorized occupant or unauthorized object in a host vehicle; a foldable bicycle, including the frame, with inflatable segments; and an electronic parking brake system with selectable modes. But perhaps the most innovative patent was filed in June 2014: a concept for an electric automobile powered by in-wheel electric motors that could turn into a unicycle (U.S. 9211932 B1):

> A self-propelled unicycle is selectively engaged with a vehicle for use with the vehicle and is selectively disengaged with the vehicle for independent use. The self-propelled unicycle includes a hub and a wheel rotatably coupled to the hub. A motor is supported on the hub and is coupled to the wheel for rotating the wheel relative to the hub. The hub includes an engagement feature for selectively engaging and disengaging the vehicle.

Then there is the skateboard. From 1899, the French chocolate manufacturer Gaston Menier produced a series of colored postcards, predicting what life would be like in Paris in the future; one of these shows something like a motorized skateboard. More than seventy years later, along came the gasoline-engine skateboard, invented by Jim Rugroden, a student in Berkeley, California, in the garage of his brother's home in the South San Francisco Bay Area town of Campbell while on break from his physics studies in summer 1975. The Motoboard evolved from a simple push-start prototype to a precision automatic shaft-driven sport vehicle capable of reaching 30 miles per hour. However, it was ultimately banned in California due to its noise and pollution. In 1999, Louie J. Finkler and Andrea Furia of Seal Beach, California, obtained a patent for a wireless electric skateboard. Speed was controlled by a hand-held throttle or weight-sensor controls, and the direction of travel was adjusted by tilting the board to one side or the other. Finkler was president of RSG Security in Signal Hill, manufacturing fire and security equipment and advanced electric motor development. But he was too early for the arrival of the ubiquitous lithium-ion battery. Since 2009, the ZBoard has been developed by Geoff Ellis Larson and Benjamin Swanberg Forman of Intuitive Motion Inc. at Hermosa Beach, California; it is a hands-free, footpad-controlled electric skateboard with a top speed of 20 miles per hour and a 20-mile range. Its lithium battery also provides energy for LED headlights and taillights.

The 250-watt-motor/252-watt-hour-battery Michelin E-System was developed by David Olsommer and Olivier Essinger at Michelin's R&D center in Givisiez, Fribourg (Michelin).

Kyle Doerksen of Santa Cruz grew up in the Canadian Rockies as an avid snowboarder and wanted to bring the feeling of snowboarding to the pavement. With multiple engineering degrees from Stanford University, Doerksen began to figure out a better way of walking to work. He spent 8 years perfecting what he called the Onewheel, a single-wheeled, self-balancing electric skateboard. The prototype used a brushless DC motor and a 24-volt lead-acid battery. The Future Motion company was formed in 2013 and by CES 2018 was shipping orders for the Onewheel+ XR: perhaps this could be an invitation to another e-sport?

Then there is the roller skate. In 1863, James Plimpton from Massachusetts invented the "rocking" skate and used a four-wheel configuration for stability, along with independent axles that turned by pressing to one side of the skate or the other when the skater wanted to create an edge. This was a vast improvement over the previous Merlin design, and it drove the huge popularity of roller skating, dubbed "rinkomania" in the 1860s and 1870s, which spread to Europe and around the world and continued through the 1930s.

In 1911, 27-year-old Hugo Gernsback of New York, then starting off his career as one of the 20th century's most visionary sci-fi writers, self-published a novel titled *Ralph 124C 41+: A Romance of the Year 2660*, in which appeared the following passage:

> Ralph bade Alice sit down on a chair in the vestibule. He pressed a nearby button twice and a servant brought two pairs of what appeared to be roller-skates. In reality they were Tele-motor-coasters. They were made of alomagnesium and each weighed only about one and a half pounds. Each had three small, rubber-covered wheels, one in front and two in the rear. Between the wheels was a small electric motor—about the size of a lemon; this motor could only be operated by high frequency currents and, despite its small size, could deliver about one-quarter horsepower.

In 1926, Gabor Vass of Cleveland, Ohio, took out a patent for roller skates, "the invention having more particular reference to a novel type of electrically driven roller skates ... the electric motor, of common construction, is attached to the heel element, and is operatively connected to a train of reduction gears, so as to drive the rear wheels, the gear being rigidly attached to the shaft and meshing with the train of reduction gears."[5]

In 1980 when Akira Kuwahara of Tokyo applied for a patent for a motorized device for pushing or pulling a roller skates, he added, "It should be noted here that, in the foregoing embodiment, although a gasoline engine is employed for the prime mover with a gasoline tank therefore being mounted on the frame, an electric motor may be employed for the prime mover by substituting a battery for the gasoline tank." In 1995, David H. Staelin and Jeffrey H. Lang were working at MIT's Department of Electrical Engineering and Computer Science and the Research Laboratory of Electronics when they decided to develop novel electric-scooter technology. They applied for a patent for a powered roller skate, including a foot support, multiple wheels mounted to the foot support, and a motor coupled to at least one of the wheels. This powered roller skate further includes an active control system with a sensor located on the skate and a controller. The controller receives

11. Variations on a Theme

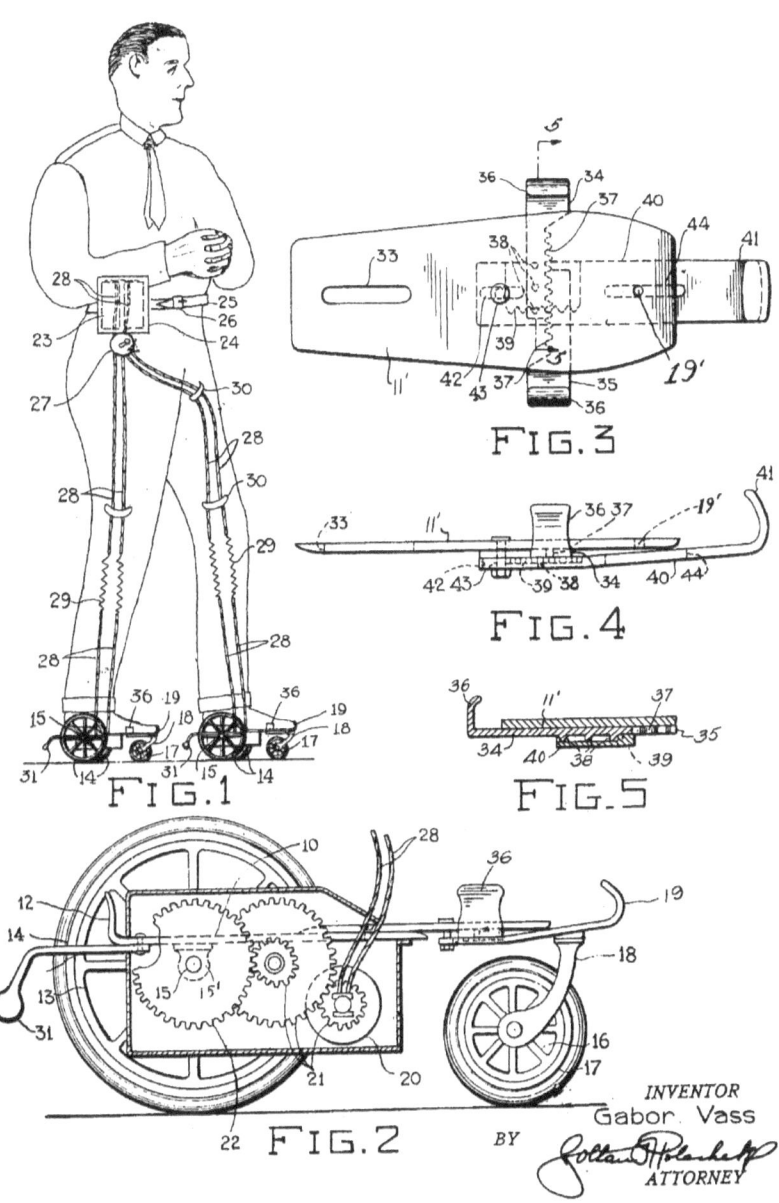

The 1926 patent for Gabor Vass of Cleveland, Ohio's motorized roller skate.

electrical signals from the sensor and electrical signals from the motor, which indicate the state of the motor. In response to those signals, and in accordance with a control mechanism, the controller sends electrical signals to its motor. To manufacture the device, Staelin and Lang developed EMPower, which was later purchased by Gary Starr of ZAP in Sebastopol, California.

SpnKiX is a pair of strap-on e-motorized *shoes* with wheels and wireless handheld remote control that has been developed Peter Treadway, who says that the idea for the shoes was conceived after he had trouble finding parking in Mountain View, Los Angeles, California. From 2007, Treadway, who founded Action Inc., went through many prototypes of this wearable mobility device until he was satisfied. With the latest version, called RocketSkates, the wearer can accelerate up to 12 miles per hour.

Then there are the double-round electric skates (motorized circles, one for each foot), of which one example is the OrbitWheel invented by Shane Chen's daughter Ywanne. While at a trade show to showcase her father's Solowheel, Ywanne got bored and decided to ride two Solowheels at the same time. While watching her, Shane got a crazy idea. He decided he was going to make a cross between a skateboard and a pair of inline skates. OrbitWheel stands alongside the Chen family of innovations: UltraDrainer, Lunicycle, Solowheel and Hovertrax.

Kuniaki Sato of Tokyo, Japan, has set up Cocoa Motors to make his WalkCar, an aluminum and carbon-fiber personal electric transporter that has a look and weight similar to a laptop—hence it is small enough to be carried in a shopping bag, taken out, and placed on the ground for scooting around town at speeds of up to 10 miles per hour for one hour. The device is known as "Japan's car-in-a-bag." However, its launch for September 2017 was postponed, due to engineering changes to improve some functionalities.

In June 2018, Segway-Ninebot launched the Segway Drift W1 electric skates, while they prepared a new kit to convert electric scooters to drivable go-karts.

From July 2018, Denmark allowed speed pedelecs on cycle paths with a speed limit of 25 kph and requiring a driving license as with a moped or automobile.

The online retailer evoMAG expanded its portofolio with a new category of products: electric scooters, bikes, skateboards and monocycles. In total, the shop will bring 300 models of this devices and was expecting to have a revenue of over EUR 300,000 by the end of the year. evoMAG also provides customers with the opportunity to test products in the new category, being the only online store in Romania to offer this.

It seems that with one or more good brushless motors and a lithium battery, almost anything is possible. The only risk is obesity!

12

Return of the Electric Three-Wheeler

As seen in chapter 1, the electric motorcycle initially resorted to three-wheelers due to the weight of lead-acid batteries.

Flashback: In 1976, a wealthy American orthodontist named Harold D. Kesling presented the world with his egg-shaped light electric vehicle—the Yare. There was one eight-inch wheel at the front and an identical one at the rear. They operated together to steer the car in and out of very tight spots. With 12-inch wheels on each side, the total 144-inch wheel base offered a stable and comfortable platform for the Yare's four passengers. With Robert A. Rocke, Kesling (based in LaPorte, Indiana) had innovated a device called the "Tooth Positioner" and built his dental concern around it, which made him a millionaire. A great believer in nature, Kesling had built his office building from fieldstones he had collected from the surrounding countryside. Like Paul Arzens of Paris, with his Oeuf Electrique of some thirty years earlier, Kesling believed that nature had delegated curves to moving things and that the shape of his vehicle should be like the forms of nature: birds, animals and fish, which move about in groups without interfering with one another. Working with an electronics engineer, Edward Arnold, Kesling spent three years developing his Yare ("Yare" is a nautical term meaning ready, complete, eager, lively, prepared, quick to move, easily worked, manageable, active). But unlike Arzens, who had relied on aluminum, Kesling was able to mold his vehicle's teardrop bodywork in glass-fiber and shatterproof Lexan windows. There were no conventional bumpers, ornamental trim or other protruding parts. The 14-foot car with twin gullwing doors was powered by a 12-horsepower General Motors unit. Energy came from 12-volt Trojan lead-acid batteries (normally used in golf carts), which also powered a fan to cool the motor, a speed controller, lights and a heater, giving a total weight of 2,550 pounds. It could go from zero to 55 miles per hour in 12 seconds. A diamond pattern wheel arrangement accommodated the design Kesling had patented in 1952.

In 1976, orthodontist-industrialist Dr. Harold D. Kesling of LaPorte developed the Yare e-tricycle prototype, using materials such as fiberglass and Lexan (La Porte County Historical Society Museum).

A low center of gravity allowed a tilting suspension system, which, when coordinated with the steering, permitted the Yare to lean into turns, enhancing both maneuverability and stability. Although the yellow Yare received a great deal of attention in Philadelphia's Civic Center during the International Electric Vehicles Show, none of the ten hoped-for orders were placed.[1] However, Dr. Kesling, 78, continued to believe that electrics would be the wave of the future, considering it a private victory if Detroit would take more notice of what he thought was the perfect shape for most motor vehicles. He died in 1979.

Kesling's and Arzen's vision was taken up in Switzerland some eight years later. For the 1988 Swiss Tour de Sol, Kaspar Villiger, one of the sponsors, wanted an LEV to follow the pack. He turned to Max Horlacher of Möhlin, near Basel, already known for having pedaled Pelargos, a 101-pound (46 kg) human-powered airplane, into the air for a few minutes. Since 1962, Horlacher's small firm had specialized in the manufacture and development of products made from fiber-reinforced plastics and composite materials. Horlacher, in his fifties, now conceived a lightweight three-wheeler with a self-supporting body composed of prefabricated, dimensionally stable body elements, including a door that was mounted so as to slide linearly along one side wall of the compartment and obliquely thereto. The 100-inch Egg (GL-88) ("Ei" in German) was propelled by an 8-kilowatt BRUSA AMC 200, asynchronous motor developed by Axel Krause, winner of the 1987 Tour de Sol. The energy came from 11 LevoGT55 12-volt lead-acid batteries. There were 3 disc brakes with aluminum calipers for regenerative braking. Villiger was able to drive the Egg up to 50 miles per hour with a range of 62 miles. Unlike Dr. Kesling's Yare, Horlacher's Egg went into production, with some 32 being built until 1990 and beloved by a club of loyal drivers. Horlacher would build 14 prototypes in the years that followed, mostly four-wheelers.

In 1997, Ian Wood, publican at the Bell Inn at Bath, England, and his business partner Tom Nesbitt set to work designing and producing a lighter, faster version of the classic rickshaw or trishaw. For the optional power assist, Cycles Maximus first turned to Cedric Lynch, then to Heinzmann for the motor.

In 2000, a hand-picked team of expert engineers, veteran designers, seasoned management, and environmental specialists was assembled by Korean-born Ki Nam in Corona, California, to design and develop a 3-wheel electric standup vehicle. With its innovative patent for a swappable battery system, charger, configuration and communication system between them, the T3 Patroller was launched in 2006 and very soon became very popular across the United States in stadiums, airports, convention centers, department store parking lots, college campuses and other settings that require security personnel to cover a large area. The New York Police Department acquired twelve units for in use in the subway, public-housing projects, Yankee Stadium and Citi Field. In October 2008, USPS letter carriers began testing three-wheeled T3s in Florida, California, and Arizona. The T3s were equipped with a small trailer that added to their storage capacity, and they had a reported 40-mile range per charge. Thirteen of the test vehicles were still in use in 2014, but no further vehicles were purchased due to their vulnerability to weather and a maximum speed limit of 5 miles per hour. In 2010, T3 ESVs were deployed as the environmentally friendly patrol solution at the Tour de France in Paris, the World Cup in South Africa, and the G20 Summit in Seoul, South Korea, as well as the Rose Parade and Super Bowl in 2011. For luxury clients, T3 Motion launched the R3 sit-down two-seater, with its dashboard built around a Samsung Galaxy pad, a range of 80–100 miles, and a top speed of 70 miles per hour; it will be classified as a motorcycle. The company also launched the Power Sport, with a top speed of 12 miles per hour and a range of up to 40 miles, which will be available in a range of colors and custom paint job or logo options. By 2012, more than 3,000 T3 series vehicles had been deployed in more than 30 countries worldwide, including 50 of the world's largest international airports.

Cree AG (Creation Engineering Ecology) was founded in Switzerland in 1996 with the aim of developing a contemporary vehicle for local use. In 2001, the company unveiled the "Sam," a 3-wheeled electric vehicle for two people seating in a tandem style. Powered by 14 lead-acid batteries that provided 168 volts to a modularized drive system (with a synchronous belt providing power to the back wheel), the vehicle had a top speed of around 52 miles per hour and a range of 31–43 miles; a full recharge took 6 hours. With two people on board, the vehicle can reach 30 miles per hour in 7 seconds. A group of former Swatch engineers in Switzerland had developed the Cree SAM/Swatchmobile tadpole three-wheeled electric car. The car seats two riders in tandem and has all of the things needed to be street legal, such as seat belts, mirrors, lights, and a windshield wiper. It also has fancy gullwing doors that fold with less fuss than those on a Tesla Model X. About 80 vehicles were produced for public testing in the Zurich and Basel area in 2001. Two years later, the company laid off all employees and applied for bankruptcy, but the shareholders (including the original designer, Daniel G. Ryhiner) bought the company and kept it running in its original three-wheeled electric form as an investment offer. In mid-2009, a Polish company, Impact Automotive Technologies (IAT, Pruszkow), was said to be developing a newer and faster version of the Cree Sam with a larger range. It was tested and received road certification in Italy, and the plan was to produce 500 cars by the beginning of 2009. It was also named after Raymond "Sam" Cree, a Northern Irish playwright.

Faced with the estimated 3.5 million gas-engine tricycles (or tuk-tuks) operating in the Philippines, the Asian Development Bank, with the Philippine government and the Department of Energy, has been transforming the public transportation sector by widely adopting electric tricycles throughout the Philippines. One solution to this problem came from the Netherlands. In 2003, some Dutch tourists had been on a backpacking trip to Thailand, where they were impressed by the rides they had in the tuk-tuks. In 2006, they decided to import fifty 11-foot three-seater tuk-tuks to Holland, which soon sold. Then they decided to electrify one. Led by Dennis Harte, formerly with TU Delft, a team converted ten tuk-tuks to an electric drivetrain, with an AC motor and a swift tray-change 72-volt lithium battery pack providing 14 kilowatts of power and a range of 60 miles after a five-hour boost with the on-board charger. Following the launch of a successful prototype and the establishment of the Tuk-Tuk Company in 2009, the first sales came in mid-2010. The first two vehicles were purchased by Anantara Bangkok Riverside Resort, and eight others were bought by individuals. TTF (Thailand) Ltd. was set up with factories in the Bang Phli area of Samut Prakan. In 2012, it stepped up production to thirty tuk-tuks, but by 2017 the new company, Thai Green Wheels Ltd., was producing 360–400 vehicles and planning to scale up production to 1,200 tuk-tuks yearly. Alongside Thailand, another market opened up in Portugal, where 90 electric tuk-tuks were sold. During this time, three students called "The Pilgreens" bought an e-tuk-tuk in Thailand and installed a larger solar-panel battery that allowed them to travel more than three hundred miles a day. Setting off in June 2015, the Pilgreens ended up in Paris in October 2015, by way of China and Russia, taking in mountains with an altitude of more than 14,700 feet. They also traveled between different cities in Europe.

In November 2007, Mark D. Frohnmayer of Eugene, Oregon, created a tandem two-seat, three-wheeled lithium-ion electric vehicle with handlebar steering he called the Arcimoto ("Future I Drive"). The prototype went through several versions until Frohnmayer and his team were satisfied. When Arcimoto revealed its fifth prototype in April 2011, actor Nathan Fillion drove the vehicle and reported that it was like driving a shark, which is where the additional name SRK came from. The eighth version, the Arcimoto SRK (generically described as a fun utility vehicle), included an expandable frame, dual-motor front-wheel drive and hand-operated regenerative braking. It has a sensible autonomy of 120 miles.

In 2010, BSA Motors, a recently formed division of the Chennai-based Tube Investments of India Ltd., promoted by the Murugappa Group, unveiled its three-wheel scooter, Roamer Able, with thoughtful touches such as a holder for crutches and a rear brake lock so that the scooter does not roll back on a slope. The rider can also engage reverse with a flick of a switch. The Roamer Able has two modes and a top speed of 25 miles per hour; in economy mode, it can clock 15.5 miles per hour. Its unique reversing feature makes parking easier for the differently abled. However, after sales peaked at 14,000 units in 2009–2010, they fell to 6,000 units in 2011–2012 as demand waned. As L. Ramkumar, MD, of Tube Investments, said in an interview, "We are going slow on that (e-scooter business). We are not sure if the country will accept e-bikes. People want faster bikes and now with the subsidy (on such electric vehicles) being withdrawn, we need a relook at what the future is."

One pedelec trike that benefits from a 100-watt solar panel is the ELF (Electric Light and Fun) developed by Robert Cotter of Organic Transit in Durham, North Carolina. In the 1980s, Cotter built and rode a streamlined recumbent pedelec trike to speeds of 60 miles per hour. Highway speeds at fractional horsepower became an obsession. A former performance engineer at Porsche, BMW and Mercedes-Benz, in 2012 Cotter teamed up with electrical engineer Don Gerhardt and materials engineer and marathon cyclist Barry Zalph to develop a solar- and human-powered hybrid car-bike for series production. The result was what they called "the most efficient vehicle on the planet," getting the equivalent of 1,800 miles per gallon. Its geared hub motor mounted mid-frame provides great torque and is protected from vibration and the elements. The ELF body, coming in bright colors (red, orange, green, etc.), is made from a rugged, re-meltable ABS composite called Trylon. By 2015, there were 300 ELFs on the road.

According to Robert Cotter:

> I think the real significance is the 900 or so that have been built have covered over 6 million miles in total. The average ELF goes about 2,500 miles per year, some going 10–12,000 miles per year. Some ELFs have 50K miles on them at this point. German immigrant, Hanna Elshoff of Chatfield, Minnesota has been riding her white ELF up and down the east coast of the US for a few years, putting in about 40 miles per day, with no set schedule, stopping at local Lions club chapters to raise money for the Lions' Leader Dogs for the Blind program; not bad for a 75 year old who had suffered a debilitating stroke a couple of years earlier.[2]

In 2013, Toyota introduced its personal mobility vehicle at the Geneva Motor Show. Called the i-ROCK, i-ROLL, or i-ROAD, the electric tricycle seats two passengers in a comfortable enclosed environment and uses an active lean technology to enable riders to lean to the right or to the left as they corner, like a motorcycle.

Helen Lee of Gotech International in Hong Kong, author of *Tao of Beauty*, has launched the Helix, a fully enclosed two-passenger, urban e-tricycle. Helen is the co-inventor of the dynamic control steering system, an electronic steering and tilt-by-wire patent filing, utilizing her experience with the flawed hydraulic mechanism approach taken by others. This system is a very advanced technology borrowed from aircraft engineering and modern robotic technology to automatically select the correct tilt angle based on speed and other vehicle and road conditions. The resulting driving experience is entirely new, safe, and exhilarating. Helix Motors spent 3 years developing a cutting-edge technology through partnerships with global innovation firms like Bosch engineering, IDIADA, and SensoDrive. In June 2014, the company partnered with Istituto Europeo di Design, one of the world's leading creative design schools with nine campuses worldwide, engaging students from campuses in Barcelona, Spain and Turin, Italy. The Helix will have a 100-mile range in the base model, a top speed of 95 miles per hour, and the ability to go from zero to 60 miles per hour in 6 seconds while realizing more than 300 miles per gallon gasoline equivalent of fuel efficiency. Helix will also integrate many, if not all, of the features of the safest cars on the road today, such as seat belts, airbags, roll cage, ABS, and more.

A classic producer of three-wheelers is Morgan Motor Company, based in Malvern Link, Worcester, England. Between 1908 and 1952, this company had manufactured 1,600 three-wheel V-twin open sports cars, until it went over to four-wheelers. In 2011, Morgan announced that it would be launching a "retro" three-wheeler. Four years later, backed by a consortium including the UK government to the tune of £6 million, Morgan developed the liquid-

12. Return of the Electric Three-Wheeler

cooled AC rear-engine EV3. Weighing less than 1,102 pounds (500 kg), the all-electric three-wheeler has a range of 150 miles. Early indications suggested it would take less than 9 seconds to go from zero to 62 miles per hour, with a top speed in excess of 90 miles per hour. Eco mode uses regenerative braking and limits throttle response to increase range. Encased within the tubular space frame chassis is a 20-kilowatt-hour lithium-ion battery and a liquid-cooled 46-kilowatt motor driving the rear wheel. Designer Jonathan Wells, inspired by the aero cars of the 1930s and motorcycles sporting an asymmetric headlight layout in the following decades, even gave the "retro" EV3 the steering wheel of a 1940s Ford pick-up truck and Lucas-style headlamps. However, its burnished brass bars up front actually serve as conductive cooling fins for the battery, while carbon fiber has been used for its hood, tonneau cover, and side panels, although a traditional ash wood frame still sits underneath.

Sôki was designed by Daniel Pavez, founder of the Chilean outfit VoZE EV; the first ten examples were expected to go into production in March 2016, with financial help from the Chilean Economic Development Agency. Named after the number 2 in a local Patagonian language—the number of passengers it seats—this particular prototype is currently traveling around various cities

Jonathan Wells, Morgan's head of design, driving the first prototype EV3 at Castlemorton Common in Malvern in summer 2016. The car was the launch edition vehicle, produced in association with the department store Selfridges to celebrate British craftsmanship, design and engineering (Morgan).

in its native land, building interest and sales. Powered by a slight 10-horsepower (7 kW) motor, the Sôki is electronically limited to a top speed of 37 miles per hour (60 kph). Its 7-kilowatt-hour lithium battery offers a range of 37 miles (60 km), thus making it more appropriate for an urban environment.

In 2015, Thomas Grübel of Munich, a pioneer pedelec engineer whose Govecs scooters were already successful, linked up with multi-utility company Trefor in Kolding, Denmark, to produce the Govecs TRIPL delivery three-wheel scooter with a carrying capacity of 198 gallons (750 liters) and 441 pounds (200 kg). In 2017, Hermes ran a pilot program using TRIPL three-wheelers in Gottingen to deliver parcels to customers in the inner-city area, where there are restrictions on conventional commercial vehicles.

Asserting that his uncle's C5 (see chapter 4) was ahead of its time, in 2017 Grant Sinclair unveiled the 121-pound (55 kg) pedelectric Iris E-Trike with a top speed of 30 miles per hour. Built on a Chromoly steel chassis, with the outer body being a super-light monocoque Quantum Foam EPP construction, the Iris has a hinged aviation acrylic canopy to protect the rider from the elements, something its predecessor did not offer. Four feet high, it is more visible to other road users than the C5. The Iris is equipped with a dedicated LCD display for access to the speed, distance, battery charge level, and power mode; it also has LED headlights, a rear brake light, turn signals and a camera at the back that can stream a rearview feed to the driver's docked smartphone in the cockpit. There are two versions, the Eco and the Extreme, with the main difference being that the Eco model has a 250-watt electric motor with just pedal-assist, while the Extreme model employs a 750-watt motor with throttle control for higher speeds (and presumably quicker acceleration). Both models use a 48-volt, 20-amp-hour lithium-ion battery for a potential range of up to 50 miles on a single charge, which is reported to take just one hour, and a regenerative braking feature is said to be able to recoup some of the energy for recharging the battery. Both models are fitted with Shimano Tannus puncture-proof tires and include a lockable rear compartment with a capacity of up to 13 gallons, which might make these trikes desirable as light delivery vehicles or for service calls; since they do not require a license or insurance to operate, they could lower costs for those applications as well. Grant Sinclair believes that the development of cycle tracks and electric vehicles has prepared the way for acceptance of the Iris. It will be launched in 2018.

Other companies are also pursuing the electric trike dream. Quantya (a Lugano-based company active for almost a decade in the production of motorcycles, scooters and electric snowmobiles) has designed and built three-wheeled drift vehicles, creating the electric recumbent DriftTrike for racing go-kart style. In contrast, the 45-kilowatt triple-engine Estonian-built NOBE

12. Return of the Electric Three-Wheeler

2017: Grant Sinclair's Iris trike prototype, a much-improved version of the C5 developed by his uncle, Sir Clive Sinclair, in the 1980s (courtesy Cassiel Sinclair).

is based on a late 1950s to early 1960s European automotive design. MIT graduate Ryan Anderson's 25-kilowatt Raht Racer is an enclosed cockpit pedelec trike capable of going 100 miles per hour with the rider protected by an airbag. Financing has been raised by Emmy Award–winning TV producer Rich Kronfeld of Minneapolis and fitness entrepreneur Scott Olson, founder of Rollerblade and RowBike and SkyRide.

In 2017, at the EICMA, Christophe Cornillon and Frédéric de Maneville of Eccity (based in Grasse in the France's Alpes Maritimes), already manufacturers of the two-wheeled Artelec 670 and 870 e-scooter range, unveiled their 419-pound (190 kg) three-wheel electric scooter with its two wheels at the rear. It will have a range of around 75 miles and a speed of 62 miles per hour. The wheels recline at 37 degrees due to a patented original system that allows only one damper to work laterally between the two separate oscillating arms. This is only permitted by each 5-kilowatt motor located in each of the wheels and not a central motor with belt or chain drive, as can be found on a Quadro4. Using a dealership network called Eccity Club, the Grasse firm is hoping to sell 3,000 units by 2020.

Last but not least, Campagnia Motors of Boucherville, Quebec, is developing an electric version of the T-REX 16SP gas three-wheeler, using a powertrain, motors, batteries and controllers from Zero Motorcycles of Santa Cruz. The gasoline version, powered by a 160-horsepower BMW 1649cc engine, can hit 0–60 miles per hour in under 4 seconds and corner with 1.3G of lateral acceleration. The first electric prototype was unveiled at the Montreal Electric Vehicle Show in April 2018, while a second, more advanced prototype was planned for the summer of 2018.

In 2015, Henry Reisner of Intermeccanica in Turin, Italy, and Jerry Kroll, former race-car champion and former CEO of CRAiLAR Technologies, founded Electra Meccanica in Vancouver, Canada, to produce the Solo three-wheeler, whose 16.1 kilowatt-hours gives it a range of almost 100 miles (160 km). Launched in 2017, it has been followed by the Super Solo and the Tofino convertible. A number of pre-production units were delivered in the Vancouver area, New York and southern California, and the vehicle awaits certification from U.S. and Canadian regulators. In 2018, Electra Meccanica worked with Ricardo PLC of Santa Clara, California, to integrate Qualcomm's Halo wireless charging technology into the Solo to give it an autonomous recharging option. Halo uses resonant magnetic induction to transfer energy wirelessly from a ground-based pad to a pad on the vehicle without action by the user.

13

Secret Weapon?

If the motor can be installed in the wheel, then why not discreetly *inside* the tubular framework?

In 1979 a Monsieur Gouzy, a former engineer at the Institute of Arts et Metiers, adapted Bari, a racing bike, with batteries and a miniature electric motor installed in the vertical tube of the framework, activated by a small on-off switch and using pedalling to regenerate the batteries. In a broadcast made by the French TV channel Rhone Alpes Regions 3, former racing cyclist Monsieur Barry demonstrated the prototype which had speed of 45 kph and an autonomy of three quarters of an hour.

In May 2005, Karl Schweitzer was a panel member on the Tyrolean Future Strategy Committee. He had an idea: an ultra-light power unit for e-bikes. The idea immediately won that year's Adventure X Business Award. In 2003, the unit's inventor, Reinhold Gruber, applied for a patent, "Fahrrad mit einem Hilfsantrieb," granted in 2004. Here was the world's lightest electric motor. Together with Gruber, Schweitzer and his daughter Monika founded Gruber Antrieb GmbH & Co KG, based in Wörgl, in the Tyrolean mountains of Austria. By March 2006, the "Gruber Assist" Sattelrohrmotor was ready to enter the market. In 2011, Gruber further reduced the sound of the motor with the Assist 3.15. Demand was sufficient for the company to build a new factory in Wörgl and to change its name to Vivax Assist, although the concept had not changed except for a redesigned motor and easier assembly by the buyer. Gruber described its device as follows:

> Sophisticated motor power is hidden in the bike's seat tube. It weighs only 1.8 kg, including the battery. Press the button and the motor delivers 200 watts to the crankshaft. Press the button again and the motor stops. Without motor power the bike functions as normal without any kind of resistance. The lithium-ion manganese high-performance battery, which fits into a conventional saddlebag, provides motor-assisted cycling lasting for 60 minutes (with a 6 Ah pack) or 90 minutes (with a 9 Ah pack). The special design of the drive unit allows it to be built into any bicycle frame with the requisite seat tube internal diameter of 31.6 mm or 30.9 mm and is therefore invisible

Weighing only 3.96 pounds (1.8 kg), the Vivax-Assist is the lightest electric motor for a pedelec, fitting inside a bicycle tube (Vivax-Assist).

on the bicycle—except the on/off switch, which is unobtrusively located on the bar end.

Unknown to the Schweitzers, over in Hungary, Istvan "Stefano" Varjas had been building concealed bike motors for more than a decade, using what he called an electromagnetic wheel: neodymium magnets concealed within the sidewall of a deep-section carbon rim generate an induction force when they rotate past battery-charged electromagnets housed within the bike's chainstays and/or seatstays. Varjas claimed that he had first designed a motor to fit inside a bike frame in 1998; an anonymous buyer paid him $2 million for it, which included a deal not to work on such motors, speak of them or sell them for 10 years.

13. Secret Weapon?

Fazua was founded by Johannes Biechele in Ottobrunn, Bavaria, in 2012 to develop a light and almost invisible e-bike drive. Evation is a compact drive system for all type of pedelecs that can be clicked in and out from the downtube at any time. The battery is hidden inside the frame, making it only slightly bigger (patent number: 9777774). Overall, the drive weighs in at no more than 3.3 pounds (1.5 kg), including a battery for a range of around 30 miles (50 km).

Although many of these discreet motors have been fitted by amateurs to increase the pleasure of cycling, others have used them for more devious ends. Suspicions of "mechanical doping" first emerged in 2010, with further reports focusing on several mysterious bike and wheel changes during major races; an allegation was made against Fabian Cancellara for using an electric motor to achieve his wins in the 2010 Paris-Roubaix and Tour of Flanders. In 2015, Femke Van den Driessche, a 19-year-old professional Belgian cyclist, was caught by the Union Cycliste Internationale (UCI) using a hidden electric motor at the Cyclo-Cross World Championships. The device was discovered when officials began using a magnetic resonance scanner to examine the bicycle frames for radio frequencies that match electric motors. Van den Driessche was banned for six years and had to pay a significant fine of 20,000 Swiss francs. In this way, the term "mechanical doping" came into being.[1]

During a cycling race in Italy in March 2016, a television camera crew used a disguised forward-looking infrared camera to detect whether there were any unexplainable heat signatures, which might indicate that hidden electric motors were being used. They declined to reveal who had been in the images, but six riders had a suspicious heat image, with a warm lower seat-tube. For the 2016 Tour de France, UCI officials made as many as 4,000 unannounced bike checks, using a combination of thermal imaging cameras, their own magnetic field scanner, and a mobile X-ray machine on loan from the French government.

In the UCI Rulebook for 2017, Article 1.3.010 states, "The bicycle shall be propelled solely, through a chain-set, by the legs (inferior muscular chain) moving in a circular movement, without electric or other assistance." The addition of mechanical or electrical systems that serve to assist the rider is prohibited. The use of an electronic unit solely to change gears is authorized provided that the attachment to the bicycle does not contravene any regulations.

Thus, the racing bicycle has come full circle—from Adolphe G. Pingault's electrifying a triplet pacing tandem in the 1890s to the prohibition of electrical systems in the 21st century.

14

Riding into the Future

In December 2017, Motorcycle.com's Brent Jaswinski wrote an article titled "The Rise of Electric vs. Gas-Powered Motorcycles: How long will it be before most of us are plugging our bikes into the wall at night?" In it, he stated,

> As futuristic as the future may one day be, I'll be the guy hoarding all the loud, leaky, inefficient, fossil-fueled motors that most of the world will consider to be boat anchors and giant paperweights—call it my Redneck 401k. One day they might be considered old-fashioned, but there's just something extremely gratifying about an internal combustion engine that an electric motor could never replicate. Mostly it's the sound and feel, obviously, and it used to be about the performance, but electric motorcycles have evolved and come a long way in recent years.

Apart from the disruptive progress described in previous chapters, even more approaches are en route for a different way to move around on one or more powered wheels.

Battery Alternatives

When, in May 2018, this author asked the electrochemist who led the successful quest for the lithium-ion battery, Professor John Goodenough (then 95), his view of the future, he replied:

> Modern society runs on the energy stored in a fossil fuel; this dependence is not sustainable. A fossil fuel, once burned, is not recyclable, and the gaseous exhausts of their combustion add to global warming and are already choking large populations in China and India. The Li[thium]-ion battery of the wireless revolution will not provide an all-electric road vehicle that is competitive in safety, cost, and convenience with today's road vehicles powered by a fossil fuel in an internal combustion engine. However, we and others are working on the development of an all-solid-state lithium or sodium battery that will compete, I believe, with the internal combustion engine to get rid of the distributed air pollution from the highways of the world as well as

14. Riding into the Future

Captain Gary Pylant and Mark Rumsey of Spring, Arizona, look to the future with their Fly-B electric-powered flying bicycle: an electric powered ultra-light airplane *and* recumbent bicycle all in one. It has still to be built (artist's impression by Mark Rumsey).

> the oceans and many other applications. I believe the new battery products will become available within 5 years, which is why the automotive industry is panicking about how to plan for the future.

Here Professor Goodenough is referring to work carried out at the Cockrell School of Engineering, University of Texas at Austin, with Portuguese physicist Maria Helena Braga. In the laboratory they have developed a battery made entirely from a special glass that can handle up to 15,000 recharge cycles, is not flammable and offers three times as much energy density.

But Professors Goodenough and Braga are not alone in seeking improvements. In November 2013, Elton Cairns, a faculty senior scientist at Lawrence Berkeley National Laboratory, with co-workers Min-Kyu Song (Molecular Foundry, Berkeley Lab) and Yuegang Zhang (Suzhou Institute of Nano-Tech and Nano-Bionics, Chinese Academy of Sciences), announced the innovation of an advanced lithium/sulfur (Li/S) cell that can provide 500 watt-hours per kilogram, more than twice that of a lithium-ion battery, and they have already shown that it can go through 1,500 charge cycles without significant deterioration. This is a sulfur-graphene oxide nanocomposite with styrene-butadiene-carboxymethyl cellulose copolymer binder.

In June 2017, researchers at the Argonne National Laboratory and Oregon State University in the United States made a new cathode architecture for lithium-sulfide batteries that consists of crystalline dilithium-sulfide nanoparticles encapsulated in few-layer graphene. Lithium-sulfur batteries are promising for future energy-storage applications thanks to their extremely high theoretical energy density of 2,600 watt-hours per kilogram, which is three- to five-fold higher than that of state-of-the-art lithium-ion batteries.

Henrik Fisker Nanotech of Los Angeles, California, has applied for a patent for a new solid-state electrode that could enable a battery with two and a half times the energy density of lithium-ion batteries and could be recharged in less than 10 minutes. Based on graphene super-capacity technology, it is destined for the 500-mile-range Fisker Emotion automobile planned for 2023, though it would certainly be useful for motorcycles.

Alternet Systems Inc., directed by Randall Torno, also has major plans for the next-generation lithium battery in the Asia Pacific region, which, as detailed in the chapter on China, is the largest motorcycle, scooter and moped market in the world. The global market for motorcycles, scooters and mopeds in 2018 is expected to exceed 130 million units.

Johann Hammerschmid of Bad Leonfelden runs Nordfels, a small Austrian factory near the Czech border that makes factory lines for the food, drug and farm industries, such as a machine that toasts 5,000 sandwiches per hour. In 2007, Hammerschmid, 56, first thought of an electric motorcycle, and it took shape over the years as essentially a weekend project. Hammerschmid founded Johammer e-mobility GmbH and, with Georg Hochreiter, innovated a battery pack development involving more than 1,200 round cells in rows with a total of 12 kilowatt-hours. The electric motor and controller are integrated into the rear wheel. The Johammer's extremely torsion-resistant aluminum main frame is covered by an aerodynamic bodywork, designed by Leonie Lawniczak and Jean-Marie Lawniczak of Yellow in Linz, that has been likened to a cuttlefish, or a giant peanut, or a pre-war Junkers airplane, or even a medieval jousting steed. The Johammer model numbers J1.150 (11 kW) and J1.200 (16 kW) refer to their range in kilometers. The first bike was released in 2014, and to date some 60 Johammers have been sold in Europe, one of which covered more than 185 miles on a single charge.

Elon Musk's demand for better and more cylindrical batteries for Tesla's e-automobile range pushed Panasonic, Sony, Samsung and LG to improve their technology. First they worked on the 18650 cells, increasing capacity from 2.2 amp-hours to 3.5 amp-hours. The next step was the 21700 battery cell, as evidenced in the 3Tron battery presented by BMZ of Karlstein-am-Main in September 2016. The 3Tron battery has 60 percent more capacity while being able to use 400 percent more discharge current at the same time, thus increasing battery life up to 12 years. This result would give a pedelec a roughly 125-mile range. These batteries are now in production at the BMZ Gigafactory. In 2014, BMZ production reached about 1 million pedelec batteries (batteries from 6 to 17 amp-hours). In September 2017, BMZ announced that it would assemble a center called E.volution, employing 150 researchers to work on innovative energy storage systems while planning to establish a total output of up to 34 gigawatt-hours of batteries per year by 2028. In July 2018, Panasonic and Honda launched a joint project in Indonesia, where Panasonic's detachable, lithium-ion batteries are being used on Honda's electric motorcycles to test efficiency. The Japanese government-run New Energy and Industrial Technology Development Organization is subsidizing the project.

MG Energy Systems is utilizing its brand-new line of batteries based on NCA chemistry (lithium-nickel-cobalt-aluminum oxide, LiNiCoAlO2), with 2.5- and 5-kilowatt-hour-capacity batteries weighing 33 and 59.5 pounds (15 and 27 kg). Their energy densities are 6 kg/kWh, and for the double-capacity (and therefore more weight-efficient) battery, no more than 5.4 kg/kWh. The maximum discharge current is 1.5 C, and maximum charge current is 1 C, with a 2,000-cycle lifetime. Electric outboard manufacturer Deutz-Torqeedo's 2.7-kilowatt-hour battery, weighing 53.3 pounds (24.2 kg), has an energy density of 9 kg/kWh, and Torqeedo's BMW3i 33-kilowatt-hour battery weighs 7.8 kg/kWh. Until now, the industry standard weight (except for MG, whose special Solar Challenge lithium packs were always super light at around 4.5 kg/kWh) was between 7.4 and 11 kg/kWh; such new products are breakthroughs.

Researchers at Bar Ilan University in Israel have developed a water-based aluminum-air battery in which the hydrated aluminum oxide is recycled to create an anode, a process that enables a closed and sustainable life cycle or recharge. Phinergy Ltd. in Lod has patented a "nano-porous silver-based catalyst," which allows oxygen into the electrode and the cell while also blocking carbon dioxide. The company claims that this invention enables its battery cathode to sustain 25,000 working hours while significantly reducing weight. An EV fitted with these batteries motored for 1,000 miles (1,600 km) before needing a recharge. In February 2018, Eviation of Israel teamed up with Kokam of South Korea to provide a 900-kilowatt-hour battery pack for its Alice aircraft, giving it a range of 650 miles (1,047 miles). Such batteries would eliminate any range anxiety for a motorcycle.

In 2018, Winston Chung, the Shenzen battery millionaire, acquired six companies in California, creating more than 3,000 new jobs. They will manufacture two couples: The first is a rare earth lithium-sulfur battery with an energy density already up to 1,000 watt-hours per kilogram, which means a car could drive 620 miles after 5 minutes of charge. Second is a rare earth yttrium-lithium storage battery with a monomer cell already up to 700–10,000 amp-hours. Both products are at the forefront of worldwide innovation. Chung also donated $10 million to University of California, Riverside, to support the new energy research, which is the university's largest single donation ever received. Chung has likewise announced his decision to install these batteries in pure electric vehicles, including taxis, buses, luxury cars, boats and motorcycles.

For those motorcyclists who like making miles, a fast-charging station for automobiles could be staked out: the Tesla Supercharger network is a system of 480-volt DC fast-charging stations built by American vehicle manufacturer Tesla Inc. to allow longer journeys for their all-electric manufactured vehicles (Model S, 3 and X) through quick charging of the vehicle's battery packs. As of December 2017, there were 1,045 stations globally, with 7,496 chargers. E.ON has announced that it is building a chain of 180 charging points from Norway to Italy, while BMW, Daimler, Ford, Volkswagen, Audi and Porsche (Volkswagen Group) are preparing Ionity, a network of 400 ultra-fast charging stations that will be in service by 2020. Although both are incompatible, it will only be a matter of time before e-motorcycles can use similar networks.

In 2017, Amazon obtained a patent for an electric-car charging drone. The drone deploys only if drivers do not have sufficient electric range to reach their destinations. The car requests the Amazon drone via a server, which dispatches the flying charging station to the target car. This mechanism could be adapted to other e-vehicles, including motorcycles.

En-route recharging is also a distant possibility. Shanhui Fan and a team at Stanford University have succeeded in transmitting electricity wirelessly to a moving LED lightbulb. However, the experiment was limited, involving only a one-milliwatt charge, whereas electric vehicles tend to require tens of kilowatts of energy to function. Scaling up would involve embedding electric induction pads into both roads and the two-, three- and four-wheelers that travel along them.

Equally, recycling lead batteries is a mature and sophisticated industry with collection and processing rates approaching 100 percent in both the developed world and emerging nations. However, recycling lithium batteries is proving a challenge, as the value of the elements contained within the battery is generally minimal; disposal is obligatory and the cost of smelting prohibitive. As a rough rule of thumb, the cost of disposal is around 10 percent of the value of the new battery—thus, a $5,000 lithium battery will cost $500 to recycle. The cost of lithium battery recycling will come down with economies of scale but will continue to be prohibitive unless a new technology emerges that can recycle these batteries without the huge cost of energy required in smelting.[1]

Fuel Cells

Following Karl Kordesch's almost prophetic fuel-cell prototype motorcycle, research and development has continued on into this power source.

In 2000, *Hydra*, the world's first hydrogen fuel cell electric boat, began to give demonstrations along the Ketelvaart and Leie Canals of Ghent, Belgium. In 2001, Paul MacCready and his team at AeroVironment applied for a patent for a fuel-celled flying wing.

For half a century, Aprilia in Noale, Italy, had been making small-capacity gas motorcycles such as the Aprilia RS250, a liquid-cooled 249cc two-stroke sport bike. In 2000, Aprilia, working with Dr. Arthur Koschany of Manhattan Scientifics, built its first prototype fuel cell moped. Installed with a 700-watt PEFC cell developed by Manhattan Scientifics, compressed hydrogen was stored in a half-gallon metal canister housed in the frame. Derived from the pedelec Enjoy, the ApriliaFC had a top speed of 20 miles per hour, weighed 20 percent less than regular electrics and traveled twice as far (about 43 miles) before it needed more power. It was presented at the Bologna Motor Show in December 2000. The ApriliaFC was seen being ridden by five-time Tour de France winner Miguel Indurain and was awarded *Time* magazine's "Invention of the Year" in 2001. The following year, Manhattan Scientifics and Aprilia unveiled their MOJITO FC at the International Paris Fair, claiming that production models should be capable of covering 120 miles with a single refueling at a speed of at least 35 miles an hour. In 2004, Koschany received U.S. Patent No. 6,808,834 for "Fuel Cell Stack with Cooling Fins and Use of Expanded Graphite in Fuel Cells," which was called the NovArs unit, for use in the pedelecs with a range of several hundred miles.

The path toward a British fuel cell motorcycle began at Loughborough University during the late 1980s, when Peter Hood and Paul Adcock led a team in investigating proton exchange membrane fuel cell technology, with the project name Intelligent Energy. By 2005, they had announced a 50-miles-per-hour fuel cell motorcycle dubbed ENV (for "emissions neutral vehicle") with a range of 4 hours and 100 miles (160 km). To realize this goal, they converted a Suzuki Burgman 650 scooter that had been around for twenty years. In 2009, Toru Eguchi and Kazuyuki Hirota of the Suzuki Motor Corporation applied for a patent for a scooter-type motorcycle equipped with fuel cell system (U.S. 8622163 B2).

Intelligent Energy now worked with Suzuki to develop the Suzuki Burgman fuel cell scooter, which they presented at the 41st Tokyo Motor Show. Two years later, the Suzuki Burgman became the first fuel cell vehicle to get European Whole Vehicle Type Approval—namely, a license to start mass production. The European Joint Research Centre "well-to-wheels" report for 2014 states that the production of hydrogen from natural gas reforming and its use in fuel cell vehicles has the potential to save as much greenhouse gas emissions as substituting coal with natural gas in power generation. Approval and tests on public roads in Japan were planned to begin in 2016, and the government worked on safety standards to secure hydrogen tanks in case of accidents. Starting in September 2017, the London Metropolitan Police began testing three Burgman scooters as part of a wider program to reduce emissions. They have been based at Alperton Deployment Centre during the 18-month trial and are being used by police community support officers within the Road and Transport Policing Command. The scooters were refueled from a private filling station, provided by Fuel Cell Systems. They have a range of around 75 miles on a single tank. Suzuki is working toward commercial production of this scooter. In that same year, the Burgman was issued with the world's first two-wheel-vehicle certification for a fuel cell two-wheeled vehicle by the Japanese government.

In 2000, Asia Pacific Fuel Cell Technologies (APFCT) Ltd. set up in Zhunan, in the province of Miaoli, Taiwan. In 2002, Jefferson Y. S. Yang, Te-Chou Yang and Yao-Sheng Hsu developed and patented a fuel cell scooter. They then entered into collaboration with Stefano Catanorchi (University of Pisa) and Michele Piana (Acta SpA, Italy), who had developed an innovative distributed hydrogen electrolyzer solution, to build the ZES. With a grant from the Taiwan Bureau of Energy subsidy program, APFCT built a fleet of 10 fuel cell scooters. This fleet was tested in the Demonstration and Verification Program of the Hydrogen Energy Industry. Under this program, six scooters were allocated to an on-road test drive of 3,100 miles (5,000 km). In February 2011, three ZES scooters completed a 170-mile (280 km) drive to appear at the 5th National Conference on Hydrogen Energy and Fuel Cells in Taiwan. The conference—at National Cheng Kung University in Tainan—hosted a showcase of Taiwanese fuel cell technology demonstration and validation projects. One scooter was durability tested for around 3,100 miles (5,000 km) by the Taiwan Automotive Research and Testing Center, which was completed in October. The remaining three scooters must each complete 9,320 miles (15,000 km) on the road. APFCT has also established what it claimed was the world's first low-pressure hydrogen canister exchange station for light electric vehicles such as fuel cell scooters. Soon afterward, APFCT began a project to build a fleet of 80 scooters for further demonstration and validation. Years earlier, in August 2012, the Hawaii-based Aloha Motor Company, a joint venture by H2 Technologies and APFCT, launched the world's first commercial off-grid solar hydrogen refueling station in Honolulu; it will be used to fuel the ZES.

The canister system, called the STOR-H, was developed by Michael F. Levy and a team at AAQIUS, headquartered in Switzerland, for their H2 scooter.

The COP22 climate change conference held in November 2016 at Marrakech saw a demonstration of the ZES with the STOR-H fast refuel system and its vending machines. In May 2017, at the Airport Show Dubai, Levy explained the advantages of STOR-H technology to His Highness Sheikh Ahmed Bin Saeed Al Maktoum, president of the Dubai Civil Aviation Authority, who has entered into a partnership to integrate the STOR-H system into the Emirate.

In 2004, Yohei Makuta, Yoshiyuki Horii, and Kuniaki Ikui of Honda adapted their company's fuel cell and stack structure to a scooter, the FCX, based on a 125cc scooter of the kind popular with commuters worldwide. Space was conserved by placing the electric drive system on the rear-wheel swing arm and by placing the Honda FC Stack fuel cell in the center of the vehicle, with auxiliary systems compactly arranged around it. The result was a scooter comparable in size to an internal-combustion-engine vehicle of the same class. In 2008, Honda released the Clarity, an innovative fuel cell electric vehicle, in limited numbers in the United States and Japan. In 2017, Honda and General Motors announced that together they will mass-produce fuel cells starting in 2020. The joint venture, which will be called Fuel Cell System Manufacturing, LLC, will build the fuel cells at GM's existing Brownstown, Michigan–based battery pack construction facility, where it currently assembles battery packs for its Volt and Bolt EVs. In 2018, a Honda patent application showed a conventionally designed motorcycle with a shaft-driven powertrain, but with a hydrogen fuel cell placed under the seat.

In 2005, the Fuel Cell Institute of Kebangsan University in Malaysia developed the Serendit II prototype with 200-watt fuel cell power. The Italian company Alcatronics developed a 3-kilowatt fuel cell motorbike, whose range was limited by two Bologna 200-bar 2.5-liter H2 steel cylinders to about 43.5 miles (70 km).

By early 2018, sales of the Toyota Mirai hydrogen fuel cell four-wheeler had surpassed 3,000 units in California. Having reached this new milestone, Mirais made up more than 80 percent of all hydrogen fuel cell vehicles in the United States. In addition, Toyota is building a new Tri-Gen facility at the Port of Long Beach that will use biowaste sourced from California's agricultural industry to generate water, electricity and hydrogen. Honda's Clarity fuel cell and Hyundai's Nexo SUV are also going into serious production. Motorcycles will follow. Honda, like other Japanese companies in the fray, has redoubled efforts to develop hydrogen filling stations.

Solar Power

At present, most owners of LEVs are criticized because their energy source comes from nuclear or fossil-fueled power stations, even though a rapidly increasing number of hydro-solar-wind stations are changing this situation. Solar power has been well proven both afloat (by *Turanor Planet Solar*, which cruised twice around the world) and in the air (by *Solar Impulse 2*, which flew once around the world), but what of on-board solar-powered motorcycles or scooters?

In 2007, Joán Orus of the Quimera Project in Barcelona, Spain, developed the SunRED solar-powered bike, which, as the Urban Solar Motorcycle, was awarded the innovation prize at the Barcelona Motor Show. The 3.1-square-meter solar panel, shaped like an armadillo, provided energy to power an electric motorcycle up to a speed of 31 miles per hour (50 kph) and with a range of 12.5 miles (20 km). Once completed, it would have been capable of recharging through both solar panels and plug-in electricity. However, the bike project was abandoned, although the name SunRED (Sun Race Engineering Development S.L.) was used by the Spanish-based auto-racing team and constructor.

In 2010, Tony "Danger" Coiro of South Bend, Indiana, a student at Purdue University, retrofitted a 1978 Suzuki to run solar energy. He bought the motorcycle for $50 and spent $2,500 on conversion, obtaining a range of 24 miles at a top speed of 45 miles per hour. But this effort was another one-off.

In 2009, Huan Canrong of China took out patent CN 101574990 for "a Wind-energy solar-energy power generation electric motorcycle." At speed, an on-board wind turbine would recharge the battery pack, as would the solar panels on the bike. No evidence has been found to indicate that this prototype was built and tested, although Dale Martin Walter-Robinson of Guilford, Connecticut, has invented a similar in-flight energy cell regenerative system for electric airplanes.

In 2012, Jesper Ørntoft Frausig of Hvidore, near Copenhagen, Denmark, opted to incorporate his e-bike's solar panels and battery into the wheels and central frame, respectively, thus reducing aerodynamic drag. A 500-watt electric motor was mounted by the pedal assembly, while a tube-like container affixed to the main frame housed the lithium-ion battery pack, fed by disc-shaped arrays of solar panels mounted inside the wheel spokes. While the solar bike stood still, it also recharged the battery. By 2015, Frausig built a second prototype, claiming that it had a 43-mile (70 km) range and a maximum speed of 30 miles per hour (50 kph) and a standard speed of 15 miles per hour.

The remarkable adventures of the Sun Trip organized by Florian Bailly can be found in chapter 9, but even these participants tow a solar panel behind them that is not fully integrated into the body shape.

In March 2018, Thammasat University in Bangkok, Thailand, launched its all-electric motorbike taxi project at the Rangsit Campus, expecting to deploy 150 electric motorbikes by the end of the year. Thammasat has teamed

Rob Cotter of Organic Transit, inventor of the ELF solar pedelec tricycle, alongside one in wasabi green livery. Since 2012, some 900 ELFs have been built and sold worldwide (courtesy Rob Cotter).

up with solar-panel manufacturer Star 8 Thailand Co. to provide 50 SolaRyde motorbikes to serve the university's students, staff and visitors—roughly 7,000 passengers per day.

The Water-Fueled Motorcycle?

According to the *Dallas Morning News* of September 8, 1935, Charles H. Garrett allegedly demonstrated his water-fueled car "for several minutes." As can be seen by examining Garrett's patent for an "electrolytic carburettor" (U.S. 2006676 A), the car generated hydrogen via electrolysis. "Dad" Garrett was something of an inventor; in 1920, he set up WRR in Dallas (the world's first municipal radio station) and was its first announcer. He was also the first man to build a radio in his car, and he developed radio transmission from cars for police use. He also invented an automatic electric traffic signal, possibly the nation's first. A few months later, Pathé News filmed his car driving along Garland Road, with the driver stopping at White Rock Lake to fill the fuel tank with water before cruising off. Nothing else was ever heard of it after that.

In 1980, Stanley Meyer claimed that he had built a dune buggy that ran on water, although he gave inconsistent explanations as to its mode of operation. In some cases, he claimed that he had replaced the spark plugs with a "water splitter," while at other times it was said to rely on a "fuel cell" that split the water into hydrogen and oxygen. The "fuel cell," which he claimed was subjected to an electrical resonance, divided the water mist into hydrogen and oxygen gas, which would then be combusted back into water vapor in a conventional internal-combustion engine to produce net energy. Meyer's claims were never independently verified, and in an Ohio court in 1996 he was found guilty of "gross and egregious fraud." He died of an aneurysm in 1998, although conspiracy theories claim that he was poisoned.

In 2015, Brazilian Ricardo Azevedo of São Paulo, a civil servant with a mechanical background, claimed to have invented a water-powered motorcycle engine called Moto Power H2O. According to Azevedo, the motorcycle (a retrofitted Honda NX 200) covered 310 miles (500 km) on one liter of water, or 1,171 miles per gallon! Most scientists and engineers saw a hydrogen motor built in this way as a "perpetual motion machine"—that is, a fantasy—because the amount of power needed to extract energy from water is equal to the energy output. Some, however, believe that a process similar to what Azevedo described could become part of a hybrid engine that would burn hydrogen, increasing fuel efficiency by 40–300 percent and reducing the amount of pollution emitted. Whether the future or fake news, water-powered bikes still have to prove themselves.

Aerodynamics

Colin Russell, a British aviation electrician/mechanic, has recorded the lowest aerodynamic coefficient of drag for a motorcycle in a wind tunnel. A faired gas motorcycle such as the Suzuki Hayabusa with a top speed of 188–194 miles per hour (303–312 kph) has a drag coefficient of about 0.55–0.60, while Russell's eMonoliner recorded 0.21.

Cedric Lynch comments:

> I think the future of electric motorcycles depends on doing something about aerodynamics. A normal motorcycle has rather less than half the frontal area of a car, but twice the drag coefficient. This means it uses about three-quarters the power of a car going at the same speed in order to overcome air drag, so 10 to 20 kilowatts at 110 to 130 km/h = about 100 or more watt-hours per kilometre. This means you need a 30 KW/H battery to get a decent range. Such a battery will weigh well over 100 kg and cost at least £10,000. There is an aircraft called the Piaggio Avanti that carries 11 people at 740 km/h on 1700 horsepower (which is about as fast as a late-model Spitfire carrying one person would go on slightly more power). The power required to overcome air drag is proportional to the cube of the speed, so this is as good as carrying

11 people at 74 km/h on 1.7 horsepower (which would be less than 5 watt-hours per person-kilometre). No road vehicle gets anywhere near this efficiency although obviously it is possible. What is needed is for an expert in aerodynamics and a stylist to work in collaboration to make something that is efficient and also attractive in appearance. The first firm to crack this will make a fortune.

Others are thinking very differently. The Boxx is a rectangular suitcase-shaped two-wheeled personal transportation vehicle that is ridden in the same way as a moped or a bicycle and is said to be just as easy and simple to operate on the road. Around 39 inches long, the 120-pound aluminum "bike" has a top speed of 35 miles per hour and can haul up to 300 pounds. Yet, despite that compact footprint, the BOXX Corporation has not skimped on tech, as the vehicle boasts traction control, anti-lock brakes and even LED lights. It is available in ten different colors.

Construction Materials

The lighter the motorcycle, the better the power/weight ratio and range.

With the increasing global awareness of the harmful effects of traditional plastic, various bio-based or bioplastic approaches are under development. They are not, however, new. During the 1930s, Henry Ford of Dearborn, Michigan, was looking for a project that would combine the fruits of industry with agriculture. He proclaimed that he would "grow automobiles from the soil," and he even had over 12,000 acres of soybeans for experimentation. His team, led by a former slave, scientist/botanist George Washington Carver, came up with the idea of an automobile made of tubular steel, whose 14 panels were made from a chemical formula that, among many other ingredients, included soybeans, wheat, hemp, flax and ramie. Weighing just 2,000 pounds (1,000 pounds lighter than a steel automobile), the "Soybean Car" was unveiled by Ford on August 13, 1941, at Dearborn Days, an annual community festival. However, the outbreak of World War II suspended all auto production, as well as the biodegradable plastic car experiment. A second unit was in production at the time that war broke out, but the project was abandoned.[2]

During the early 1950s, engineers at the Sachsenrig Automobilwerke in Zwickau, East Germany, in working to resolve the problem of steel shortage, came up with a way to recycle waste cotton and wool from the Soviet Union, mixing it with wood fibers and phenol resins from the dye industry to make Duroplast. Using this organic-based plastic for its bodywork, the affordable Trabant people's car remained in production from 1957 until the collapse of the Eastern Bloc in 1990.

In 2006, Good Natured Products Inc., a Canadian green chemistry start-up, began to make Solegear, the first 100 percent natural bioplastic (derived from plants). Its completely biodegradable moldable Polysole product could be used to replace the hard plastic parts of a car or a motorcycle or bicycle.

In 2008, to raise environmental awareness and reflect what the 69,000 employees of Siemens USA were doing to help America stay on the cutting edge of tomorrow's green economy, Siemens approached Paul Teutul, Sr., of Orange County Choppers and asked him to custom-build an electric chopper using recycled steel and aluminum, LED lighting and environmentally friendly water-based paints. Based on a Ducati Monster 1100, the Siemens Smart Chopper featured a 27-horsepower, 8-inch brushless motor with 72–96 volts of peak electrical output, good for a top speed in excess of 100 miles per hour, and enough battery life for a 60-mile range. The Siemens Smart Chopper was unveiled at the Time Warner Center in New York on August 12, 2009. It was then auctioned off, with the proceeds going to a charitable cause that helped benefit the environment. After that, Siemens purchased back the bike so the company could show it at tradeshows and conferences. It was also kept clean with a biodegradable cleaning fluid.

Since 2013, Kevin M. Murray, a naturopathic physician and acupuncturist in South Deerfield, Massachusetts, has been working with his son Nevin on the PEBL, a pedelec velomobile, whose innovative bodywork is made of 100 percent hemp cloth and soy epoxy resin made from resourced plant oils. The body sits on a corrosion-resistant aluminum "tadpole"-style frame that is the most stable three-wheel configuration, good for the rain, snow and dirt roads of the demanding New England climate. Such an approach could also be applied to an e-bike.

Christopher P. Lacson and Banatti in the Philippines have built the *Green Falcon* electric bicycle, using a one-piece marine-lacquered bamboo for the framework. The Filipino Department of Environment and Natural Resources is planting a ton of bamboo between now and 2020—as much as 15,000 hectares—for CO_2 control and soil erosion prevention. Banatti hopes to hand-build an initial 111 units.

In July 2018, the Japan-Sri Lanka Comprehensive Partnership secretariat and T-PLAN launched a venture to manufacture electric tuk-tuk three wheelers on the island, to replaced the existing one million-plus gas-powered versions. That same month, both Bird and Lime launched electric scooters on the sidewalks of the Paris's 1st and 6th arrondissements.

In August 2018, ZIV (Zweirad Industrie Verband) of Germany announced the R200 standard to measure the range of all electric-assist bikes of all makes and will act like a neutral, level playing field for all the brands in the segment. In this ZIV were helped by some of the biggest names in the industry, with Accell, Bosch, Shimano and Velotech. If a rider's pedal power is 100 watts, the range of the bike will be calculated with the electric motor providing 200 percent of this value. Hence, the total hybrid power rating would reach 300 watts, measured in accordance with variable factors, such as terrain type, bike weight, weather conditions and much more. Also in August, the San Francisco Municipal Transportation Agency awarded a one-year permit to two electric scooter companies, Scoot and Skip, while telling Lime and Bird that they had failed in their applications.

Titanium, much lighter than steel, is another approach. In 2007, Donald Atchinson, a road racer/engineer from Denver, Colorado, made a gas motorcycle called the Ecosse Titanium FE Ti XX Series, so called because of its all-titanium frame and carbon-fiber wheels. It has a 200-horsepower, 2150cc polished billet aluminum V-twin engine with an individual brake pad for each of the 12 brake pistons. Overall weight is only 440 pounds. Only 13 units of this limited edition series were made, each at a price of $300,000. At the other end of the spectrum is the 28.66-pound (13 kg) titanium-frame Budnitz Model E pedelec, with the motor and battery sealed into the polished rear hub. Developed by Paul Budnitz of Burlington, Vermont (founder of Superplastic, the world's premiere creator of art toys and accessories), Model E is also equipped with a Gates Carbon Drive belt, 30 percent lighter than a chain. Its lightness gives it a range of 100 miles. Budnitz, a passionate cyclist, began building titanium bicycles for his own use in 2002. Almost immediately, people began stopping him on the street to ask where they could buy a bicycle just like the one he was riding; in 2010, a production company was set up.

In 2015, Professors Hansoo Kim and Nack J. Kim at the Graduate Institute of Ferrous Technology at Pohang University of Science and Technology in South Korea created an alloy that is as strong as titanium, lighter than ordinary steel, and cheap to boot. The new alloy is created by combining the steel with aluminum—this lightens the steel, but also makes it weak. To counter that weakness, the team added a dash of manganese and a sprinkle of nickel, while modifying the way the metal crystals form at the nanometer scale. This new alloy is referred to as High Specific Strength Steel (nanotwinned Al-Fe). The Pohang University researchers worked with the South Korean company Posco, one of the world's largest steel manufacturers, to scale up their technology.

From home décor to medical prosthetics, robotic parts to aircraft interiors, 3D printing is the future of manufacturing. APWorks of Ottobrunn, Bavaria, a 100 percent subsidiary of Airbus Group, has been working at the forefront of additive layer manufacturing (ALM) and advanced materials since its launch in 2013. APWorks produces bionically optimized metal parts for a wide range of industries, from aerospace to automotive and robotics. In 2016, APWorks launched Light Rider, the world's first 3D-printed motorcycle, whose "organic exoskeleton," based on natural growth, is made from Scalmalloy®, a corrosion-resistant, high-strength aluminum-magnesium-scandium alloy. With its power system, Light Rider weighs just 77 pounds

Airbus APWorks' Light Rider is the world's first 3D-printed motorcycle, whose "organic exoskeleton" is made from Scalmalloy. It weighs 77 pounds (35 kg), 30 percent lighter than conventionally manufactured e-motorcycles (APWorks).

(35 kg), 30 percent lighter than conventionally manufactured e-motorcycles. Its complex and branched hollow structure could not have been produced using conventional technologies such as milling or welding. A 6-kilowatt electric motor powers the vehicle from zero to 50 miles per hour (80 kph) in 3 seconds, although its range is limited to 37 miles. Numbers are strictly limited, with a price tag of €50,000.

Xioafan Luo of Polymaker in Shanghai has teamed up with JAC Motors to make a city-ready production LSEV, with 57 of its component parts made using 3D printing. Doors, bumpers, and window housings, as well as most other visible parts, are 3D printed in fused filament fabrication (FFF) using Polymaker material. Weighing just 992 pounds (450 kg), the LSEV can reach a top speed of about 43 miles per hour with a range of 93 miles on a single charge. Production time is reduced by about 70 percent, taking around three days to complete both interior and exterior components. With units leaving the plant by 2019, Poste Italiane (the Italian postal, communication, logistics, and financial services company) has placed an order for 5,000 cars, and ARVAL (a vehicle leasing branch of BNP Paribas) has ordered 2,000. And what works for four wheels must, therefore, work for three, two and one.

For the smartphone-controlled UJet foldable electric scooter, developed by Mariana and Timo Grehl and Patrick David of Leudelange, Luxembourg, its asymmetrical construction of the mixed magnesium alloy and carbon-fiber frame is helped along by the 14-inch hubless wheels, with integrated suspension and large-diameter disc brakes. The rear wheel houses the 5.4-horsepower/65-pound-foot motor that keeps the scooter rolling forward for up to 93 miles (150 km) per charge and provides regenerative braking. UJet also has an ultra-lightweight nano-augmented tire technology, a rubber compound enhanced with Tuball single-wall carbon nanotubes.

In 2014, after two years of development and four prototypes, Eloi Fugère and Cédrick Levesque-Baker of Drummondville, Quebec, reached their goal by creating the first infusion-molded carbon-fiber/epoxy-resin electric bike frame kit. Their Nyx unit can accommodate all types of batteries, hub motors and controllers for an electric bike. Wheels up to 26 inches in diameter and 3 inches in width, as well as disc brakes between 6.3 and 8 inches, can be coupled to the aluminum aerospace graded swing arm. Its unique design allows riders to run one speed without chain tensioners.

In sharp and traditional contrast, Unplugged Design of Barcelona has launched the 71-pound (32 kg) hand-made Rocsie with a laminated bent-beech wood frame, a custom leather saddle, an inverted suspension fork, 4-piston brakes with titanium discs and a choice of four frame colors. Wood, at least, is recyclable.

Artificial Intelligence

Regarding the use of AI on e-bikes, the possibilities are pretty daunting. In 2006, a Suzuki Bandit was developed with something called Intelligent Speed Adaptation, which used GPS data to electronically limit the speed of the bike to the speed limit.

In 2012, after several years of research, Carlos Felipe of Alicante, Spain, set up the Electric Mobility Company to create a fully assisted scooter-electric bike with full iPhone integration, which he called the Xkuty One, a new concept in sustainable urban mobility. A free app enables its rider to connect their smartphone via Android or iOS (iPhone) with the scooter and set parameters such as maximum speed, acceleration style and battery consumption. The phone then clips to the center of the handlebars to act as a speedometer and monitor battery life. The phone's gyroscope also monitors orientation and angular momentum, and the app can be programmed to call an emergency contact if it senses a collision or fall. The integrated helmet enables hands-free conversations and allows the rider to listen to favorite music. The Xkuty One recognizes several languages. The Electric Mobility Company also added SPARK, a solar-powered recharging station for the Xkuty One.

Yamaha presented its MOTOROiD at the 2017 Tokyo Motor Show. According to Yamaha, technology allows the bike to identify and interact with its rider like a living creature. The MOTOROiD is effectively a horse on two wheels, ready in the garage for its rider, connected to their home and their personal devices, fully aware of their movements, their plans for the day and their immediate needs. Unlike John Wayne, you will not even need to whistle for your steed to come out to the front of the house because it will already know and be able to ride around to meet you. Then you hop on, secure in the knowledge that the bike has enough intelligence to keep you as safe as possible while still being able to enjoy the thrill of the (relatively) open road. Not only does the MOTOROiD have gesture and facial recognition, but it also incorporates a rider interface that includes a haptic (i.e., sense of touch) device that further promotes the rider's sense of unity with the bike.

In October 2017, Hiroshi Saijo, CEO and managing director at Yamaha Motor Ventures & Laboratory Silicon Valley, set up the Motobot, a motorcycle ridden by a robot. At Thunderhill Raceway in California's Sacramento Valley, he pitted it against a motorcycle ridden by Valentino Rossi, one of the most successful motorcycle racers of all time, with nine Grand Prix world championships to his name. The Motobot hit a speed of 124 miles per hour (200 kph). When rounding the track, though, its lap time came to 117.50 seconds—nearly 32 seconds short of Rossi's best, 85.74 seconds. However, the robot sensed the environment, calculated what to do, kept the bike stable, and managed acceleration and deceleration—all while factoring in road conditions, air resistance, and engine braking. At CES 2018, Yamaha presented both the MOTOROiD and MOTOBOT Version 2 to attract new partners from multiple fields, creating technological innovation and new businesses through open innovation.

Meanwhile, Kawasaki is developing "Rideology," a natural language dialogue system that will allow the rider to talk to their motorcycle (and the vehicle to talk back), possibly via a Bluetooth intercom paired with the motor's computers. In this way, the vehicle could help the rider stay abreast of the traffic situation and monitor attentiveness. It could also locate itself to within 2.5 centimeters using a combination of inertial measurement and GPS-RTK (GPS with real-time kinematics), which would mean augmenting GPS by referring to a signal from a radio station.

Honda's Riding Assist-e electric motorcycle uses a computer-controlled system to make tiny steering adjustments such as staying upright when moving at a snail's pace and even when at a dead stop.

BMW Motorrad is preparing an electric scooter called the C-Evolution and the Concept Link, as well as the eRR, the electric version of its supersport motorcycle S 1000 RR. With BMW's Vision Next 100 motorcycle, the rider can ride with no hands and will not even require a helmet (or any other protective gear, for that matter), as the bike, with its retracting/projecting pedals, self-balances and is able to suggest and make corrections in case of impending danger. The bike is stripped down almost entirely, with most information provided to the rider via an augmented reality headset (the visor) that shows speed, navigation and the rear mirrors. To indicate turning right or left, the rider need only stretch out their arm and point, and the indicator light will respond and start flashing. Powering everything is a zero-emission electric drivetrain.

The 100-miles-per-hour Emflux e-motorcycle prototype, made in Bengal, India, by a 25-person team led by Vinay Raj Somashekar, is also AI. It is fitted with single rear cameras, built-in navigation systems, Bluetooth, Wi-Fi and 4G connectivity and a custom-designed Emflux NEXT user interface, all built around an NVIDIA Jetson TK1 brain—a device designed to assist drones and other compact devices in machine learning. The Jetson TX1 is the first embedded computer designed to process deep neural networks, which gives it the ability to not only recognize objects but also interpret information. The Emflux motorcycle unveiled at the 2018 Auto Expo in New Delhi is said to update and upgrade itself via over-the-air updates (much like a smartphone).

Mitsubishi Electric Corporation has developed Maisart-brand high-performing automotive camera technology that detects various object types at distances of up to about 330 feet, which will enable riders to receive advance warning for enhanced riding safety and help to prevent accidents.

At this time, BMW is working with Honda and Yamaha to form the Connected Motorcycle Consortium (CMC) so brands can work together to standardize the intelligent systems they are developing—much like what has happened with cars. All three brands are looking to have cooperative-intelligent transportation systems on motorcycles, most probably electric by the year 2020.

BMW Motorrad's concept for tomorrow's motorcycle (BMW).

But it could go even further. In November 2016, *Wired*'s Jack Stewart, wearing an electrode cap developed by Santosh Mathan, an engineer with Honeywell Aerospace, used his mind to fly a Beechcraft King Air C90 above Seattle. With what Stewart describes as "a tiny amount of practice in a simulator," he could make the twin turboprop climb, descend and turn simply by focusing on certain areas of a tablet screen.

Dr. Lucian Gheorghe at the Nissan Research Center in Atsugi, Japan, is perfecting "Brain-to-Vehicle technology" (B2V), which provides the world's first system for real-time detection and analysis of brain activity relating to driving (or riding or piloting). It includes activity in advance of intentional movement (e.g., steering), known as movement-related cortical potential, and activity that reveals the variance between what the driver expects and what they are experiencing (e.g., a car moving too fast for comfort), known as error-related potentials. The system would detect when the rider is about to initiate an action, from stepping on a pedal to turning the handlebars, and would start this motion ahead of contact, improving the two-wheeler's reaction time by 0.2–0.5 seconds. Brain-controlled motorcycles may also become an option in the future.

The earliest electric vehicles were modifications of horse-drawn carriages or, indeed, a simple change from horses to two wheels. Compared with man's age-old companion, the horse (which has been with us for 4,000 years), AI motorcycles still have a way to go. They will need a delicate sense of smell and touch, extended hearing range, 360-degree night/color vision and sophisticated-response body language. They will have to move sideways as well as forward/backward. In addition, they must be capable of taking sleeping riders home, across a desert, through the surf of a beach, across a river or through mud or snow without breaking down.

Silence Not Allowed

In November 2016, *Verge* journalist Andrew J. Hawkins reported, "Electric cars are now required to make noise at low speeds so they don't sneak up and kill us."

In the United Kingdom, the Locomotive Act of 1865 required self-propelled vehicles to be led by a pedestrian waving a red flag or carrying a lantern to warn bystanders of the vehicle's approach.

> Firstly, at least three persons must be employed to drive or conduct such locomotive, and if more than two waggons or carriages be attached thereto, an additional person must employed, to take charge of such waggons or carriages. Secondly, one of such persons, while any locomotive is in motion, shall precede such locomotive on foot by not less than sixty yards, and shall carry a red flag constantly displayed, and shall

warn the riders and drivers of horses of the approach of such locomotives, and shall signal the driver thereof when it shall be necessary to stop, and shall assist horses, and carriages drawn by horses, passing the same.[3]

In his research, this author came across an uncorroborated report of how, in the early 1900s, the driver of an electric vehicle in New York City was tried for a double manslaughter. Driving forward, he had run over an unsuspecting pedestrian and reversed, only to run over a second unsuspecting pedestrian.

When, in the 1980s, those promoting the Electric Boat Association (EBA) attempted to persuade narrowboat owners on the British Canal System to convert to silent electric power, the owners complained that they would no longer enjoy the "dugga-dugga-dugga" of their Gardener or Lister oil engines. The EBA suggested that they take an audio-cassette player on board with them that would play the sound they feared missing. This, of course, was only a joke.

For 20 years the objective has been to make cars and motorcycles quieter. Now things have become too quiet, and EVs are obliged to become louder. Beginning in summer 2019, electric and hybrid-fuel cars, as well as scooters and motorcycles, in the United States will be required to produce noise when traveling at low speeds under a new rule issued by the U.S. National Highway Traffic Safety Administration. This is to prevent these vehicles from injuring pedestrians, especially people who are blind or are visually impaired. The new rule requires all newly manufactured electric vehicles weighing 10,000 pounds or less, including motorcycles, to make an audible noise when traveling forward or in reverse at speeds of 19 miles per hour or less. NHTSA says the sound alert is not required at higher speeds because other factors, such as tire and wind noise, "provide adequate audible warning to pedestrians." It doesn't explain what kind of alert automakers should use, so whether it's a fake engine noise or a "beeping" noise will be up to the manufacturers of electric vehicles, who have already been working on the challenge for almost a decade.

Psycho-acousticians at the Technical University of Munich are building up the potential sounds. It should sound like a motorcycle—yet not precisely the same as a gas motorcycle. Advanced-technology cars available on the market with manually activated electric warning sounds include the Nissan Leaf, Chevrolet Volt, Honda FCX Clarity, Nissan Fuga Hybrid/Infiniti M35, Hyundai Sonata Hybrid, and Toyota Prius (Japan only).

There are different approaches to this problem. ECTunes is developing a system that utilizes directional sound equipment to emit noise when and where it is needed. According to the company, its technology sends audible signals only in the direction of travel, thus allowing the vehicle to be heard by those who may be in motorcycle's path. By contrast, SoundRacer AB of

Sweden has presented its Electric Vehicle Electronic Engine Sound System, which uses only real engine sound recordings as the base for the sounds.

As for silent motorcycles, although the traditional steel was replaced by aluminum, the final drive to the wheel was by a belt, typical of gasoline Harley-Davidsons. For the LiveWire electric range, Harley-Davidson has added a housing that creates a resonance when in operation, a whirring sound somewhere between a jet turbine and an oversized vacuum. It will be interesting to see how Zero, Energica, and other electric motorcycles will follow suit.

Afloat and Airborne

Personal watercraft or water scooters (sometimes known as Jet Skis, after the popular Kawasaki model) have been annoying beach lovers with their gasoline roar for almost forty years. It was inevitable that they, too, would convert to electric. In 2010, a Frenchman, Jérémy Benichou, persuaded the Mayenne Laval Technopole, based in France's Loire region, to back him in developing a silent electric waterbike. Setting up Aqualeo, he produced the Gliss-Speed, an 8-foot (2.49 m) two-seater, joystick-controlled electric water go-kart that manages a speed of almost 19 miles per hour, using a 2.5-kilowatt motor and 3-kilowatt lithium-ion battery pack. Autonomy is between 2 and 4 hours. Benichou has set up a distribution network in the Caribbean, Dubai and Oman, resulting in the sales of more than 300 Gliss-Speeds. With the Gliss-Speed's speed increased to 28 miles per hour (45 kph), Benichou has announced that waterjet versions will be available starting in 2019.

In September 2013, LGM Inc., a subsidiary of Leo Motors Ltd., was granted 70 million won ($63,000) by the Korean Ministry of Maritime Affairs and Fisheries to research electric propulsion for small boats. The following year the company received a further subsidy from the government to develop an electric jet ski (forthcoming).

Jordan Darling of Free Form Factory in Sacramento, who has developed an advanced polymer material called Hulklite, teamed up with Zero Motorcycles to use their powertrains to make an electric personal watercraft called the Gratis X1. Power comes from a ZF 75-5 permanent-magnet, brushless, liquid-cooled motor and ZF 6.5-kilowatt-hour intelligent, liquid-cooled power pack, giving the Gratis X1 about 30–45 minutes of run time with 46 horsepower and a top speed of 40 knots (46 mph/74 kph), which is actually faster than it appears when on water. As with Zero motorcycles, customers can choose to add an additional Z-Force ZF 3.3-kilowatt-hour power pack (sold separately) for about 20 more minutes of run time. In 2017, Free Form was purchased by Salt Lake City–based Nikola Motor Co. Nikola is aiming to produce a sit-down personal watercraft that will outperform the top internal-combustion versions on the water and provide up to five hours of ride time with zero emissions and less noise.

What about a pedelec afloat? Guy Howard-Willis always had a passion for cycling and watersports, which drove him to found Torpedo7, New Zealand's leading outdoor and adventure sports multi-channel retailer. In 2010, Guy became fascinated with the introduction of hydrofoils in America's Cup, which tripled the yacht's speed, ultimately revolutionizing high-speed sailing. Guy met Roland Alonzo, another passionate cyclist who also happened to be an accomplished bicycle designer. They came up with a 400-watt pedelec aluminum/carbon-fiber hydrofoil they called the Manta 5. The cyclist can adjust one of the foils when in use to get greater lift.

In *Electric Aircraft and Drones*, this author defined an electric aircraft as a vehicle that, with or without a pilot and/or passenger(s), is regularly capable of taking off from the ground, rising to a height of no less than 100 feet and no more than 80,000 feet, and then flying for between 4 minutes and 4 years, using electric or hybrid-electric propulsion. This book is about electric vehicles with one or more wheels that use roads or tracks to move along. So is there such a vehicle as an air-cushioned wheeler?

Since 1989, Lexus in Lima, Peru (part of the Toyota Motor Corporation), has employed Haruhiko Tanahashi as its chief engineer, innovating the Lexus LFA supercar and, more recently, the 25.35-pound (11.5 kg) SLIDE, a bamboo and carbon-fiber electric hoverboard that relies on superconductors and magnets that combine to repel the force of gravity to ride just above the ground. With superconducting temperatures at -321°Fahrenheit (-197°C), the SLIDE is cooled by reservoirs of liquid nitrogen. The fact that the maglev SLIDE's rider can only run on a track containing permanent magnets severely limits its use, though the manufacturer envisions the introduction of slide parks (like skateboard parks).

In contrast, the ArcaBoard, built and developed by Bucharest-born Dumitru Popecu at the ARCA Space Corporation in Las Cruces, New Mexico, can travel anywhere. It is lifted by 36 high-power electric ducted fans, occupying 90 percent of the space inside the board with a maximum thrust of 430 pounds (200 kgf). Using an iOS or Android smartphone, the rider can control the ArcaBoard via Bluetooth, with the stabilization system either on or off. When the stabilization system is on, the rider need only sit on ArcaBoard and move the phone with their hand, and the ArcaBoard will replicate the rider's movements. Popecu, a former theology student turned aeronautical engineer, is also involved with space rockets and UAVs—and drones.

The Hoversurf Scorpion 3, a quadcopter "motorcycle," is the brainchild of Alexandr Atamanov, IT businessman and aviation enthusiast of Moscow and Los Angeles. Its wooden rotors enable it to fly up to 13 feet. After two years of research and development, this third-generation e-hoverbike was publicly launched in December 2016. Scorpion 3—which was demonstrated at the Moscow Raceway, 60 miles (97 km) from the city—can withstand 275 pounds (125 kg) and is capable of reaching 37 miles per hour (60 kph). Its battery capacity allows it to stay in the air for 15 minutes.[4] In October 2017, it was announced that Dubai was planning to add Scorpion 3s to its police fleet.

Also from Russia, weapons manufacturer Kalashnikov Concern, known for its AK-47 machine gun (the world's most used weapon), demonstrated its unnamed 8 double-prop prototype, calling it a "Hovercycle." The batteries appear to be located under the rider linked to the rotors; the flying car has a seat and is maneuvered by using a joystick. Is this Russia's new cavalry? Indeed, there is another project for a quadcopter with sub-machine gun and 100-round magazine control by a smart tablet.

Virtual Reality

One application of the fast-growing hobby of virtual reality is avoiding the need to physically go on a motorcycle ride.

In Steven Lisberger's *Tron*, a 1982 American science-fiction action-adventure film, computer hacker Kevin Flynn (played by Jeff Bridges) is transported inside the software world of a mainframe computer, where he interacts with programs in his attempt to escape. In the movie, light cycles are vehicles resembling motorcycles that are driven by programs in the Game Grid. Upon being rezzed in by a program's rod, a light cycle completely covers the driver—who is forced into a riding position—with a protective canopy.

In 2005, Cruden BV of Amsterdam built its first professional-grade simulator, and the company has been improving it ever since for use by manufacturers, universities, race teams and road safety organizations. The now widespread availability of head-mounted displays from companies like Oculus, HTC, and Sony has catapulted virtual reality into the mainstream. Once a gauzy fantasy, VR is now reality. VR computer motorcycle games enable players to race the world's greatest circuits next to Valentino Rossi or ride trails through the Rockies and perform stunts greater than those of Robbie Maddison. At the Auto Expo 2016, Nextwave created a 3D VR racing stall using real TVS RTR bikes rigged up to the controls that gave the rider an extremely realistic effect. Riders got the choice of two environments: Dirt Ace, where they could tear up a super cross track, or Hill 'n' Dale, where they found themselves testing their skills racing against the forces of nature. Using an Oculus Rift allows the player to look around seamlessly as in real life! Haptics will take VR users beyond sight and sound, adding motion, touch, and force feedback to virtual experiences. Force feedback means that virtually generated forces are exerted onto the player's skin and into their body. For Google's Daydream headset and the Samsung Gear VR, it's already on the smartphone slotted into the headset. Of course, VR headsets are powered by a rechargeable battery, like an electric motorcycle or pedelec.

In Steven Spielberg's sci-fi film *Ready Player One* (2018), set in the year 2045, Wade Watts is joined in his quest by Art3mis, who is basically a warrior-goddess who rides the motorcycle from the 1989 anime film *Akira* and has an equally formidable knowledge of all things nostalgic.

Appendix: Electric Motorcycle and Battery Builders (Past and Present)

Motorcycles

AeroVironment
Agni
Alta
Aqualeo
Arcimoto
Auranthetic
Bafang
Bell Custom Cycles
BK Tech
BMW
Bowen
Brammo
BRD
Brompton
BSA
Corbin
Cranes
Cree
Curtiss
Ducati
Eicher
Electric Bicycle Company
Electric Motorbike Inc.
Electricross
Electrotherm
E-Max
Emflux
Emmerich
Energica
EPS
EV Global
EVantage
Evoke
Ford
Free Form
GeoOrbital
Giant
Gogoro
Harley-Davidson
Heinzmann
Hercules
Honda
Intelligent Energy
JD
Jiangsu Xinri
Johammer
Kalkoff
Karbon Kinetics Ltd.
Kinetic
Lito
Luyuan
Lynch
Michelin
Modern Times Ltd.
Momentum Electric
Morgan
MotoCzyzs
Motorino
Mylane
Nikola
Organic Transit
Panasonic
Peugeot
Quantya
Riese & Müller
Rool'in
Ryan
Ryno
Saietta
Sanyo
Saroléa
Schachner

Segway
Sinclair
Small Antelope
Socovel
Solar Bike
Solowheel
Sparta
Superpedestrian
T3
Tacita
Terra Motors
Tork
Tuk-Tuk
UM
Vectrix
Velocity
Vespa
Vivax Assist
Vmoto
Voxan

VoZE
WaveCrest
Winston Shenzen
Yadea
Yamaha
Zero

Batteries

A123
Asia Pacific Fuel Cell
   Technologies
Banner
BionX
BMZ
Bosch
East Penn
Exide
Farasis
Fulmen

Kokam
LG
Lucas
MG
Molycell
Mylion
Optima
Ovonic
Panasonic
Prest-O-Lite
Saft
Samsung
Sonnenschein
Sony
Spitfire
Trojan
Tudor
Valence
Winston Shenzen

Chapter Notes

Foreword

1. George Bernard Shaw, *Man and Superman* (New York: Brentano's, 1903), 238 ("Maxims for Revolutionists").

Chapter 1

1. Indeed, today there is a company in the area named the Electric Bike Store.
2. "Died in the Saddle," *Boston Daily Globe*, June 2, 1896, p. 1.
3. In October 2010, a Roper steam cycle was auctioned for the record amount of more than $500,000.
4. Henri de Parville, *The Official*, April 20, 1881.
5. L'Abbé Moigno, *Les Mondes*, May 20, 1881.
6. Bibliothèque centrale du Conservatoire national des arts et métiers (Paris), Fonds Godin, correspondance de Jean-Baptiste André Godin, FG 15 (21); Claudine Cartier, *Des machines au service du peuple: Godin et la mécanique* (Guise: Editions du Familistère, 2017).
7. Georges Dary, *A travers l'électricité* (Paris: Vuibert et Nony, 1895), 456.
8. *Telegraph Journal and Electrical Review* 11, no. 258 (November 4, 1882).
9. "The Vienna International Electric Exhibition," *La Nature*, November 4, 1883.
10. Advertisement in *Sussex Advertiser*, November 28, 1887.
11. "An Electric Dog-Cart Friday," *St. James's Gazette*, January 6, 1888.
12. Conrad Volk, *Magnus Volk of Brighton* (Chichester, UK: Phillimore, 1971).
13. "Mr Magnus Volk's 81st Birthday. Pioneer of Electricity," *Sussex Biographies*, November 22, 1932.
14. "The Vaughan-Sherrin Electric Tricycle and Boat," *Electrical Engineer* 6, October 3, 1890.
15. *Corriere di Garfagnana*, Year VII, no. 537, October 1, 1891, p. 2.
16. Kevin Desmond, *The Electric Boat and Ship: A History* (Jefferson, NC: McFarland, 2017).
17. Canton City Directory, 1892–1893.
18. Details provided by Tom Haas, volunteer researcher at the McKinley Presidential Library & Museum; Canton City Directories, 1895–1902; Edward Heald, *The Stark County Story*, Vol. III (Canton, OH: Stark County Historical Society, 1950).
19. Documentation researched by Liza Sanchez (Center for Local & Global History, Cleveland Public Library, Ohio).
20. *La Lumière Electrique*, October 1, 1892, p. 48.
21. *Automotor and Horseless Vehicle Journal*, June 1897.
22. http://www.historywebsite.co.uk/Museum/Engineering/engineeringhall.htm.
23. "Scott and Janney, Electrical Manufacturers," *Wheeling Daily Intelligencer*, May 31, 1898.
24. *Le Journal*, February 11 and May 30, 1897.
25. "Albert Champion," *Le Petit Braquet*

Chronique, no. 95, http://www.lepetitbraquet.fr/chron95-Champion-Albert-II.html.
  26. *La Presse*, September 24, 1898.
  27. "Voitures Automobiles Electriques," Ch. Mildé Fils, Constructeurs-Electriciens, rue Desrenaudes, avenue Niel, Paris, May 1900.
  28. Erwin Maderholz, "Elektrofahrzeuge in Postdienst," *Archive für deutsche Postgeschichte*, Heft 2 (1981).

Chapter 2

  1. Halwart Schrader, *Deutsche Autos 1885–1920* (Stuttgart: Motorbuch Verlag, 2002).
  2. "Elektromobilität anno 1900," motoped.info.
  3. Theo de Kogel, "De elektrischefiets van Philips," *De Oude Fiets*, no. 2003/4 and 2004/1.
  4. Maurice Victor, "L'Œuf électrique," *La revue de l'aluminium français*, no. 122 (May 1946): 168–73.

Chapter 3

  1. J. Kupelian and J. Sirtaine, *Belgische Motoren* (Overijsse: Kupélian, 1983), 129–31.
  2. One of these is preserved at the Musée Henri-Malartre in Rochetaillée-sur-Saône.
  3. "The Motor Cycle Introduces 'An Electric Motor Cycle,'" *The Motorcycle*, April 18, 1946.

Chapter 4

  1. "News and Views: Britain's Electric Vehicles," *Autocar* 127, no. 3729 (August 3, 1967): 55.
  2. Communication from Cedric Lynch, 2017.
  3. "The Electric Bike in Search of Money," *New Scientist*, February 21, 1985.

Chapter 5

  1. With a 20-strong workforce, Schachner sells more than 12,000 units per year.
  2. Communication from Ray Morgan, February 23, 2018.
  3. "Pedal Power Gets a Boost," *Yamaha News*, October 1, 1993, No 5.
  4. Communication from Jon Geffen, March 16, 2018.

Chapter 6

  1. The *NuVinci* name represents a "tip of the hat" to Leonardo da Vinci, who in 1490 sketched what is considered the first documented continuously variable transmission.
  2. "Is This the End of the Petrol-Powered Motorcycle?" *Motor Cycle News*, July 28, 2017.
  3. Communication from Cedric Lynch, April 3, 2018.

Chapter 7

  1. Zero Motorcycles website.
  2. Regulations TT Zero, 2010 International Tourist Trophy, Isle of Man, May 29–June 11, 2010, p. 27.
  3. Communication from Cedric Lynch, December 21, 2017.
  4. Ibid.
  5. "Bruce Anstey Takes SES TT Zero Win for Mugen," *TT*, June 9, 2017.
  6. Patrick Leary, "Harley-Davidson CEO Levatich Weighs in on Electric Bikes, KC Plant Closure," *Milwaukee Business Journal*, January 30, 2018.
  7. Kevin Desmond, *Gustave Trouvé: French Electrical Genius* (Jefferson, NC: McFarland, 2015), 114.
  8. Sam Sims, "50+ Departments Fight Crime on Zero Police Motorcycles," *Ultimate Motorcycling*, May 29, 2015.
  9. Kelsey D. Atherton, "Special Forces Are Getting a Stealth Motorcycle That's Silent and Deadly," *Popular Science*, May 26, 2017.

Chapter 8

  1. Jamerson and Benjamin, *Electric Bikes Worldwide Report*, several volumes.
  2. Binchun, *Chengcha Biji (Travels*

Abroad) 1866/68 (Beijing: Yuelu shushe, 1985).
   3. Peter Fairley, "China's Cyclists Take Charge Electric Bicycles Are Selling by the Millions Despite Efforts to Ban Them," *IEEE Spectrum*, June 1, 2005; J. Weinert, C. Ma, and C. Cherry, "The Transition to Electric Bikes in China: History and Key Reasons for Rapid Growth," *Transportation* 34, no. 301 (2007).
   4. Information supplied by Zhejiang Luyuan Electric Vehicle Co., Ltd., March 2018.
   5. Ivana Kottasová, "China Accused of Flooding Europe with Cheap E-bikes," *CCNTech*, October 2, 2017.

Chapter 9

   1. "Japanese Man to Travel 'Around-the-Globe' on Electric Scooter," Agence France-Presse, March 9, 2004.
   2. Communication from Florian Bailly, February 14, 2018.
   3. Ken Foxe, "Riding Team Plans Longest-Ever Electric Motorcycle Expedition," *Lonely Planet*, February 14, 2018.

Chapter 10

   1. Comunication from Richard Hatfield, December 2017.
   2. Wikipedia plus revions by Chip Yates.
   3. Communication from Paul Thede, February 2018.
   4. *Electric Racing News.*
   5. Zack Courts, "Thunder and Lightning: Gasoline versus Electricity at the Pinnacle of Performance," *Motorcyclist*, November 2017.
   6. Communications from Bill Dubé and Eva Håkansson.

Chapter 11

   1. *La Vie de l'Automobile*, no. 134 (April 23, 1904): 260.

   2. "Study on the Stability and Motion Control of a Unicycle: Part I: Dynamics of a Human Riding a Unicycle and Its Modeling by Link Mechanisms," *JSME International Journal*, June 1995.
   3. Communication from Ralf Luther, February 1, 2018.
   4. Nick Bilton, "Start-Up Reinvents the Bicycle Wheel," *New York Times* "Bits" Blog, October 21, 2013.
   5. "Roller Skates and the History of Roller Skating," planetonwheels.com.

Chapter 12

   1. The Yare is on display at the LaPorte County Museum.
   2. Communication from Robert Cotter, February 15, 2018.

Chapter 13

   1. Daniel McMahon, "A 19-Year-Old Belgian Cyclist Got Caught Cheating at the World Championships after Racing a Bike That Had a Motor Hidden in the Frame," *Business Insider UK*, February 1, 2016.

Chapter 14

   1. Communication from Mike Halls, editor of *Batteries International*, April 2018.
   2. Rusty Davis, "Henry's Plastic Car: An Interview with Mr. Lowell E. Overly," *V8 Times* (1988): 46–51.
   3. "Parliamentary Intelligence: House of Commons," *The Times*, April 27, 1865.
   4. Loz Blain, "Safety Last: Russian Hoverbike Is Equally Amazing and Horrifying," *New Atlas*, February 21, 2017.

Selected Bibliography

Books

Adamson, Ian, and Richard Kennedy. *Sinclair and the "Sunrise" Technology.* Harmondsworth, UK: Penguin, 1986.
Dale, Rodney. *The Sinclair Story.* London: Gerald Duckworth, 1985.
Dary, Georges. *A travers l'électricité.* Paris: Vuibert et Nony, 1895.
Desmond, Kevin. *Electric Boats and Ships: A History.* Jefferson, NC: McFarland, 2017.
_____. *Gustave Trouvé: French Electrical Genius (1839–1902).* Jefferson, NC: McFarland, 2015.
_____. *Innovators in Battery Technology: Profiles of 93 Influential Electrochemists.* Jefferson, NC: McFarland, 2016.
Galbiati, Fermo, and Nino Ciravegna. *La bicicletta.* Milan, Italy: Be-Ma, 1989.
Jamerson, Frank, and Ed Benjamin. *Electric Bikes Worldwide Report.*
Neupert, Hannes. *Spezial Historie.* Tanna, Germany: Extra Energie, 2011.
Schrader, Halwart. *Deutsche Autos, 1885–1920.* Stuttgart: Motorbuch Verlag, 2002.
Tragatsch, Erwin. *The Illustrated Encyclopedia of Motorcycles.* New York: Chartwell, 1989.
Volk, Conrad. *Magnus Volk of Brighton.* Chichester, UK: Phillimore, 1971.

Journals and Websites

Autocar
Automotor and Horseless Vehicle Journal
Boston Daily Globe
Business Insider UK
Elecdrive.com
Electrical Engineer
Electricbike.com
ExtraEnergy
GeekWire
Gizmag
IEEE Spectrum
Le Journal
JSME International Journal
La Lumière Electrique
Milwaukee Business Journal
Les Mondes
Mother Earth News
Motor Cycle News
The Motorcycle
Motorcyclist
La Nature
New Atlas
New Scientist
New York Times
De Oude Fiets
Le Petit Braquet Chronique
Popular Science
Powerinflux.wordpress.com

La Presse
St. James's Gazette
Sussex Advertiser
Telegraph Journal and Electrical Review
Transportation
Ultimate Motorcycling
La Vie de l'Automobile
Wheeling Daily Intelligencer
Wired
Yamaha News

Index

Numbers in **bold italics** indicate pages with illustrations

Accell **99**, 100, 134, 218; Haibike **99**
Ace Trikes 100
Action Incorporated 192; RocketSkates 192; SpnKiX 192
aerial bicycle 13, **14**
AeroVironment 74, 82–83, 211
Agility Motors *see* Saietta
Agni Motors 117–118, 137; Agni-Suzuki 117; Agni X01 117; Agni Z2 118
Albert Champion Company 37
Alfa Romeo 133
Al-Hallaj, Sai 97
All-Cell Technologies 97
Alonzo, Roland 227
Alta Motors (formerly BRD Motorcycles) 121–122, 126, 131; Motocross MX 121; Redshift MX (later changed to Alta) 121, **121**; Supermoto (SM) 121
Alternet Systems Incorporated 208
Amigo Mobility International Incorporated 67; Amigo 67
Ananthakrishna, Anil 99
Anchor bicycles *see* Flying Pigeon
Anderson, Ryan 201; Raht Racer 201
Aprilia 211; Aprilia RS250 211; ApriliaFC 211; MOJITO FC 211
Arcade Cycles 103
Arzens, Paul 48–49, **50**, 54, 60, 193–194
Askenazi, Abe 128
Atamov, Alexandr 227
Atchinson, Donald 219
Audi 145, 210
Auranthetic Corporation 68; Auranthetic Charger 68
AV Charger 83
Ayrton, William Edward 11–12, **12**, 13
Azevedo, Ricardo 216

Bafang Motor Company 143
Bailly, Florian 148–150, **149**, **214**; *see also* Sun Trip

Bänziger, Benno 83
Barceló, Marc 138
Battery Automated Transportation International (BAAT) 89
battery makes: Cylon 90; Edison 43, 45; Eneloop 100; EPS 16; Eveready 65, 85; Exide 68, **69**, 157; Exxon 85; Faure-King 29; Fulmen 48; Impact 82; Ironclad-Exide 45; Kokam 87, 117, 209; LevoGT 55 195; Lucas 59, 71; Molicel 117; Oldham 77; Optima 90, 94, 163; Panasonic 107, 109, 184; Pharos 93; Planté 11; Prest-O-Lite 53, **55**; Pulsar Power Pack 160; SAFT 91, **92**, 161; Sellon-Volckmar 11; Svenska Ackumulator AB Jungner 45; Thunder Sky 87–88, 143, 164; Torqeedo 209; Trojan 193; Tudor 53, 55; Turnigy A123 134; Varta 48; VX-1 Li/Li 113; Zero ZF6.5 129; Zero ZF9 128; ZETA II 92
battery types: alkaline dry cell 65; aluminium air 209; chlorine-zinc flow 20; deep-cycle 69; hydrazine 66; lead-acid 11, 15, 43, 57, 59, 68, **69**, 71, 73, 75, 78, 82, 87, 90, 92, 94, 96, 142, 157–158, 160, 163, 190, 193, 195–196; lithium 84–85, 87, 91, 143, 145, 164, 196, 200, 208; lithium cobolt 134; lithium-cobalt-aluminium-oxide 209; lithium ion 85, **85**, 87–88, 97–98, 101, 106–107, 113–115, 117, 120, 124, 121, 126, 134–136, 138, 154, 162–163, 177, 184, 186, 188–189, 197, 199–200, 206–209, 214; lithium-ion manganese 203; lithium ion polymer 87, 96, 127, 133; lithium iron phosphate 149; lithium-manganese 97, 115; lithium nano-phosphate 163, 165, **172**, 173; lithium sulphide 207; lithium sulfur 207; manganese dioxide 65; nickel-cadmium **66**, 66, 69, 75, 78, 81, 91, **92**, **93**, 93, 160–161; nickel-iron 45, **45**; nickel-metal hydride NiMH 83–84, **84**; 96, 98, 100, 113, 183; nickel-zinc 158; rare earth lithium sulfur 209–210; rare earth yytrium-lithium sulfur 210; silver-zinc 157; sodium

Index

206; solid state lithium 206; ultracapacitor 98; valve regulated lead-acid VRLA 89, 105; voltaic 5, 30; zinc-air 89; zinc-carbon 18
Battery Vehicle Society 71–72
Bell, Alexander Graham 7
Bell, Christopher 126
Bell Custom Cycles (BCC) 126; Brutus Café 126; Brutus V9 126; V2 Rocket 126
Benichou, Jérémy 226
Benjamin, Edward 89
Bersey, Walter C. 30, *31*
Bersey Rhodin 65
Bertone 154
bicycle railroad 28
Biderman, Assaf 186
Biechele, Johannes 205; Evation 205
bike sharing 110–111; EcoBici 110
Bingegeli, Thomas 102
Bion X 93
Bjorge, Johannes 43–44, *44*
BK Tech 93
Bland, Aaron T. 126–127
Blood Sales Company Incorporated 49, *51*
BMW 96, 131, 136, 145, 197, 202, 210, 222, *223*; C-Evolution 222; ConceptLink 222; eRR 220; Motorrad 222, *223*; Vision Next 100 222–223
BMZ 208–209; E.volution 209; 3Tron 208–209
Bolton, Ogden, Jr. 22–23, *24*
Bonneville Salt Flats 158, 160, 164–165, *166*, 167–168, 172–174, *174*
Bosch GmbH 46, 97, 101, 107, 198
Bowden, Benjamin George "Ben" 60–62, *61*, *62*
BOXX Corporation 217
Boynton, William 28
Braga, Maria Helena 207
Brammo Enertia 126; Empulse R 126–127
Bramscher, Craig 126
BRD Motorcycles *see* Alta Motors
Brompton 105–106, *106*
Brüsch, Suzanne *80*, 89, 94–95, *94*, *151*
Brush, Charles E. 14–15; Brush Electric Company 15
BSA Motors 197; Roamer Able 197
Budnitz, Paul 219; tuk-tuk 218
Buell, Erik 128
Buell Motorcycle Company 128
Bulls 102
Burtov, Michael 184, *185*; GeoOrbital 184–185, *185*
Butler-Adams, William 106, *106*

Cairns, Elton 207
Campagnia Motors 202; T-REX 16SP 202
Canary 64
Capital Pacific Pty Limited 101
Carli, Giuseppe 18, 20
Cassez, Micha'l 161
Castilioni, Giovanni 136
Catalan Motor Industry Consortium 138
Catanorchi, Stefano 212
Cevolini, Livia 123, *124*
Champion, Albert 37; Champion Ignition Company 37
charging/re-charging 107, 110, 124–125, 152, 156, 210, 212, 221; Amazon 210; Enertech 160; E.ON 210; Fortnum 110; Ionity 210; Tesla Supercharger 210
Chen, Shane 183; Hovertrax 192; Lunicycle 192; OrbitWheel 192; Solowheel 183; UltraDrainer 192
Chiang, Yet-Ming *172*, 173
China Electric Bicycle Association 143
Ching, Winston 143
Chizuru 143
Chrysler 83, 90
Chung, Winston 87, 209–210
Cochard, Benjamin 109
Cocoa Motors 192; WalkCar 192
Colombo, Nicola 154
construction materials 217–221; Airbus AP Works Lightrider 219–220, *220*; Banatti Green Falcon 218; Budnitz Model E 219; Ecosse Titanium FE Ti XX 219; JAC Motors 220; Nyx 221; 3D printing 219–220, *220*; Ujet 220–221; Unplugged Design Rocsie 221
Copenhagen Wheel 186–187, *187*
Corbin 157–158; Corbin Electric 68, *69*, 157; Corbin XLP-1 160; Lightning 157; Quicksilver 157–158, *159*
Corbin, Mike 68, 69, 157, *159*, 160
Cornillon, Christophe 201
Cotter, Robert 197–198, *215*
Coventry Lever 8
Coventry Rotary 8
Cranes Electric Vehicle Company 142–143
Cree AG 195–196; Cree SAM Swatchmobile 195; Sam 195
Cronk, Scott 89–90
CRP Racing 123; eCRP 123; eCRP 1.0 123; eCRP 1.4 123; Ego 123–125; Ego 45 124; Energica 123–125 *124*; Energica Eva 124; Esse Esse 9 124–125
Currie, Dr. Malcolm R. 88, 100
Currie Technologies 100
Curtiss 132–133, 161; Curtiss Hercules 133; Zeus 133
Curtiss, Glenn 132
Cyclemaster Limited 184
cyclemotors and bicycle adapters 183–184; DK City Wheel 187; eBici 184; electron Wheel 187; FlyKly Smart Wheel 187; Mercury 184; Michelin E-System 188; Omni-Wheel 185; Phillips 184; Rabeneick 184; Rool'in 187; Vincent Norman 184; Zehus Bike+ 187; *see also* Copenhagen Wheel Cycles Maximus 195
Czysz, Michael 168

Index

d'Acremon, Antoine 187–188
Daimler-Benz 114, 210
Daluge 143
dandy-horse 5
Daniell, Professor John 5
Darling, Jordan 226
Darracq, Pierre Alexandre 32, 35–37
David, Patrick 221
Davin, Patrick Dennis 101
Davis, J.C. 156
Dayun 147
Decker, Dakota 184, *185*
Defense Advanced Research Projects Administration (DARPA) 131–132; SilentHawk 131–132
de Limelette, Albert 53–54, *55*
de Limelette, Maurice 53–54, *55*
de Maneville, Frédéric 201
Desbarats, Guy 76
Dick, Claudio 122
DiCostanzo, Don 83
Doerksen 189
dog-cart 16, *17*, 20, 29–31, 37, *38*
Dolphin *80*
Dorresteyn, Derek 121, *121*
drag racing 113, 160, 162–163, 165, 169–171
Dubé, Jean Yves 96
Dubé, William 161–162, 169, 171–174, *174*; Ewetwik Wabbit 162; Green Envy 175; Killacycle 162–163, 163, 168, 171; Killajoule 168, 171–175, *174*
Ducati 133, 136, 168, 186
Duffield, Marshall "Duffy" 66–67

Eagle III 64
Eastman, Henry F. 31–32
Eastman Automobile Company 32
Eberhard, Martin 122
Eccity 201; Artelec *650* 201; Artelec *850* 201; Quadro4 201
eCycleElectric LLC 89
Edison, Thomas Alva 32, 39; Edison Electric Company 32; Edison Manufacturing Company 42
Eguchi, Toru 211
Eicher Motors 122; Royal Enfield Bullet 500 122–123
Eko Vehicles Pvt. Limited 99; Cosmic 99; Eko-Strike 99; ET-100 99; EV-60 99; Velocity 99
Eleck Rider RC 69
Electra (1991) 81–82, *81*
Electra (1993) 83
Electra Bicycle Company (1993) 83
Electra Cycle Company (1911) 43
Electra-Meccanica 202; Solo 202; SuperSolo 202; Tofino 202
Electra PFA 54, 57
electrathons 161–162
Electric Bicycle Company 88–89
Electric Construction Company 29

Electric Mobility Company 221; Xkuty 1 221; SPARK 221
Electric Motorbike Incorporated 90
Electric Power Storage Company Limited 13, 29
Electric Propulsion Systems (EPS) 96
Electrical Accumulator Company 15
Electrical Vehicle Institute of China Electrotechnical Society 142
Electricross *see* Zero Motorcycles
Electricycle 49–50, *51*
ElectroCat *see* Håkansson, Eva
Electrocyclette 46
Electrotherm 104; YO EXL 104–105; YObyke 104–105
Elektra 43
E-Max 97–98, 101; E-Max 140L 97
EM Power 191, 192
Emflux 223; Emflux NEXT 223
E.M.I. (N.V. Elektrotechnische Mechanische Industrie) 48
eMotion Motors 137; Surge 137
Eneloop 100
Erforth, Jeano 83
Essinger, Olivier 188
Estelle 90, *91*
European Bicycle Manufacturers Association (EBMA) 146
EV Global Motors 90, 98
EV Rider Incorporated 89; EV Warrior 88, 90, 100
EVantage *see* Polaris
Eviation 209
Evoke Motorcycles 134; Urban Classic 134; Urban S 134
Evolve Motorcycles 134; Xenon 134
Expedition Electric 950 KTM 156
ExtraEnergy 82, 94–95
Exxon Enterprises 85; Exxon Research and Engineering Company 84, *85*
Eyeball Engineering 160; Ampeater 160; Kawashoki 160
eZee Solar Delta Longabike 150

fake noise 224–226; ECTunes 225; Soundracer AB 225–226
Faure, Camille 11
Faure, Pierre 54, 57
Faure Electric Accumulator Company 11
Fazua 205
Felipe, Carlos 221
Fenigstein, Marc 122
Ferrari 133
FIAT 134
Finkler, Louie J. 189
Fitzgerald, Desmond Gerald 30
FLX 102
Flyer 81
flying bicycle 207; Fly-B *207*
Flying Pigeon 141–142
folding vehicles 46, 89, 93, 97–98, 101, 104–

Index

106, *106*, 114, 188 220–221; eZee 97; Quando 97; Sahel Compact 104; WiLL 97; YikeBike 106–107
Ford Motor Company 83, 90, 108–109, 210; OjO 108–109
Frausig, Jesper Ørntoft 214
Fritz Heinzmann GmbH 90–91, *91*, 100, 104, 195
Frohnmayer, Mark D. 197; Arcimoto SRK 197
Froma, Benjamin Swanberg 189
fuel cells 211–213; AAQIUS 212; Alcatronics 213; Aloha Motor Company 212; Fuel Cell System Manufacturing 213; Fuel Cell Systems 212; Fuel Cell Technologies (APFACT) Limited 212; H2 Technologies 212; Serendit II 213; STOR-H 212–213; ZES 212–213
Fugère, Eloi 221
Fumagalli, Valerio 154
Fuoriserie Evoluzione Alloy 134
Furia, Andrea 189
Furukawa Battery Company Limited 113
Future Motion 189; Onewheel 189–190; Onewheel+ ZR 190

Gardner, Fulton 18, *19*
Garrett, Charles H. 215
Geha 43
Gelhard, Egon 74
General Motors (GM) 43, 82, 83, 88–89, 109, 134, 193, 213; Maven Merge 109; Merge 109
Gerhardt, Donald 197
Giant 107; Lafree 107
Godin, Jean-Baptiste 10
Gogoro Incorporated 107; Smartscooter 107
go-kart 54, 192, 200
Gold Peak 113
golf cart 64–65
Goodenough, Prof. John B. 85, *85*, 206–207
Gotech International 198; Helix 198
Govecs GmbH 101; e-Schwalbe 101
Grehl, Mariana 221
Grehl, Timo 221
Grübel, Thomas 97, 101, 200; Govecs 200; Govecs TRIPL 200
Gruber, Reinhold 203
Gruber Antrieb GmbH & Company KG 203; Gruber Assist 203; Gruber Assist 3.15 (Vivax Assist) 203, *204*
Grulke, Carl A. 65–66, *66*; GT370 64
GT371 64
Guidicci, Antonin 109

Hachenberger, G. P. *14*
Håkansson, Eva 169–175, *172*, *174*; ElectroCat 170
Halske, Johann 8
Hammerschmid, Johann 208
Haojue 147
Harbilt 64–65
Harley-Davidson 41, 43, 68–69, 102, 108, 125– 126, 128, 131, 226; H-D Revelation 126; Livewire 226
Harte, Dennis 196
Hatfield, Richard 163–165, 168–169
Hayes, Hector H. 31–32
Heiko, Müller 101
Henrik Fisker Nanotech 208
Hercules 81–82, *81*
Hero-Eco 100–101; A2B Metro 101
Hershner, Terry "Electric Terry" 151–152, *153*
Hippomobile 5
Hirota, Kazuyuki 211
HNG 184; Radmeister 184
Hochreiter, Georg 208
Hoffmann, Christopher J. 177
Honda 87, 93, 103, 108; 118–119, 127, 209, 213, 222–223; Clarity 213; Mugen Roku 119–120; Mugen Shinden San 119–120; SuperCub 108
Horlacher, Max 194–195; Egg (Ei) 195
hoverbike 227–228; Hovercycle 228; Hoversurf Scorpion 3 227–228
hoverboard 227; Arcaboard 227; Toyota SLIDE 227
Howard-Willis, Guy 227; Manta 5 227
Hsu, Yao-Sheng 212
Hu, Jihong 144
hybrid 20, *66*, 66, 74, 85, 99–100, 108, 131, 197, 216, 218–219, 225
Hyundai Nexo 213

Iacocca, Lee 90
ID Bike 93
IDIADA 198
Impact Automotive Technologies 196
Indian Motorcycle Company 41, 43, 67, 102
Intelligent Energy 211–212
Intuitive Motion Incorporated 189; Z Board 189
Inventist Incorporated 182; Hovertrax 182; Solowheel 182
Isle of Man Tourist Trophy (TT) 116–117, 122; Time Trial Extreme Grand Prix (TTXGP) 117–118, 122–123, 126; TT Zero 118–120, 125, 135, 168

La Jamais Contente 2 (JC2) 161
Jambon-Buerre 109–110; Gloria 110
Jamerson, Frank E. 88–89
Janney, William S. 32
Japan Storage Battery Company Limited 87
jet-skis 226–228 ; Aqualeo Gliss-Speed 226; Gratis X1 226; LGM Incorporated 226; Nikola Motor Company 226–227
Jiangsu Xinri E-Vehicle Company Limited 145; SUNRA 145
Johammer e-mobility GmbH 208; J1.150 208, J1.200 208

Kalishnikov 136–137, 228; IZH Ovum 137
Kalkhoff 104
Kamen, Dean L. 105, 178; iBot 178

Karbon Kinetics Limited 99–100; Gocycle 99–100; Gocycle G2 100; Gocycle G3 100
Kawasaki 160–161, 169, 222
Kesling, Harold D. 193–195, *194*
Killacycle *see* Dubé, William
kinetic energy recovery system (KERS) 167
Kinetic Motors 100; Kinetic Luna 100
Klawitter, Remo 154
Klever Mobility Incorporated 107–108
Ko, Johnson 74
Koga 102
Kohlbrenner, Philippe 79
Kong, Ji Joon 87
Kordesh, Karl V. 65–66, *66*, 211
Kriéger, Louis Antoine 28
Krieger, Michael 102
Kroll, Jerry 202
Kutter, Michael 79, *80*
Kuwahara, Akira 190
Kwang Yang Motor Company Limited 107; Queen 107
KYMCO 108; iONIX 108
Kynast *70*

Lafree 84, *84*
Lal, Siddhartha 123
Lamborghini 154
Lancia 134
Lang, Jeffrey H. 190, 192
Larson, Geoff Ellia 189
LaStella, Joseph P. 89
Lee, Helen 198
Legris, Jean-Pierre 127
LeJay Manufacturing Company 47; LeJay GoBike 47
Levesque-Baker, Cédrick 221
LG 208
Libbey, Dr. Hosea Wait 25–27, *26*, *27*
8881 165; LS218 168–169
LIN 1 72
LITO Green Motion Incorporated 127; LitoSora 127
Liu, King 84, *84*
Lo, Tony 84, *84*
Logos Tchnologies 131
LSA Autonomy 132; Nightmare 132
Lucas Industries plc 71; Lucas Electrics Limited 71
Luke, Horace 107
Luyuan Electric Vehicle Company 144–146
Lynch, Cedric 70–74, *73*, 78, 87–88, 94, 105, 117, 137–139, 195, 216
Lynn, Danell 156

Ma, Guilong 143
MacCready, Dr. Paul 74, 82, 211
MacGowan, Andrew J. 112
MacLeod, Bruce 151
Mahindra and Mahindra Limited 100
Major, Jeff *166*

Marazzi, Lawrence 137
Marquis, Raoul "Marquis Henri de Graffigny" 20, *21*
Martin, Guy 119
Maserati 134
Maslove, Boris A. 98
Maxim, Sir Hiram 42
McArthur, Charles 159, 160
McBride, Larry "Spiderman" 163; Lawless Electric Rocket 163
McGreen, James 82
Meijs, Ronald Josef Maria 108
MEIJS Motorman 108
Mercedes-Benz 84, 197
MG Eneergy Systems 209
Mildé, Charles 37–39, *38*, *39*
Miloshev, Milo 97
Mishra, Rajeev 135
Mitsubishi Electric Corporation 87, 223
Mobivia 188
Modkovich, Boris 185
Modkovich, Yevgeniy 185
Momentum Electric 103; Model-T 103; VIT-S 103
monocycle 176–177, 182–183, 188, 192; Airwheel X3 177; Gotway MSuper 18 177; Kiwano KO1 177; Ninebot OneE+ 177
Monteil, Jean-Francois 161
moped 67–68, 76, 79, 82, 93, 100–103, 108, 184, 192, 208, 211, 217
Morgan Motor Company 198–199, *199*; EV3 199
Mossay, Paul Alphonse Hubert 44–45
Motobécane 68
MotoCzysz 118; MotoCzysz E1 118; MotoCzysz E1pc 168
motor makes: ACEC 53, *55*; Agni 120, 134; Agni/Saietta 137–138; Baldor 68; Bion X 96; Bosch 67, *70*, 78, 151; Briggs & Stratton 115; Brose 134; BRUSA AMC200 195; CargoPower RN-111 104; Dyno 59; EVO Electric AFM 173; GoSwiss Drive 151; Greffe 39; Immisch 16; J&H 160; Les Etablissements R.B. 57, *58*; Lister 42; Machubi 70; Moës 53, *55*; Morris 59; Motorino 97; Nidec 103; Paris-Rhone 57; Parker GMV 126; Prestolite MTC 160; SIBA 73; Zero-Emission Transport Accessory (ZETA) 92
motor types: air-cooled 129; asynchronous 195; battery electric 7; brushless airgap DC 112–113; brushless DC 184, 190; brushless permanent magnet 226; electric-hub brushless 98, 142, 183; interior permanent magnet 126, 129, 135; permanent magnet 75; permanent magnet synchronous 107; PMDC 68; rare earth neodymium 115; three phase AC permanent magnet 124; two-stroke liquid hydrocarbon 5
Musk, Elon 122, 208
MUTE 101

244　Index

Nam, Ki 195; Power Sport 195; T3 ESV 195; T3 Motion 195; T3 Patroller 195
NASA 98, 114, 161
National Bicycle Industrial 87
Nelson & Collin Limited 63, **64**
Neupert, Hannes 82, 89, 94
New Map 57, **58**
Nezu, Kota 129
Nielson, Glenn E. 163; Silver Bullitt 163
Ninebot Incorporated *see* Segway Incorporated
Nissan 87, 123, 173, 224–225; Riding Assist 222
Nissan Motors 87
NOBE 201
Norton Motorcycles 41

L'Œuf Electrique 49, **50**, 54, 60, 192
Olsommer, David 188
Optima Corporation 101
Organic Transit 197, **215**; ELF 197–198
Orus, Joán 214
Outram, Christine Louise 186
Ovonic Battery Company 83
Ovshinsky, Stan 83
Ozrelic, Tony 177

Panasonic 68, 81, 87, 93, 97, 100, 208–209
parallel bicycle 177
Parker, Thomas Hugh 29–30
Pastor, Gildo Pallanca 134–135
Patroller 83
Paupe, Roger 57, **58**
Pavez, Daniel 199
pedelecs 72, 75, 78, **80**, 82–84, **84**, 89, **91**, 93–95, **94**, 96–98, 100–101, 102–105, 107, 109–110, 112, 149, 151, 185–186, 188, 192, 197, 200, **204**, 205, 209, 211, **215**, 218–219, 227, 229; Delta 186; Foldable Quest 186; Galaxy Cruiser 186; Ion-pedelec 98; iZip-Express 100; Wayscral 188
pedelectrics *see* pedelecs
Perreaux, Louis-Guillaume 6–7, 10
Perry, John 11–12, **12**, 13
Petrocelli, Dr. Americo W. **159**, 160
Peugeot 57, 91–92, **92**, 113, 134, 161
Philips 48, 76
Phynergy limited 209
Piana, Michele 212
Pingault, Adolphe G. 32, **33**, 34–35
Plyant, Captain Gary **207**
Polaris Industries 101–102, 127; Brammo 102, 127; Empulse TT 127; EVantage 102; Meridian 102; Polaris 1.0 102; Polaris 2.0 102; Strive 102; Victory 102, 127
Polutnik, Aleksander 183; eniCycle 183
Popecu, Dumitru 227
Porsche 163–164, 197, 210
Pratt, Philip W. 15
Propella Electric Bikes 109
PUES Corporation 74
Pyntikov, Alex 98

quadricycle 74–5
Quantya 122, 200; DriftTrike 200; FMX 122; Strada 122

Rabadia, Arvind 72–73, **73**, 117, 137–138
Rachmuhl, Stéphanie 187
Racoon Compo 93–94
Raleigh Bicycle Company 93, 100
Rambola 46–47
Rannberg, Ed 160
Ransomes, Sims & Jeffries 44–45, **45**
Ratner, Donald 109
Ratti, Carlo 186
Razor 74
Razor USA 74
Reckenzaun, Anthony 13
Red Flag 143
Redshift MX *see* BRD Motorcycles
Reise, Markus 101
Reise and Müller 101–102; Delite GT 101; Delite Hybrid 500S 101; Packster 101
Reisner, Henry 202
ReVolt Electric Motorcycles 136
Rhodin, John Gustaf Adolf 30–31, **31**
Rich, Ben 152–153
Rieju 138
Riether, Chris Lee 134
Rigo, Pierpaolo 133
Riker, Andrew Lawrence 20–21; Riker Electric Motor Company 20–21
Ritchie, Andrew 105
Road Torpedo 41–42
Robbens, Bjorn 135
Robbens, Torsten 135–136
roller skates 190–192, **191**
Roper, Sylvester Howard 5–7
Rossi, Valentino 222, 228
Royal Enfield 41; Royal FZR750 69–70; Royal Salvo 8; *see also* Eicher Motors
Rugroden, Jim 189
Rumsey, Mark **207**
Ryan, Grant 106
Ryan, Shaun 106
RYNO Motors 177

Saietta 137–138; Next Generation Saietta (NGS) 138; Saietta R 138; Saietta S 138
Saiki, Neal T. 114–115, **116**, 120, 128; Locker-Cycle 120; NTS SunCycle 120
Sam Ever Industry Company 107; Ever 107
Samsung 208
Sand, Jeff Waldo 121, **121**
Sanyo **84**, 87, 100; Enacle 75
Saroléa 135–136; MANX7 136; Saroléa SP7 136
Sato, Kuniaki 192
Sauve, Dennis N. 89
Schuckert, Johann 39; Schuckertwerke 39–40
Schultz, Horst 13
Schweitzer, Karl 203, 204
Schwinn 108

Index

science fiction 21–22, 75, 123, 134, 190, 229
Scoot'Elec 92, *92*
scooters 41, *42*, 54, 57, 67, 74, 89, 91, 96–97, 101, 103–104, 107–109, 111, 113, 120, 137, 142–143, 145, 148, 178, 184, 190, 192, 197, 200, 201, *208*, 212–213, 218–219, 221–222, 225; Bird 218–219; Lime 218–219; Scoot 219; Skip 219
Scutum 138
Searles, Mark Aubrey 96; Cytronex C1 96; Cytronex Cannondale Capo 96; Cytronex Cannondale Super Six 96; Cytronex Trek FX 96
Segway Incorporated (later Segway-Ninebot Incorporated) 105, 178–182; Loomo bot 182; Loomo Go 182; Segway Advanced Personal Robot 182; Segway Drift W1 192; Segway polo 179–181, *181*; Segway PT 178–180, 182; Segway X2 Golf 179
Seiden, Dale 109
Selman, Jan Robert 97
SensoDrive 198
Shapiro, Alan 109
sharing services 107, 109–110, 151
Shelke, Kapil 122
Shenzen Battery Limited 87, 143
Shkondin, Vassily 100
sidecar 29, 45, 54, 136, 172–173
Siemens 40; Siemens Smart Chopper 218
Siemens, Werner 8
Simeray, Janick 182–183
simerLab 182
Sinclair, Sir Clive 75–76, *77*, 78, 92, *201*; C1 (Clive One) 76; Excaliber ZETA III 92; Sinclair Research 76; Sinclair Vehicles 76, 78; Zike 78
Sinclair, Grant 200–201; Iris 201; Iris E-Trike Eco 200; Iris E-Trike Extreme 200
Sinclair C5 75–78, *77*, 92, 200, *201*
Siy, Nathan 134
skateboard 189–190, 192
Small Antelope 143
Smart 114
Smith, Grey 156
Smith Electric Vehicles 115
Snug Design 129; Zec00 129
Socovel (Société pour l'étude et la Construction de Vehicules Electriques) 52–54, *55*, *56*, *58*, 59–60
solar 74–5, 82, 120, 137, 139, 148–150, 156, 168, 173, 197, 213–214, *215*, 221; Quimera SunRED 214; SolaRyde 215
Solo Electra 67–68
Solocar 63, *64*
Somashekar, Vinay Raj 223
Song, Min-Kyu 207
Sony Corporation 85–87, 208
Spacelander 62
Sparta 93, 98, *99*; Country tour 98; Double-E 98; E-Kargo 98; E-Motion 98; Fold-E 98; Granny 98; Pick-up 98

Staelin, David H. 190, 192
Starley, James 8
Starley, John Kemp 15
Starley Salvo *9*
steam power 5–7, 13
Steffens, Commodore Matthew Joseph 37
Stellmar Pedelec 78
Step Compo 94
Stevens, Brooks 68–69
StreetScooter 104
Strom World Tour 154, *155*; STORM Wave 154, *155*
Stromer 102; ST1 102
Sun Trip *150*, 214; Sun Trip Company 150; Sun Trip Tour 151
Sunraycer 82
Sunrise No. 1 149
Superpedestrian Incorporated 186–187
Suzuki Motor Corporation 69, 87, 211–212, 214; Bandit 221; Suzuki RG 134

Tacita 133; T-Race Enduro 133; Tacita T-Cruise 133
Tan, Yin Tsao 103
tandem 32–35, *33*, *35*, *36*, 41, 46, 98, 157, 205
Tarassoli, Behyad Ben 109
Tarpenning, Marc 122
Taylor, Matthew 107
Taylor-Dunn Manufacturing Company 63–64
Terra Motors 103; A4000i 103
Tesla 121–122, 126, 130, 196, 208, 210; Model S 152
Thede, Paul 165–166, *166–167*
Thieme, Allan R. 67
Thomson-Houston Electric Company 15
Thorpe, Richard Brian 99–100
three-wheeler 5, 7–9, *9*, 10–12, *12*, 13, 15–16, 18, *19*, 20–21, *21*, 22–23, 28–31, *31*, 36–37, 39–41, 43, 46, 49, 51, 54, 57, 63, 65, 68, 72, 74–76, 78, 104–105, 113, 137, 145, 147, 149, 157, 193–202, 210
Thunderchild 89–90
TidalForce 98; iO-750 Cruiser 98; M-750 98; S-750 98
Tinmouth, Jenni 118
Tokushige, Torun 103
Tork Motorcycles 122
Törpsch, Andreas 103
Torqeedo 115
Torrot Electric 138
Toyota 65, 94, 164, 168, 198, 227; EX-II 65; i-ROCK 198; i-ROAD 198; i-ROLL 198; Mirai 213
Treadway, Peter 192
Trefecta 151
Trice 75
tricycle *see* three-wheeler
Trident 63–64
triplette 35–36
Triumph 41, 43

Index

Trouvé, Gustave Pierre 7–9, *9*, 10–13, 15, 20, 131, 157
Tsai, Gino 74
TT Zero *see* Isle of Man Tourist Trophy
TTXGP *see* Isle of Man Tourist Trophy
tuk-tuks 196–197; Green Wheels Limited 196; TTF (Tailand) Limited 196; Tuk-Tuk Company 196

UK Electric Vehicle Association 64
UM Motorcycles 134; Renegade Duty Ace 135; Renegade Duty S 135; Renegade Thor 135
unicycle *see* monocycle
Union Carbide Corporation 65

Vanguard Motorcycles 102
VanguardSpark 102–103; Speedbike 103
Vass, Gabor 190, *191*
Vaughan-Sherrin, John 18
Vectrix 112–114, 152; MAXI 113; VX-1 112–113; VX-2 113; VX-3 113
Vedovelli, Eduardo *38*
velocipede 5–8, 10, 32
Velocipedrome 25–26, *26*
Velocity *80*
Velocity Dolphin 79
Vespa 108; Vespa Elettrica 108; Vespa LX50 108; Paggio X8125 108, 120
Victory *see* Polaris
Victory bicycles *see* Flying Pigeon
Villiger, Kaspar 194–195
Violet-Violent 160–161
virtual reality 228–229
Vmoto 101
Voiture Legère de Ville 57
Volk, Magnus 15–18, *17*
Volkswagen Group 133, 210
Volt Motorcycle Company 154; Lacama 154
Volta Motorbikes 138; My Volta 138; Volta BCN City 138; Volta Sport 138
Voxan 134–135; Voxan Wattman 134–135
VoZE EV 199; Sôki 199–200

Wang, Qinghua 143
WaveCrest Laboratories 98

Wells, Jonathan 199, *199*
Westinghouse Electric and Manufacturing Company 44
Westinghouse Machine Company 21
Wheatley, William B. "Bill" 49–50, *51*
Whittingham, M. Stanley 84, *85*
Willard Storage Battery Company 32
Williams, Earle 57, 59
Wismann, Brian 126–127
Woodward, Robert 109

Yadea Technology Group Company Limited 145; Z3 e-scooter 145
Yamaha 87, 93, 103, 108, 148, 164, 223; Motobot 222; MOTOROiD 222; Passol electric scooter 148; PED1 108; PES2 108; power assistance system (PAS) **86**, 93, 142; R1 120
Yang, Jefferson Y.S. 212
Yang, Te-Chou 212
Yardney Electric 157–158, *159*, 160
Yare 193–195, *194*
Yates, William Morrison III "Chip" 164–167, *166*, 168
Yongjui 143

Zalph, Barry 197
ZAP Power Systems 82, 143; ElectriCruiser 82; Powerbike 82; S&W Patrol Bike 82; ZAP DX 82; ZAP SX 82; Zappy microscooter 82; ZAPTRIKE 82
Zedify 105
Zero Motorcycles (formerly Electricross) 102, 105, 114–120, **116**, **119**, 128–131, **132**, 133, 151, **152**, 202, 226; charge tank 154; Drift 115; power packs 129–130; Zero Agni 118; Zero DS 128, 130–131; Zero DSP 131; Zero DSR 129–130; Zero DSR ZF14.4 Black Forest 130, 154; Zero DS ZF7.2 130; Zero FX 129; Zero FXS 129; Zero MMX 131; Zero MX 128; Zero MXD 128; Zero S 128, 130–131, 152; Zero S ZF6 128; Zero S ZF9 151; Zero SR 128, 130, 152; Zero SR ZF13.0 130; Zero X 116, 128; Zero XD 128; Zero XU 117, 128
Zhang, Yuegang 207
Zike 92
Zongshen 147

www.ingramcontent.com/pod-product-compliance
Lightning Source LLC
Chambersburg PA
CBHW021351300426
44114CB00012B/1182